EWALD FLÜGEL.
PALO ALTO. CAL.

# COLLECTION

## OF

# BRITISH AUTHORS.

### VOL. CLXXXIX.

CRITICAL AND HISTORICAL ESSAYS
BY
THOMAS BABINGTON MACAULAY.

IN FIVE VOLUMES.

VOL. V.

# Critical and Historical Essays: Diary and Letters of Madam D'arblay. the Life and Writings of Addison. the Earl of Chatham. Index

Baron Thomas Babington Macaulay Macaulay

**Nabu Public Domain Reprints:**

You are holding a reproduction of an original work published before 1923 that is in the public domain in the United States of America, and possibly other countries. You may freely copy and distribute this work as no entity (individual or corporate) has a copyright on the body of the work. This book may contain prior copyright references, and library stamps (as most of these works were scanned from library copies). These have been scanned and retained as part of the historical artifact.

This book may have occasional imperfections such as missing or blurred pages, poor pictures, errant marks, etc. that were either part of the original artifact, or were introduced by the scanning process. We believe this work is culturally important, and despite the imperfections, have elected to bring it back into print as part of our continuing commitment to the preservation of printed works worldwide. We appreciate your understanding of the imperfections in the preservation process, and hope you enjoy this valuable book.

# CRITICAL

## AND

# HISTORICAL ESSAYS,

CONTRIBUTED TO

THE EDINBURGH REVIEW.

BY

THOMAS BABINGTON MACAULAY.

COPYRIGHT EDITION.

IN FIVE VOLUMES.

VOL. V.

LEIPZIG

BERNH. TAUCHNITZ JUN.

1850.

219818

824.6
M117cr
v.5

# CONTENTS

## OF VOLUME V.

|  | PAGE |
|---|---|
| DIARY AND LETTERS OF MADAME D'ARBLAY | 1 |
| THE LIFE AND WRITINGS OF ADDISON | 68 |
| THE EARL OF CHATHAM | 162 |
| INDEX | 263 |

# CRITICAL AND HISTORICAL ESSAYS

CONTRIBUTED TO

THE EDINBURGH REVIEW.

---

## MADAME D'ARBLAY. (JANUARY, 1843.)

*Diary and Letters of Madame D'Arblay.* Five vols. 8vo.
London: 1842.

Though the world saw and heard little of Madame D'Arblay during the last forty years of her life, and though that little did not add to her fame, there were thousands, we believe, who felt a singular emotion when they learned that she was no longer among us. The news of her death carried the minds of men back at one leap over two generations, to the time when her first literary triumphs were won. All those whom we had been accustomed to revere as intellectual patriarchs seemed children when compared with her; for Burke had sate up all night to read her writings, and Johnson had pronounced her superior to Fielding, when Rogers was still a schoolboy, and Southey still in petticoats. Yet more strange did it seem that we should just have lost one whose name had been widely celebrated before any body had heard of some illustrious men who, twenty, thirty, or forty years ago, were, after a long and splendid career, borne with honour to the grave. Yet so it was. Frances Burney was at the height of fame and popularity before Cowper had published his first volume, before Porson had gone up to college, before Pitt had taken his seat in the House of Commons, before the voice of Erskine had been once heard in Westminster Hall. Since the appearance of her first work, sixty-two years had passed; and this interval had been crowded, not only with political, but also with intellectual revolutions. Thousands of reputations had, during that period, sprung up, bloomed, withered, and disappeared. New kinds of composition had come into fashion, had gone out of fashion, had been derided, had been forgotten. The fooleries of Della Crusca, and the fooleries of Kotzebue, had for a time bewitched the multitude, but had left no trace behind them; nor had misdirected genius been able to save from decay the once flourishing schools of Godwin, of Darwin, and of Radcliffe. Many books, written for temporary effect, had run through six or seven editions, and had then been gathered to the novels of Afra Behn, and the epic poems of Sir Richard Blackmore. Yet the early works of Madame D'Arblay, in spite of the lapse of years, in spite of the change of manners, in spite of the popularity deservedly obtained by some of her rivals, continued to hold a high place in the public esteem. She lived to be a classic. Time set on her fame, before she went hence, that seal which is seldom set except on the fame of the departed. Like Sir Condy Rackrent in the tale, she survived her own wake, and overheard the judgment of posterity.

Having always felt a warm and sincere, though not a blind admiration for her talents, we rejoiced to learn that her Diary was about to be made public. Our hopes, it is true, were not unmixed with fears. We could not forget the fate of the Memoirs of Dr. Burney, which were published ten years ago. That unfortunate book contained much that was curious and *interesting*. Yet it was received with a cry of disgust, and was *speedily consigned* to oblivion. The truth is, that it deserved its doom. It was written in Madame D'Arblay's later style, the worst style that has ever been known among men. No genius, no information, could save from proscription a book so written. We, therefore, opened the Diary with no small anxiety, trembling lest we should light upon some of that peculiar rhetoric which deforms almost every page of the Memoirs, and which it is impossible to read without a sensation made up of mirth, shame, and loathing. We soon, however, discovered to our great delight that this Diary was kept before Madame D'Arblay became eloquent. It is, for the most part, written in her earliest and best manner, in true woman's English, clear, natural, and lively. The two works are lying side by side before us; and we never turn from the Memoirs to the Diary without a sense of relief. The difference is as great as the difference between then atmosphere of a perfumer's shop, fetid with lavender water and jasmine soap, and the air of a heath on a fine morning in May. Both works ought to be consulted by every person who wishes to be well acquainted with the history of our literature and our manners. But to read the Diary is a pleasure; to read the Memoirs will always be a task.

We may, perhaps, afford some harmless amusement to our readers if we attempt, with the help of these two books, to give them an account of the most important years of Madame D'Arblay's life.

She was descended from a family which bore the name of Macburney, and which, though probably of Irish origin, had been long settled in Shropshire, and was possessed of considerable estates in that county. Unhappily, many years before her birth, the Macburneys began, as if of set purpose and in a spirit of determined rivalry, to expose and ruin themselves. The heir apparent, Mr. James Macburney, offended his father by making a runaway match with an actress from

Goodman's Fields. The old gentleman could devise no more judicious mode of wreaking vengeance on his undutiful boy than by marrying the cook. The cook gave birth to a son named Joseph, who succeeded to all the lands of the family, while James was cut off with a shilling. The favourite son, however, was so extravagant, that he soon became as poor as his disinherited brother. Both were forced to earn their bread by their labour. Joseph turned dancing master, and settled in Norfolk. James struck off the Mac from the beginning of his name, and set up as a portrait painter at Chester. Here he had a son named Charles, well known as the author of the History of Music, and as the father of two remarkable children, of a son distinguished by learning, and of a daughter still more honourably distinguished by genius.

Charles early showed a taste for that art, of which, at a later period, he became the historian. He was apprenticed to a celebrated musician in London, and applied himself to study with vigour and success. He soon found a kind and munificent patron in Fulk Greville, a highborn and highbred man, who seems to have had in large measure all the accomplishments and all the follies, all the virtues and all the vices, which, a hundred years ago, were considered as making up the character of a fine gentleman. Under such protection, the young artist had every prospect of a brilliant career in the capital. But his health failed. It became necessary for him to retreat from the smoke and river fog of London, to the pure air of the coast. He accepted the place of organist, at Lynn, and settled at that town with a young lady who had recently become his wife.

At Lynn, in June, 1752, Frances Burney was born. Nothing in her childhood indicated that she would, while still a *young woman*, have secured for herself an honourable and *permanent place* among English writers. She was shy and

and silent. Her brothers and sisters called her a dunce, and not without some show of reason; for at eight years old she did not know her letters.

In 1760, Mr. Burney quitted Lynn for London, and took a house in Poland Street; a situation which had been fashionable in the reign of Queen Anne, but which, since that time, had been deserted by most of its wealthy and noble inhabitants. He afterwards resided in Saint Martin's Street, on the south side of Leicester Square. His house there is still well known, and will continue to be well known as long as our island retains any trace of civilisation; for it was the dwelling of Newton, and the square turret which distinguishes it from all the surrounding buildings was Newton's observatory.

Mr. Burney at once obtained as many pupils of the most respectable description as he had time to attend, and was thus enabled to support his family, modestly indeed, and frugally, but in comfort and independence. His professional merit obtained for him the degree of Doctor of Music from the University of Oxford; and his works on subjects connected with his art gained for him a place, respectable, though certainly not eminent, among men of letters.

The progress of the mind of Frances Burney, from her ninth to her twenty-fifth year, well deserves to be recorded. When her education had proceeded no further than the hornbook, she lost her mother, and thenceforward she educated herself. Her father appears to have been as bad a father as a very honest, affectionate, and sweet tempered man can well be. He loved his daughter dearly; but it never seems to have occurred to him that a parent has other duties to perform to children than that of fondling them. It would indeed have been impossible for him to superintend their education himself. His professional engagements occupied him all day. *At seven in the morning he began to attend his pupils, and,* when London was full, was sometimes employed in teaching till eleven at night. He was often forced to carry in his pocket a tin box of sandwiches, and a bottle of wine and water, on which he dined in a hackney coach, while hurrying from one scholar to another. Two of his daughters he sent to a seminary at Paris; but he imagined that Frances would run some risk of being perverted from the Protestant faith if she were educated in a Catholic country, and he therefore kept her at home. No governess, no teacher of any art or of any language, was provided for her. But one of her sisters showed her how to write; and, before she was fourteen, she began to find pleasure in reading.

It was not, however, by reading that her intellect was formed. Indeed, when her best novels were produced, her knowledge of books was very small. When at the height of her fame, she was unacquainted with the most celebrated works of Voltaire and Molière; and, what seems still more extraordinary, had never heard or seen a line of Churchill, who, when she was a girl, was the most popular of living poets. It is particularly deserving of observation that she appears to have been by no means a novel reader. Her father's library was large; and he had admitted into it so many books which rigid moralists generally exclude that he felt uneasy, as he afterwards owned, when Johnson began to examine the shelves. But in the whole collection there was only a single novel, Fielding's Amelia.

An education, however, which to most girls would have been useless, but which suited Fanny's mind better than elaborate culture, was in constant progress during her passage from childhood to womanhood. The great book of human nature was turned over before her. Her father's social position was very peculiar. He belonged in fortune and station *to the middle class.* His daughters seemed to have been suffered to mix freely with those whom butlers and waiting maids call vulgar. We are told that they were in the habit of playing with the children of a wigmaker who lived in the adjoining house. Yet few nobles could assemble in the most stately mansions of Grosvenor Square or Saint James's Square, a society so various and so brilliant as was sometimes to be found in Dr. Burney's cabin. His mind, though not very powerful or capacious, was restlessly active; and, in the intervals of his professional pursuits, he had contrived to lay up much miscellaneous information. His attainments, the suavity of his temper, and the gentle simplicity of his manners, had obtained for him ready admission to the first literary circles. While he was still at Lynn, he had won Johnson's heart by sounding with honest zeal the praises of the English Dictionary. In London the two friends met frequently, and agreed most harmoniously. One tie, indeed, was wanting to their mutual attachment. Burney loved his own art passionately; and Johnson just knew the bell of Saint Clement's church from the organ. They had, however, many topics in common; and on winter nights their conversations were sometimes prolonged till the fire had gone out, and the candles had burned away to the wicks. Burney's admiration of the powers which had produced Rasselas and The Rambler bordered on idolatry. Johnson, on the other hand, condescended to growl out that Burney was an honest fellow, a man whom it was impossible not to like.

Garrick, too, was a frequent visitor in Poland Street and Saint Martin's Lane. That wonderful actor loved the society of children, partly from good nature, and partly from vanity. The ecstasies of mirth and terror, which his gestures and play of countenance never failed to produce in a nursery, flattered him quite as much as the applause of mature critics. He often exhibited all his powers of mimicry for the amusement of the little Burneys, awed them by shuddering and crouching as if he saw a ghost, scared them by raving like a maniac in Saint Luke's, and then at once became an auctioneer, a chimney-sweeper, or an old woman, and made them laugh till the tears ran down their cheeks.

But it would be tedious to recount the names of all the men of letters and artists whom Frances Burney had an opportunity of seeing and hearing. Colman, Twining, Harris, Baretti, Hawkesworth, Reynolds, Barry, were among those who occasionally surrounded the tea table and supper tray at her father's modest dwelling. This was not all. The distinction which Dr. Burney had acquired as a musician, and as the historian of music, attracted to his house the most eminent musical performers of that age. The greatest Italian singers who visited England regarded him as the dispenser of fame in their art, and exerted themselves to obtain his suffrage. Pachierotti became his intimate friend. The rapacious Agujari, who sang for nobody else under fifty pounds an air, sang her best for Dr. Burney without a fee; and in the company of Dr. Burney even the haughty and eccentric Gabrielli constrained herself to behave with civility. It was thus in his power to give, with scarcely any expense, concerts equal to those of the aristocracy. On such occasions the quiet street in which he lived was blocked up by coroneted chariots, and his little drawing-room was crowded with peers, peeresses, ministers, and ambassadors. On one evening, of which we happen to have a full account, there were present Lord Mulgrave, Lord Bruce, Lord and Lady Edgecumbe, Lord Barrington from the War Office, Lord Sandwich from the Admiralty, Lord Ashburnham, with his gold key dangling from his pocket, and the French Ambassador, M. De Guignes, *renowned for his fine person and for his success in gallantry. But the great show of the night was the Russian Ambassador,*

Count Orloff, whose gigantic figure was all in a blaze with jewels, and in whose demeanour the untamed ferocity of the Scythian might be discerned through a thin varnish of French politeness. As he stalked about the small parlour, brushing the ceiling with his toupee, the girls whispered to each other, with mingled admiration and horror, that he was the favoured lover of his august mistress; that he had borne the chief part in the revolution to which she owed her throne; and that his huge hands, now glittering with diamond rings, had given the last squeeze to the windpipe of her unfortunate husband.

With such illustrious guests as these were mingled all the most remarkable specimens of the race of lions, a kind of game which is hunted in London every spring with more than Meltonian ardour and perseverance. Bruce, who had washed down steaks cut from living oxen with water from the fountains of the Nile, came to swagger and talk about his travels. Omai lisped broken English, and made all the assembled musicians hold their ears by howling Otaheitean love songs, such as those with which Oberea charmed her Opano.

With the literary and fashionable society, which occasionally met under Dr. Burney's roof, Frances can scarcely be said to have mingled. She was not a musician, and could therefore bear no part in the concerts. She was shy almost to awkwardness, and scarcely ever joined in the conversation. The slightest remark from a stranger disconcerted her; and even the old friends of her father who tried to draw her out could seldom extract more than a Yes or a No. Her figure was small, her face not distinguished by beauty. She was therefore suffered to withdraw quietly to the background, and, unobserved herself, to observe all that passed. Her nearest relations were aware that she had good sense, but seem not to have suspected that, under her demure and bashful deportment, were concealed a fertile invention and a keen sense of the ridiculous. She had not, it is true, an eye for the fine shades of character. But every marked peculiarity instantly caught her notice and remained engraven on her imagination. Thus, while still a girl, she had laid up such a store of materials for fiction as few of those who mix much in the world are able to accumulate during a long life. She had watched and listened to people of every class, from princes and great officers of state down to artists living in garrets, and poets familiar with subterranean cookshops. Hundreds of remarkable persons had passed in review before her, English, French, German, Italian, lords and fiddlers, deans of cathedrals and managers of theatres, travellers leading about newly caught savages, and singing women escorted by deputy husbands.

So strong was the impression made on the mind of Frances by the society which she was in the habit of seeing and hearing, that she began to write little fictitious narratives as soon as she could use her pen with ease, which, as we have said, was not very early. Her sisters were amused by her stories: but Dr. Burney knew nothing of their existence; and in another quarter her literary propensities met with serious discouragement. When she was fifteen, her father took a second wife. The new Mrs. Burney soon found out that her step-daughter was fond of scribbling, and delivered several goodnatured lectures on the subject. The advice no doubt was well meant, and might have been given by the most judicious friend; for at that time, from causes to which we may hereafter advert, nothing could be more disadvantageous to a young lady than to be known as a novel-writer. Frances yielded, relinquished her favourite pursuit, and made a bonfire of all her manuscripts.*

* There is some difficulty here as to the chronology. "This sacrifice," says the editor of the Diary, "was made in the young authoress's fifteenth year." This could not be; for the sacrifice was the effect,

She now hemmed and stitched from breakfast to dinner with scrupulous regularity. But the dinners of that time were early; and the afternoon was her own. Though she had given up novel writing, she was still fond of using her pen. She began to keep a diary, and she corresponded largely with a person who seems to have had the chief share in the formation of her mind. This was Samuel Crisp, an old friend of her father. His name, well known, near a century ago, in the most splendid circles of London, has long been forgotten. His history is, however, so interesting and instructive, that it tempts us to venture on a digression.

Long before Frances Burney was born, Mr. Crisp had made his entrance into the world, with every advantage. He was well connected and well educated. His face and figure were conspicuously handsome; his manners were polished; his fortune was easy; his character was without stain; he lived in the best society; he had read much; he talked well; his taste in literature, music, painting, architecture, sculpture, was held in high esteem. Nothing that the world can give seemed to be wanting to his happiness and respectability, except that he should understand the limits of his powers, and should not throw away distinctions which were within his reach in the pursuit of distinctions which were unattainable.

"It is an uncontrolled truth," says Swift, "that no man ever made an ill figure who understood his own talents, nor a good one who mistook them." Every day brings with it fresh illustrations of this weighty saying; but the best commentary that we remember is the history of Samuel Crisp. Men like him have their proper place, and it is a most important one, in the Commonwealth of Letters. It is by the judg-

---

according to the editor's own showing, of the remonstrances of the second Mrs. Burney; and Frances was in her sixteenth year when her father's second marriage took place.

ment of such men that the rank of authors is finally determined. It is neither to the multitude, nor to the few who are gifted with great creative genius, that we are to look for sound critical decisions. The multitude, unacquainted with the best models, are captivated by whatever stuns and dazzles them. They deserted Mrs. Siddons to run after Master Betty; and they now prefer, we have no doubt, Jack Sheppard to Von Artevelde. A man of great original genius, on the other hand, a man who has attained to mastery in some high walk of art, is by no means to be implicitly trusted as a judge of the performances of others. The erroneous decisions pronounced by such men are without number. It is commonly supposed that jealousy makes them unjust. But a more creditable explanation may easily be found. The very excellence of a work shows that some of the faculties of the author have been developed at the expense of the rest; for it is not given to the human intellect to expand itself widely in all directions at once, and to be at the same time gigantic and well proportioned. Whoever becomes preeminent in any art, nay, in any style of art, generally does so by devoting himself with intense and exclusive enthusiasm to the pursuit of one kind of excellence. His perception of other kinds of excellence is therefore too often impaired. Out of his own department he praises and blames at random, and is far less to be trusted than the mere connoisseur, who produces nothing, and whose business is only to judge and enjoy. One painter is distinguished by his exquisite finishing. He toils day after day to bring the veins of a cabbage leaf, the folds of a lace veil, the wrinkles of an old woman's face, nearer and nearer to perfection. In the time which he employs on a square foot of canvass, a master of a different order covers the walls of a palace with gods burying giants under mountains, or makes the cupola of a church alive with seraphim and martyrs. The more fervent the passion of each of these artists for his art, the higher the merit of each in his own line, the more unlikely it is that they will justly appreciate each other. Many persons who never handled a pencil probably do far more justice to Michael Angelo than would have been done by Gerard Douw, and far more justice to Gerard Douw than would have been done by Michael Angelo.

It is the same with literature. Thousands, who have no spark of the genius of Dryden or Wordsworth, do to Dryden the justice which has never been done by Wordsworth, and to Wordsworth the justice which, we suspect, would never have been done by Dryden. Gray, Johnson, Richardson, Fielding, are all highly esteemed by the great body of intelligent and well informed men. But Gray could see no merit in Rasselas; and Johnson could see no merit in the Bard. Fielding thought Richardson a solemn prig; and Richardson perpetually expressed contempt and disgust for Fielding's lowness.

Mr. Crisp seems, as far as we can judge, to have been a man eminently qualified for the useful office of a connoisseur. His talents and knowledge fitted him to appreciate justly almost every species of intellectual superiority. As an adviser he was inestimable. Nay, he might probably have held a respectable rank as a writer, if he would have confined himself to some department of literature in which nothing more than sense, taste, and reading was required. Unhappily he set his heart on being a great poet, wrote a tragedy in five acts on the death of Virginia, and offered it to Garrick, who was his personal friend. Garrick read, shook his head, and expressed a doubt whether it would be wise in Mr. Crisp to stake a reputation, which stood high, on the success of such a piece. But the author, blinded by ambition, set in motion a machinery such as none could long resist. His intercessors were the most eloquent man and the most lovely woman of that generation. Pitt was induced to read Virginia, and to pronounce it excellent. Lady Coventry, with fingers which might have furnished a model to sculptors, forced the manuscript into the reluctant hand of the manager; and, in the year 1754, the play was brought forward.

Nothing that skill or friendship could do was omitted. Garrick wrote both prologue and epilogue. The zealous friends of the author filled every box; and, by their strenuous exertions, the life of the play was prolonged during ten nights. But, though there was no clamorous reprobation, it was universally felt that the attempt had failed. When Virginia was printed, the public disappointment was even greater than at the representation. The critics, the Monthly Reviewers in particular, fell on plot, characters, and diction without mercy, but, we fear, not without justice. We have never met with a copy of the play; but, if we may judge from the scene which is extracted in the Gentleman's Magazine, and which does not appear to have been malevolently selected, we should say that nothing but the acting of Garrick, and the partiality of the audience, could have saved so feeble and unnatural a drama from instant damnation.

The ambition of the poet was still unsubdued. When the London season closed, he applied himself vigorously to the work of removing blemishes. He does not seem to have suspected, what we are strongly inclined to suspect, that the whole piece was one blemish, and that the passages which were meant to be fine, were, in truth, bursts of that tame extravagance into which writers fall, when they set themselves to be sublime and pathetic in spite of nature. He omitted, added, retouched, and flattered himself with hopes of a complete success in the following year; but in the following year, Garrick showed no disposition to bring the amended tragedy on the stage. Solicitation and remonstrance were tried in vain. Lady Coventry, drooping under that malady which seems ever to select what is loveliest for its prey, could render no assistance. The manager's language was civilly evasive; but his resolution was inflexible.

Crisp had committed a great error; but he had escaped with a very slight penance. His play had not been hooted from the boards. It had, on the contrary, been better received than many very estimable performances have been, than Johnson's Irene, for example, or Goldsmith's Good-natured Man. Had Crisp been wise, he would have thought himself happy in having purchased self-knowledge so cheap. He would have relinquished, without vain repinings, the hope of poetical distinction, and would have turned to the many sources of happiness which he still possessed. Had he been, on the other hand, an unfeeling and unblushing dunce, he would have gone on writing scores of bad tragedies in defiance of censure and derision. But he had too much sense to risk a second defeat, yet too little sense to bear his first defeat like a man. The fatal delusion that he was a great dramatist, had taken firm possession of his mind. His failure he attributed to every cause except the true one. He complained of the ill will of Garrick, who appears to have done for the play every thing that ability and zeal could do, and who, from selfish motives, would, of course, have been well pleased if Virginia had been as successful as the Beggar's Opera. Nay, Crisp complained of the languor of the friends whose partiality had given him three benefit nights to which he had no claim. He complained of the injustice of the spectators, when, in truth, he ought to have been grateful for their unexampled patience. He lost his temper and spirits, and became a cynic and a hater of mankind. From London he *retired to Hampton*, and from Hampton to a solitary and long deserted mansion, built on a common in one of the wildest tracts of Surrey. No road, not even a sheepwalk, connected his lonely dwelling with the abodes of men. The place of his retreat was strictly concealed from his old associates. In the spring he sometimes emerged, and was seen at exhibitions and concerts in London. But he soon disappeared, and hid himself, with no society but his books, in his dreary hermitage. He survived his failure about thirty years. A new generation sprang up around him. No memory of his bad verses remained among men. His very name was forgotten. How completely the world had lost sight of him, will appear from a single circumstance. We looked for him in a copious Dictionary of Dramatic Authors published while he was still alive, and we found only that Mr. Henry Crisp, of the Custom House, had written a play called Virginia, acted in 1754. To the last, however, the unhappy man continued to brood over the injustice of the manager and the pit, and tried to convince himself and others that he had missed the highest literary honours, only because he had omitted some fine passages in compliance with Garrick's judgment. Alas, for human nature, that the wounds of vanity should smart and bleed so much longer than the wounds of affection! Few people, we believe, whose nearest friends and relations died in 1754, had any acute feeling of the loss in 1782. Dear sisters, and favourite daughters, and brides snatched away before the honeymoon was passed, had been forgotten, or were remembered only with a tranquil regret. But Samuel Crisp was still mourning for his tragedy, like Rachel weeping for her children, and would not be comforted. "Never," such was his language twenty-eight years after his disaster, "never give up or alter a tittle unless it perfectly coincides with your own inward feelings. I can say this to my sorrow *and my cost*. But mum!" Soon after these words were written, his life, a life which might have been eminently useful and happy, ended in the same gloom in which, during more than a quarter of a century, it had been passed. We have thought it worth while to rescue from oblivion this curious fragment of literary history. It seems to us at once ludicrous, melancholy, and full of instruction.

Crisp was an old and very intimate friend of the Burneys. To them alone was confided the name of the desolate old hall in which he hid himself like a wild beast in a den. For them were reserved such remains of his humanity as had survived the failure of his play. Frances Burney he regarded as his daughter. He called her his Fannikin; and she in return called him her dear Daddy. In truth, he seems to have done much more than her real parents for the development of her intellect; for though he was a bad poet, he was a scholar, a thinker, and an excellent counsellor. He was particularly fond of the concerts in Poland Street. They had, indeed, been commenced at his suggestion, and when he visited London he constantly attended them. But when he grew old, and when gout, brought on partly by mental irritation, confined him to his retreat, he was desirous of having a glimpse of that gay and brilliant world from which he was exiled, and he pressed Fannikin to send him full accounts of her father's evening parties. A few of her letters to him have been published; and it is impossible to read them without discerning in them all the powers which afterwards produced Evelina and Cecilia, the quickness in catching every odd peculiarity of character and manner, the skill in grouping, the humour, often richly comic, sometimes even farcical.

Fanny's propensity to novel-writing had for a time been kept down. It now rose up stronger than ever. The heroes and heroines of the tales which had perished in the flames, were still present to the eye of her mind. One favourite story, in particular, haunted her imagination. It was about a certain Caroline Evelyn, a beautiful damsel who made an unfortunate love match, and died, leaving an infant daughter. Frances began to image to herself the various scenes, tragic and comic, through which the poor motherless girl, highly connected on one side, meanly connected on the other, might have to pass. A crowd of unreal beings, good and bad, grave and ludicrous, surrounded the pretty, timid, young orphan; a coarse sea captain; an ugly insolent fop, blazing in a superb court dress; another fop as ugly and as insolent, but lodged on Snow Hill, and tricked out in secondhand finery for the Hampstead ball; an old woman, all wrinkles and rouge, flirting her fan with the air of a miss of seventeen, and screaming in a dialect made up of vulgar French and vulgar English; a poet lean and ragged, with a broad Scotch accent. By degrees these shadows acquired stronger and stronger consistence; the impulse which urged Frances to write became irresistible; and the result was the History of Evelina.

Then came, naturally enough, a wish, mingled with many fears, to appear before the public; for, timid as Frances was, and bashful, and altogether unaccustomed to hear her own praises, it is clear that she wanted neither a strong passion for distinction, nor a just confidence in her own powers. Her scheme was to become, if possible, a candidate for fame without running any risk of disgrace. She had not money to bear the expense of printing. It was therefore necessary that some bookseller should be induced to take the risk; and such a bookseller was not readily found. Dodsley refused even to look at the manuscript unless he were entrusted with the name of the author. A publisher in Fleet Street, named Lowndes, was more complaisant. Some correspondence took place *between this* person and Miss Burney, who took the name of *Grafton,* and desired that the letters addressed to her might be left at the Orange Coffeehouse. But, before the bargain was finally struck, Fanny thought it her duty to obtain her father's consent. She told him that she had written a book, that she wished to have his permission to publish it anonymously, but that she hoped that he would not insist upon seeing it. What followed may serve to illustrate what we meant when we said that Dr. Burney was as bad a father as so goodhearted a man could possibly be. It never seems to have crossed his mind that Fanny was about to take a step on which the whole happiness of her life might depend, a step which might raise her to an honourable eminence, or cover her with ridicule and contempt. Several people had already been trusted, and strict concealment was therefore not to be expected. On so grave an occasion, it was surely his duty to give his best counsel to his daughter, to win her confidence, to prevent her from exposing herself if her book were a bad one, and, if it were a good one, to see that the terms which she made with the publisher were likely to be beneficial to her. Instead of this, he only stared, burst out a laughing, kissed her, gave her leave to do as she liked, and never even asked the name of her work. The contract with Lowndes was speedily concluded. Twenty pounds were given for the copyright, and were accepted by Fanny with delight. Her father's inexcusable neglect of his duty happily caused her no worse evil than the loss of twelve or fifteen hundred pounds.

After many delays Evelina appeared in January 1778. Poor Fanny was sick with terror, and durst hardly stir out of doors. Some days passed before any thing was heard of the book. It had, indeed, nothing but its own merits to push it into public favour. Its author was unknown. The house by which it was published, was not, we believe, held in high estimation. No body of partisans had been engaged to applaud. The better class of readers expected little from a novel about a young lady's entrance into the world. There was, indeed, at that time a disposition among the most respectable people to condemn novels generally: nor was this disposition by any means without excuse; for works of that sort were then almost always silly, and very frequently wicked.

Soon, however, the first faint accents of praise began to be heard. The keepers of the circulating libraries reported that every body was asking for Evelina, and that some person had guessed Anstey to be the author. Then came a favourable notice in the London Review; then another still more favourable in the Monthly. And now the book found its way to tables which had seldom been polluted by marble covered volumes. Scholars and statesmen, who contemptuously abandoned the crowd of romances to Miss Lydia Languish and Miss Sukey Saunter, were not ashamed to own that they could not tear themselves away from Evelina. Fine carriages and rich liveries, not often seen east of Temple Bar, were attracted to the publisher's shop in Fleet Street. Lowndes was daily questioned about the author, but was himself as much in the dark as any of the questioners. The mystery, however, could not remain a mystery long. It was known to brothers and sisters, aunts and cousins: and they were far too proud and too happy to be discreet. Dr. Burney wept over the book in rapture. Daddy Crisp shook his fist at his Fannikin in affectionate anger at not having been admitted to her confidence. The truth was whispered to Mrs. Thrale; and then it began to spread fast.

The book had been admired while it was ascribed to men of letters long conversant with the world, and accustomed to composition. But when it was known that a reserved, silent young woman had produced the best work of fiction that had appeared since the death of Smollett, the acclamations were redoubled. What she had done was, indeed, extraordinary. But, as usual, various reports improved the story till it became miraculous. Evelina, it was said, was the work of a girl of seventeen. Incredible as this tale was, it continued to be repeated down to our own time. Frances was too honest to confirm it. Probably she was too much a woman to contradict it; and it was long before any of her detractors thought of this mode of annoyance. Yet there was no want of low minds and bad hearts in the generation which witnessed her first appearance. There was the envious Kenrick and the savage Wolcot, the asp George Steevens, and the polecat John Williams. It did not, however, occur to them to search the parish register of Lynn, in order that they might be able to twit a lady with having concealed her age. That truly chivalrous exploit was reserved for a bad writer of our own time, whose spite she had provoked by not furnishing him with materials for a worthless edition of Boswell's Life of Johnson, some sheets of which our readers have doubtless seen round parcels of better books.

But we must return to our story. The triumph was complete. The timid and obscure girl found herself on the highest pinnacle of fame. Great men, on whom she had gazed at a distance with humble reverence, addressed her with admiration, tempered by the tenderness due to her sex and age. Burke, Windham, Gibbon, Reynolds, Sheridan, were among her most ardent eulogists. Cumberland acknowledged her merit, after his fashion, by biting his lips and wriggling in his chair whenever her name was mentioned. But it was at Streatham that she tasted, in the highest perfection, the sweets of flattery, mingled with the sweets of friendship. Mrs. Thrale, then at the height of prosperity and popularity, with *gay spirits, quick wit,* showy though superficial acquirements, pleasing though not refined manners, a singularly amiable temper, and a loving heart, felt towards Fanny as towards a younger sister. With the Thrales Johnson was domesticated. He was an old friend of Dr. Burney; but he had probably taken little notice of Dr. Burney's daughters, and Fanny, we imagine, had never in her life dared to speak to him, unless to ask whether he wanted a nineteenth or a twentieth cup of tea. He was charmed by her tale, and preferred it to the novels of Fielding, to whom, indeed, he had always been grossly unjust. He did not, indeed, carry his partiality so far as to place Evelina by the side of Clarissa and Sir Charles Grandison; yet he said that his little favourite had done enough to have made even Richardson feel uneasy. With Johnson's cordial approbation of the book was mingled a fondness, half gallant half paternal, for the writer; and this fondness his age and character entitled him to show without restraint. He began by putting her hand to his lips. But he soon clasped her in his huge arms, and implored her to be a good girl. She was his pet, his dear love, his dear little Burney, his little character-monger. At one time, he broke forth in praise of the good taste of her caps. At another time he insisted on teaching her Latin. That, with all his coarseness and irritability, he was a man of sterling benevolence, has long been acknowledged. But how gentle and endearing his deportment could be, was not known till the Recollections of Madame D'Arblay were published.

We have mentioned a few of the most eminent of those who paid their homage to the author of Evelina. The crowd of inferior admirers would require a catalogue as long as that in the second book of the Iliad. In that catalogue would be Mrs. Cholmondeley, the sayer of odd things, and Seward, much *given to yawning,* and Baretti, who slew the man in the Hay-*market, and Paoli,* talking broken English, and Langton, taller by the head than any other member of the club, and Lady Millar, who kept a vase wherein fools were wont to put bad verses, and Jerningham, who wrote verses fit to be put into the vase of Lady Millar, and Dr. Franklin, not, as some have dreamed, the great Pennsylvanian Dr. Franklin, who could not then have paid his respects to Miss Burney without much risk of being hanged, drawn, and quartered, but Dr. Franklin the less,

$$Aἴας\ μείων,\ οὔτι\ τόσος\ γε\ ὅσος\ Τελαμώνιος\ Aἴας,\\ ἀλλὰ\ πολὺ\ μείων.$$

It would not have been surprising if such success had turned even a strong head, and corrupted even a generous and affectionate nature. But, in the Diary, we can find no trace of any feeling inconsistent with a truly modest and amiable disposition. There is, indeed, abundant proof that Frances enjoyed with an intense, though a troubled, joy, the honours which her genius had won; but it is equally clear that her happiness sprang from the happiness of her father, her sister, and her dear Daddy Crisp. While flattered by the great, the opulent, and the learned, while followed along the Steyne at Brighton, and the Pantiles at Tunbridge Wells, by the gaze of admiring crowds, her heart seems to have been still with the little domestic circle in Saint Martin's Street. If she recorded with minute diligence all the compliments, delicate and coarse, which she heard wherever she turned, she recorded them for the eyes of two or three persons who had loved her from infancy, who had loved her in obscurity, and to whom her fame gave the purest and most exquisite delight. Nothing can be more unjust than to confound these outpourings of a kind heart, sure of perfect sympathy, with the egotism of a bluestocking, who prates to all who come near her about her own novel or her own volume of sonnets.

It was natural that the triumphant issue of Miss Burney's first venture should tempt her to try a second. Evelina, though it had raised her fame, had added nothing to her fortune. Some of her friends urged her to write for the stage. Johnson promised to give her his advice as to the composition. Murphy, who was supposed to understand the temper of the pit as well as any man of his time, undertook to instruct her as to stage effect. Sheridan declared that he would accept a play from her without even reading it. Thus encouraged, she wrote a comedy named The Witlings. Fortunately it was never acted or printed. We can, we think, easily perceive, from the little which is said on the subject in the Diary, that The Witlings would have been damned, and that Murphy and Sheridan thought so, though they were too polite to say so. Happily Frances had a friend who was not afraid to give her pain. Crisp, wiser for her than he had been for himself, read the manuscript in his lonely retreat, and manfully told her that she had failed, that to remove blemishes here and there would be useless, that the piece had abundance of wit but no interest, that it was bad as a whole, that it would remind every reader of the *Femmes Savantes*, which, strange to say, she had never read, and that she could not sustain so close a comparison with Molière. This opinion, in which Dr. Burney concurred, was sent to Frances, in what she called "a hissing, groaning, catcalling epistle." But she had too much sense not to know that it was better to be hissed and catcalled by her Daddy, than by a whole sea of heads in the pit of Drury Lane Theatre: and she had too good a heart not to be grateful for so rare an act of friendship. She returned an answer, which shows how well she deserved to have a judicious, faithful, and affectionate adviser. "I intend," she wrote, "to console myself for your censure by this greatest proof I have ever received of the sincerity, candour, and, let me add, esteem, of my dear daddy.

And as I happen to love myself more than my play, this consolation is not a very trifling one. This, however, seriously I do believe, that when my two daddies put their heads together to concert that hissing, groaning, catcalling epistle they sent me, they felt as sorry for poor little Miss Bayes as she could possibly do for herself. You see I do not attempt to repay your frankness with an air of pretended carelessness. But, though somewhat disconcerted just now, I will promise not to let my vexation live out another day. Adieu, my dear daddy, I won't be mortified, and I won't be *downed;* but I will be proud to find I have, out of my own family, as well as in it, a friend who loves me well enough to speak plain truth to me."

Frances now turned from her dramatic schemes to an undertaking far better suited to her talents. She determined to write a new tale, on a plan excellently contrived for the display of the powers in which her superiority to other writers lay. It was in truth a grand and various picture gallery, which presented to the eye a long series of men and women, each marked by some strong peculiar feature. There were avarice and prodigality, the pride of blood, and the pride of money, morbid restlessness and morbid apathy, frivolous garrulity, supercilious silence, a Democritus to laugh at every thing, and a Heraclitus to lament over every thing. The work proceeded fast, and in twelve months was completed. It wanted something of the simplicity which had been among the most attractive charms of Evelina; but it furnished ample proof that the four years which had elapsed since Evelina appeared, had not been unprofitably spent. Those who saw Cecilia in manuscript pronounced it the best novel of the age. Mrs. Thrale laughed and wept over it. Crisp was even vehement in applause, and offered to insure the rapid and complete success of the book for half a crown. What Miss Burney received for the *copyright is* not mentioned in the Diary; but we have observed several expressions from which we infer that the sum was considerable. That the sale would be great nobody could doubt; and Frances now had shrewd and experienced advisers, who would not suffer her to wrong herself. We have been told that the publishers gave her two thousand pounds, and we have no doubt that they might have given a still larger sum without being losers.

Cecilia was published in the summer of 1782. The curiosity of the town was intense. We have been informed by persons who remember those days that no romance of Sir Walter Scott was more impatiently awaited or more eagerly snatched from the counters of the booksellers. High as public expectation was, it was amply satisfied; and Cecilia was placed, by general acclamation, among the classical novels of England.

Miss Burney was now thirty. Her youth had been singularly prosperous; but clouds soon began to gather over that clear and radiant dawn. Events deeply painful to a heart so kind as that of Frances followed each other in rapid succession. She was first called upon to attend the deathbed of her best friend, Samuel Crisp. When she returned to Saint Martin's Street, after performing this melancholy duty, she was appalled by hearing that Johnson had been struck with paralysis; and, not many months later, she parted from him for the last time with solemn tenderness. He wished to look on her once more; and on the day before his death she long remained in tears on the stairs leading to his bedroom, in the hope that she might be called in to receive his blessing. He was then sinking fast, and though he sent her an affectionate message, was unable to see her. But this was not the worst. There are separations far more cruel than those which are *made by death*. She might weep with proud affection for

Crisp and Johnson. She had to blush as well as to weep for Mrs. Thrale.

Life, however, still smiled upon Frances. Domestic happiness, friendship, independence, leisure, letters, all these things were hers; and she flung them all away.

Among the distinguished persons to whom she had been introduced, none appears to have stood higher in her regard than Mrs. Delany. This lady was an interesting and venerable relic of a past age. She was the niece of George Granville, Lord Lansdowne, who, in his youth, exchanged verses and compliments with Edmund Waller, and who was among the first to applaud the opening genius of Pope. She had married Dr. Delany, a man known to his contemporaries as a profound scholar and an eloquent preacher, but remembered in our time chiefly as one of that small circle in which the fierce spirit of Swift, tortured by disappointed ambition, by remorse, and by the approaches of madness, sought for amusement and repose. Doctor Delany had long been dead. His widow, nobly descended, eminently accomplished, and retaining, in spite of the infirmities of advanced age, the vigour of her faculties and the serenity of her temper, enjoyed and deserved the favour of the royal family. She had a pension of three hundred a year; and a house at Windsor, belonging to the crown, had been fitted up for her accommodation. At this house the King and Queen sometimes called, and found a very natural pleasure in thus catching an occasional glimpse of the private life of English families.

In December 1785, Miss Burney was on a visit to Mrs. Delany at Windsor. The dinner was over. The old lady was taking a nap. Her grandniece, a little girl of seven, was playing at some Christmas game with the visitors, when the door opened, and a stout gentleman entered unannounced, with a *star on his breast*, and "What? what? what?" in his mouth. A cry of "The King!" was set up. A general scampering followed. Miss Burney owns that she could not have been more terrified if she had seen a ghost. But Mrs. Delany came forward to pay her duty to her royal friend, and the disturbance was quieted. Frances was then presented, and underwent a long examination and cross-examination about all that she had written and all that she meant to write. The Queen soon made her appearance, and his Majesty repeated, for the benefit of his consort, the information which he had extracted from Miss Burney. The goodnature of the royal pair might have softened even the authors of the Probationary Odes, and could not but be delightful to a young lady who had been brought up a Tory. In a few days the visit was repeated. Miss Burney was more at ease than before. His Majesty, instead of seeking for information, condescended to impart it, and passed sentence on many great writers, English and foreign. Voltaire he pronounced a monster. Rousseau he liked rather better. "But was there ever," he cried, "such stuff as great part of Shakspeare? Only one must not say so. But what think you? What? Is there not sad stuff? What? What?"

The next day Frances enjoyed the privilege of listening to some equally valuable criticism uttered by the Queen touching Goethe and Klopstock, and might have learned an important lesson of economy from the mode in which her Majesty's library had been formed. "I picked the book up on a stall," said the Queen. "Oh, it is amazing what good books there are on stalls!" Mrs. Delany, who seems to have understood from these words that her Majesty was in the habit of exploring the booths of Moorfields and Holywell Street in person could not suppress an exclamation of surprise. "Why," said *the* Queen, "I don't pick them up myself. But I have a servant very clever; and, if they are not to be had at the booksellers, they are not for me more than for another." Miss Burney describes this conversation as delightful; and, indeed we cannot wonder that, with her literary tastes, she should be delighted at hearing in how magnificent a manner the greatest lady in the land encouraged literature.

The truth is, that Frances was fascinated by the condescending kindness of the two great personages to whom she had been presented. Her father was even more infatuated than herself. The result was a step of which we cannot think with patience, but which, recorded as it is, with all its consequences, in these volumes, deserves at least this praise, that it has furnished a most impressive warning.

A German lady of the name of Haggerdorn, one of the keepers of the Queen's robes, retired about this time; and her Majesty offered the vacant post to Miss Burney. When we consider that Miss Burney was decidedly the most popular writer of fictitious narrative then living, that competence, if not opulence, was within her reach, and that she was more than usually happy in her domestic circle, and when we compare the sacrifice which she was invited to make with the remuneration which was held out to her, we are divided between laughter and indignation.

What was demanded of her was that she should consent to be almost as completely separated from her family and friends as if she had gone to Calcutta, and almost as close a prisoner as if she had been sent to gaol for a libel; that with talents which had instructed and delighted the highest living minds, she should now be employed only in mixing snuff and sticking pins; that she should be summoned by a waiting woman's bell to a waiting woman's duties; that she should pass her whole life under *the restraints of* a paltry etiquette, should sometimes fast till she was ready to swoon with hunger, should sometimes stand till her knees gave way with fatigue; that she should not dare to speak or move without considering how her mistress might like her words and gestures. Instead of those distinguished men and women, the flower of all political parties, with whom she had been in the habit of mixing on terms of equal friendship, she was to have for her perpetual companion the chief keeper of the robes, an old hag from Germany, of mean understanding, of insolent manners, and of temper which, naturally savage, had now been exasperated by disease. Now and then, indeed, poor Frances might console herself for the loss of Burke's and Windham's society, by joining in the "celestial colloquy sublime" of his Majesty's Equerries.

And what was the consideration for which she was to sell herself to this slavery? A peerage in her own right? A pension of two thousand a year for life? A seventy-four for her brother in the navy? A deanery for her brother in the church? Not so. The price at which she was valued was her board, her lodging, the attendance of a man-servant, and two hundred pounds a year.

The man who, even when hard pressed by hunger, sells his birthright for a mess of pottage, is unwise. But what shall we say of him who parts with his birthright, and does not get even the pottage in return? It is not necessary to inquire whether opulence be an adequate compensation for the sacrifice of bodily and mental freedom; for Frances Burney paid for leave to be a prisoner and a menial. It was evidently understood as one of the terms of her engagement, that, while she was a member of the royal household, she was not to appear before the public as an author: and, even had there been no such understanding, her avocations were such as left *her no leisure for* any considerable intellectual effort. That her *place was incompatible* with her literary pursuits was indeed frankly acknowledged by the King when she resigned. "She has given up," he said, "five years of her pen." That during those five years she might, without painful exertion, without any exertion that would not have been a pleasure, have earned enough to buy an annuity for life much larger than the precarious salary which she received at court, is quite certain. The same income, too, which in Saint Martin's Street would have afforded her every comfort, must have been found scanty at Saint James's. We cannot venture to speak confidently of the price of millinery and jewellery; but we are greatly deceived if a lady, who had to attend Queen Charlotte on many public occasions, could possibly save a farthing out of a salary of two hundred a year. The principle of the arrangement was, in short, simply this, that Frances Burney should become a slave, and should be rewarded by being made a beggar.

With what object their Majesties brought her to their palace, we must own ourselves unable to conceive. Their object could not be to encourage her literary exertions; for they took her from a situation in which it was almost certain that she would write, and put her into a situation in which it was impossible for her to write. Their object could not be to promote her pecuniary interest; for they took her from a situation where she was likely to become rich, and put her into a situation in which she could not but continue poor. Their object could not be to obtain an eminently useful waiting maid; for it is clear that, though Miss Burney was the only woman of her time who could have described the death of Harrel, thousands might have been found more expert in tying ribands and filling snuff boxes. To grant her a pension on the civil list would have been an act of judicious liberality, honourable to the court. If this was impracticable, *the next best thing* was to let her alone. That the King and

Queen meant her nothing but kindness, we do not in the least doubt. But their kindness was the kindness of persons raised high above the mass of mankind, accustomed to be addressed with profound deference, accustomed to see all who approach them mortified by their coldness and elated by their smiles. They fancied that to be noticed by them, to be near them, to serve them, was in itself a kind of happiness; and that Frances Burney ought to be full of gratitude for being permitted to purchase, by the surrender of health, wealth, freedom, domestic affection, and literary fame, the privilege of standing behind a royal chair, and holding a pair of royal gloves.

And who can blame them? Who can wonder that princes should be under such a delusion, when they are encouraged in it by the very persons who suffer from it most cruelly? Was it to be expected that George the Third and Queen Charlotte should understand the interest of Frances Burney better, or promote it with more zeal, than herself and her father? No deception was practised. The conditions of the house of bondage were set forth with all simplicity. The hook was presented without a bait; the net was spread in sight of the bird: and the naked hook was greedily swallowed; and the silly bird made haste to entangle herself in the net.

It is not strange indeed that an invitation to court should have caused a fluttering in the bosom of an inexperienced young woman. But it was the duty of the parent to watch over the child, and to show her that on one side were only infantile vanities and chimerical hopes, on the other liberty, peace of mind, affluence, social enjoyments, honourable distinctions. Strange to say, the only hesitation was on the part of Frances. Dr. Burney was transported out of himself with delight. Not such are the raptures of a Circassian father who *has sold his* pretty daughter well to a Turkish slave-merchant.

Yet Dr. Burney was an amiable man, a man of good abilities, a man who had seen much of the world. But he seems to have thought that going to court was like going to heaven; that to see princes and princesses was a kind of beatific vision; that the exquisite felicity enjoyed by royal persons was not confined to themselves, but was communicated by some mysterious efflux or reflection to all who were suffered to stand at their toilettes, or to bear their trains. He overruled all his daughter's objections, and himself escorted her to her prison. The door closed. The key was turned. She, looking back with tender regret on all that she had left, and forward with anxiety and terror to the new life on which she was entering, was unable to speak or stand; and he went on his way homeward rejoicing in her marvellous prosperity.

And now began a slavery of five years, of five years taken from the best part of life, and wasted in menial drudgery or in recreations duller than even menial drudgery, under galling restraints and amidst unfriendly or uninteresting companions. The history of an ordinary day was this. Miss Burney had to rise and dress herself early, that she might be ready to answer the royal bell, which rang at half after seven. Till about eight she attended in the Queen's dressing room, and had the honour of lacing her august mistress's stays, and of putting on the hoop, gown, and neckhandkerchief. The morning was chiefly spent in rummaging drawers and laying fine clothes in their proper places. Then the Queen was to be powdered and dressed for the day. Twice a week her Majesty's hair was curled and craped; and this operation appears to have added a full hour to the business of the toilette. It was generally three before Miss Burney was at liberty. Then she had two hours at her own disposal. To these hours we owe great part of her Diary. At five she had to attend her colleague, Madame Schwellenberg, a hateful old toad-eater, as illiterate as a chambermaid, as proud as a whole German Chapter, rude, peevish, unable to bear solitude, unable to conduct herself with common decency in society. With this delightful associate, Frances Burney had to dine, and pass the evening. The pair generally remained together from five to eleven, and often had no other company the whole time, except during the hour from eight to nine, when the equerries came to tea. If poor Frances attempted to escape to her own apartment, and to forget her wretchedness over a book, the execrable old woman railed and stormed, and complained that she was neglected. Yet, when Frances stayed, she was constantly assailed with insolent reproaches. Literary fame was, in the eyes of the German crone, a blemish, a proof that the person who enjoyed it was meanly born, and out of the pale of good society. All her scanty stock of broken English was employed to express the contempt with which she regarded the author of Evelina and Cecilia. Frances detested cards, and indeed knew nothing about them; but she soon found that the least miserable way of passing an evening with Madame Schwellenberg was at the card-table, and consented, with patient sadness, to give hours, which might have called forth the laughter and the tears of many generations, to the king of clubs and the knave of spades. Between eleven and twelve the bell rang again. Miss Burney had to pass twenty minutes or half an hour in undressing the Queen, and was then at liberty to retire, and to dream that she was chatting with her brother by the quiet hearth in Saint Martin's Street, that she was the centre of an admiring assemblage at Mrs. Crewe's, that Burke was calling her the first woman of the age, or that Dilly was giving her a cheque for two thousand guineas.

Men, we must suppose, are less patient than women; for *we are utterly at a loss to conceive how any human being could* endure such a life, while there remained a vacant garret in Grub Street, a crossing in want of a sweeper, a parish workhouse, or a parish vault. And it was for such a life that Frances Burney had given up liberty and peace, a happy fireside, attached friends, a wide and splendid circle of acquaintance, intellectual pursuits in which she was qualified to excel, and the sure hope of what to her would have been affluence.

There is nothing new under the sun. The last great master of Attic eloquence and Attic wit has left us a forcible and touching description of the misery of a man of letters, who, lured by hopes similar to those of Frances, had entered the service of one of the magnates of Rome. "Unhappy that I am," cries the victim of his own childish ambition: "would nothing content me but that I must leave mine own pursuits and mine old companions, and the life which was without care, and the sleep which had no limit save mine own pleasure, and the walks which I was free to take where I listed, and fling myself into the lowest pit of a dungeon like this? And, O God! for what? Was there no way by which I might have enjoyed in freedom comforts even greater than those which I now earn by servitude? Like a lion which has been made so tame that men may lead him about by a thread, I am dragged up and down, with broken and humbled spirit, at the heels of those to whom, in mine own domain, I should have been an object of awe and wonder. And, worst of all, I feel that here I gain no credit, that here I give no pleasure. The talents and accomplishments, which charmed a far different circle, are here out of place. I am rude in the arts of palaces, and can ill bear comparison with those whose calling, from their youth up, has been to flatter and to sue. Have I, then, two lives, that, after I have wasted one in the service of others, there may yet remain to me a second, which I may live unto *myself?*"

Now and then, indeed, events occurred which disturbed the wretched monotony of Frances Burney's life. The court moved from Kew to Windsor, and from Windsor back to Kew. One dull colonel went out of waiting, and another dull colonel came into waiting. An impertinent servant made a blunder about tea, and caused a misunderstanding between the gentleman and the ladies. A half witted French Protestant minister talked oddly about conjugal fidelity. An unlucky member of the household mentioned a passage in the Morning Herald, reflecting on the Queen; and forthwith Madame Schwellenberg began to storm in bad English, and told him that he made her "what you call perspire!"

A more important occurrence was the King's visit to Oxford. Miss Burney went in the royal train to Nuneham, was utterly neglected there in the crowd, and could with difficulty find a servant to show the way to her bedroom, or a hairdresser to arrange her curls. She had the honour of entering Oxford in the last of a long string of carriages which formed the royal procession, of walking after the Queen all day through refectories and chapels, and of standing, half dead with fatigue and hunger, while her august mistress was seated at an excellent cold collation. At Magdalene College, Frances was left for a moment in a parlour, where she sank down on a chair. A goodnatured equerry saw that she was exhausted, and shared with her some apricots and bread, which he had wisely put into his pockets. At that moment the door opened; the Queen entered; the wearied attendants sprang up; the bread and fruit were hastily concealed. "I found," says poor Miss Burney, "that our appetites were to be supposed annihilated, at the same moment that our strength was to be invincible."

Yet Oxford, seen even under such disadvantages, "revived in her," to use her own words, "a consciousness to pleasure which had long lain nearly dormant." She forgot, during one moment, that she was a waiting maid, and felt as a woman of true genius might be expected to feel amidst venerable remains of antiquity, beautiful works of art, vast repositories of knowledge, and memorials of the illustrious dead. Had she still been what she was before her father induced her to take the most fatal step of her life, we can easily imagine what pleasure she would have derived from a visit to the noblest of English cities. She might, indeed, have been forced to travel in a hack chaise, and might not have worn so fine a gown of Chambery gauze as that in which she tottered after the royal party; but with what delight would she have then paced the cloisters of Magdalene, compared the antique gloom of Merton with the splendour of Christ Church, and looked down from the dome of the Radcliffe Library on the magnificent sea of turrets and battlements below! How gladly would learned men have laid aside for a few hours Pindar's Odes and Aristotle's Ethics, to escort the author of Cecilia from college to college! What neat little banquets would she have found set out in their monastic cells! With what eagerness would pictures, medals, and illuminated missals have been brought forth from the most mysterious cabinets for her amusement! How much she would have had to hear and to tell about Johnson, as she walked over Pembroke, and about Reynolds, in the antechapel of New College! But these indulgences were not for one who had sold herself into bondage.

About eighteen months after the visit to Oxford, another event diversified the wearisome life which Frances led at court. Warren Hastings was brought to the bar of the House of Peers. The Queen and Princesses were present when the trial commenced, and Miss Burney was permitted to attend. *During the subsequent* proceedings a day rule for the same purpose was occasionally granted to her; for the Queen took the strongest interest in the trial, and, when she could not go herself to Westminster Hall, liked to receive a report of what had passed from a person who had singular powers of observation, and who was, moreover, acquainted with some of the most distinguished managers. The portion of the Diary which relates to this celebrated proceeding is lively and picturesque. Yet we read it, we own, with pain; for it seems to us to prove that the fine understanding of Frances Burney was beginning to feel the pernicious influence of a mode of life which is as incompatible with health of mind as the air of the Pomptine marshes with health of body. From the first day she espouses the cause of Hastings with a presumptuous vehemence and acrimony quite inconsistent with the modesty and suavity of her ordinary deportment. She shudders when Burke enters the Hall at the head of the Commons. She pronounces him the cruel oppressor of an innocent man. She is at a loss to conceive how the managers can look at the defendant, and not blush. Windham comes to her from the manager's box, to offer her refreshment. "But," says she, "I could not break bread with him." Then, again, she exclaims, "Ah, Mr. Windham, how came you ever engaged in so cruel, so unjust a cause?" "Mr. Burke saw me," she says, "and he bowed with the most marked civility of manner." This, be it observed, was just after his opening speech, a speech which had produced a mighty effect, and which, certainly, no other orator that ever lived could have made. "My curtsy," she continues, "was the most ungrateful, distant, and cold; I could not do otherwise; so hurt I felt to see him the head of such a cause." Now, not only had Burke treated her with constant kindness, but the very last act which he *performed on the day on which he was turned out of the Pay Office, about four years before this trial, was to make Doctor*

Burney organist of Chelsea Hospital. When, at the Westminster election, Doctor Burney was divided between his gratitude for this favour and his Tory opinions, Burke in the noblest manner disclaimed all right to exact a sacrifice of principle. "You have little or no obligations to me," he wrote; "but if you had as many as I really wish it were in my power, as it is certainly in my desire, to lay on you, I hope you do not think me capable of conferring them, in order to subject your mind or your affairs to a painful and mischievous servitude." Was this a man to be uncivilly treated by a daughter of Doctor Burney, because she chose to differ from him respecting a vast and most complicated question, which he had studied deeply during many years, and which she had never studied at all? It is clear, from Miss Burney's own narrative, that, when she behaved so unkindly to Mr. Burke, she did not even know of what Hastings was accused. One thing, however, she must have known, that Burke had been able to convince a House of Commons, bitterly prejudiced against himself, that the charges were well founded, and that Pitt and Dundas had concurred with Fox and Sheridan, in supporting the impeachment. Surely a woman of far inferior abilities to Miss Burney might have been expected to see that this never could have happened unless there had been a strong case against the late Governor-General. And there was, as all reasonable men now admit, a strong case against him. That there were great public services to be set off against his great crimes is perfectly true. But his services and his crimes were equally unknown to the lady who so confidently asserted his perfect innocence, and imputed to his accusers, that is to say, to all the greatest men of all parties in the state, not merely error, but gross injustice and barbarity.

She had, it is true, occasionally seen Mr. Hastings, and had *found his* manners and conversation agreeable. But surely she could not be so weak as to infer from the gentleness of his deportment in a drawing-room, that he was incapable of committing a great state crime, under the influence of ambition and revenge. A silly Miss, fresh from a boarding school, might fall into such a mistake; but the woman who had drawn the character of Mr. Monckton should have known better.

The truth is that she had been too long at Court. She was sinking into a slavery worse than that of the body. The iron was beginning to enter into the soul. Accustomed during many months to watch the eye of a mistress, to receive with boundless gratitude the slightest mark of royal condescension, to feel wretched at every symptom of royal displeasure, to associate only with spirits long tamed and broken in, she was degenerating into something fit for her place. Queen Charlotte was a violent partisan of Hastings, had received presents from him, and had so far departed from the severity of her virtue as to lend her countenance to his wife, whose conduct had certainly been as reprehensible as that of any of the frail beauties who were then rigidly excluded from the English Court. The King, it was well known, took the same side. To the King and Queen all the members of the household looked submissively for guidance. The impeachment, therefore, was an atrocious persecution; the managers, were rascals; the defendant was the most deserving and the worst used man in the kingdom. This was the cant of the whole palace, from Gold Stick in Waiting, down to the Table-Deckers and Yeomen of the Silver Scullery; and Miss Burney canted like the rest, though in livelier tones, and with less bitter feelings.

The account which she has given of the King's illness contains much excellent narrative and description, and will, we

k, be as much valued by the historians of a future age as

any equal portion of Pepys' or Evelyn's Diaries. That account shows also how affectionate and compassionate her nature was. But it shows also, we must say, that her way of life was rapidly impairing her powers of reasoning and her sense of justice. We do not mean to discuss, in this place, the question, whether the views of Mr. Pitt or those of Mr. Fox respecting the regency were the more correct. It is, indeed, quite needless to discuss that question: for the censure of Miss Burney falls alike on Pitt and Fox, on majority and minority. She is angry with the House of Commons for presuming to inquire whether the King was mad or not, and whether there was a chance of his recovering his senses. "A melancholy day," she writes; "news bad both at home and abroad. At home the dear unhappy king still worse; abroad new examinations voted of the physicians. Good heavens! what an insult does this seem from Parliamentary power, to investigate and bring forth to the world every circumstance of such a malady as is ever held sacred to secrecy in the most private families! How indignant we all feel here, no words can say." It is proper to observe, that the motion which roused all this indignation at Kew was made by Mr. Pitt himself. We see, therefore, that the loyalty of the minister, who was then generally regarded as the most heroic champion of his Prince, was lukewarm indeed when compared with the boiling zeal which filled the pages of the backstairs and the women of the bedchamber. Of the Regency Bill, Pitt's own bill, Miss Burney speaks with horror. "I shuddered," she says, "to hear it named." And again, "Oh, how dreadful will be the day when that unhappy bill takes place! I cannot approve the plan of it." The truth is that Mr. Pitt, whether a wise and upright statesman or not, was a statesman; and whatever motives he might have for imposing restrictions on the regent, felt that in some way *or other* there must be some provision made for the execution of some part of the kingly office, or that no government would be left in the country. But this was a matter of which the household never thought. It never occurred, as far as we can see, to the Exons and Keepers of the Robes, that it was necessary that there should be somewhere or other a power in the state to pass laws, to preserve order, to pardon criminals, to fill up offices, to negotiate with foreign governments, to command the army and navy. Nay, these enlightened politicians, and Miss Burney among the rest, seem to have thought that any person who considered the subject with reference to the public interest, showed himself to be a bad-hearted man. Nobody wonders at this in a gentleman usher; but it is melancholy to see genius sinking into such debasement.

During more than two years after the King's recovery, Frances dragged on a miserable existence at the palace. The consolations, which had for a time mitigated the wretchedness of servitude, were one by one withdrawn. Mrs. Delany, whose society had been a great resource when the Court was at Windsor, was now dead. One of the gentlemen of the royal establishment, Colonel Digby, appears to have been a man of sense, of taste, of some reading, and of prepossessing manners. Agreeable associates were scarce in the prison house, and he and Miss Burney therefore naturally became attached to each other. She owns that she valued him as a friend; and it would not have been strange if his attentions had led her to entertain for him a sentiment warmer than friendship. He quitted the Court, and married in a way which astonished Miss Burney greatly, and which evidently wounded her feelings, and lowered him in her esteem. The palace grew duller and duller; Madame Schwellenberg became more and more savage and insolent; and now the health of poor Frances began *to give way*; and all who saw her pale face, her emaciated figure, and her feeble walk, predicted that her sufferings would soon be over.

Frances uniformly speaks of her royal mistress, and of the princesses, with respect and affection. The princesses seem to have well deserved all the praise which is bestowed on them in the Diary. They were, we doubt not, most amiable women. But "the sweet queen," as she is constantly called in these volumes, is not by any means an object of admiration to us. She had undoubtedly sense enough to know what kind of deportment suited her high station, and self-command enough to maintain that deportment invariably. She was, in her intercourse with Miss Burney, generally gracious and affable, sometimes, when displeased, cold and reserved, but never, under any circumstances, rude, peevish, or violent. She knew how to dispense, gracefully and skilfully, those little civilities which, when paid by a sovereign, are prized at many times their intrinsic value; how to pay a compliment; how to lend a book; how to ask after a relation. But she seems to have been utterly regardless of the comfort, the health, the life of her attendants, when her own convenience was concerned. Weak, feverish, hardly able to stand, Frances had still to rise before seven, in order to dress the sweet Queen, and to sit up till midnight, in order to undress the sweet Queen. The indisposition of the handmaid could not, and did not, escape the notice of her royal mistress. But the established doctrine of the Court was, that all sickness was to be considered as a pretence until it proved fatal. The only way in which the invalid could clear herself from the suspicion of malingering, as it is called in the army, was to go on lacing and unlacing, till she fell down dead at the royal feet. "This," Miss Burney wrote, when she was suffering cruelly from sickness, watching, and labour, "is by no means from hardness of heart; far *otherwise*. There is no hardness of heart in any one of them; but it is prejudice, and want of personal experience."

Many strangers sympathized with the bodily and mental sufferings of this distinguished woman. All who saw her saw that her frame was sinking, that her heart was breaking. The last, it should seem, to observe the change was her father. At length, in spite of himself, his eyes were opened. In May 1790, his daughter had an interview of three hours with him, the only long interview which they had had since he took her to Windsor in 1786. She told him that she was miserable, that she was worn with attendance and want of sleep, that she had no comfort in life, nothing to love, nothing to hope, that her family and friends were to her as though they were not, and were remembered by her as men remember the dead. From daybreak to midnight the same killing labour, the same recreations, more hateful than labour itself, followed each other without variety, without any interval of liberty and repose.

The Doctor was greatly dejected by this news; but was too good-natured a man not to say that, if she wished to resign, his house and arms were open to her. Still, however, he could not bear to remove her from the Court. His veneration for royalty amounted in truth to idolatry. It can be compared only to the grovelling superstition of those Syrian devotees who made their children pass through the fire to Moloch. When he induced his daughter to accept the place of keeper of the robes, he entertained, as she tells us, a hope that some worldly advantage or other, not set down in the contract of service, would be the result of her connection with the Court. What advantage he expected we do not know, nor did he probably know himself. But, whatever he expected, he certainly got nothing. Miss Burney had been hired for board, lodging, and two hundred a year. Board, lodging, and two hundred a year, she had duly received. We have looked carefully through the Diary, in the hope of finding some trace of those extraordinary benefactions on which the Doctor reckoned. But we can discover only a promise, never performed, of a gown: and for this promise Miss Burney was expected to return thanks, such as might have suited the beggar with whom Saint Martin, in the legend, divided his cloak. The experience of four years was, however, insufficient to dispel the illusion which had taken possession of the Doctor's mind; and, between the dear father and the sweet Queen, there seemed to be little doubt that some day or other Frances would drop down a corpse. Six months had elapsed since the interview between the parent and the daughter. The resignation was not sent in. The sufferer grew worse and worse. She took bark; but it soon ceased to produce a beneficial effect. She was stimulated with wine; she was soothed with opium; but in vain. Her breath began to fail. The whisper that she was in a decline spread through the Court. The pains in her side became so severe that she was forced to crawl from the card table of the old Fury to whom she was tethered, three or four times in an evening, for the purpose of taking hartshorn. Had she been a negro slave, a humane planter would have excused her from work. But her Majesty showed no mercy. Thrice a day the accursed bell still rang; the Queen was still to be dressed for the morning at seven, and to be dressed for the day at noon, and to be undressed at midnight.

But there had arisen, in literary and fashionable society, a general feeling of compassion for Miss Burney, and of indignation against both her father and the Queen. "Is it possible," said a great French lady to the Doctor, "that your daughter is in a situation where she is never allowed a holiday?" Horace Walpole wrote to Frances, to express his sympathy. Boswell, boiling over with good-natured rage, almost forced an entrance into the palace to see her. "My dear Ma'am, why do you stay? It won't do, Ma'am; you must resign. We can put up with it no longer. Some very violent measures, I assure you, will be taken. We shall address Dr. Burney in a body." Burke and Reynolds, though less noisy, were zealous in the same cause. Windham spoke to Dr. Burney; but found him still irresolute. "I will set the club upon him," cried Windham; "Miss Burney has some very true admirers there, and I am sure they will eagerly assist." Indeed the Burney family seem to have been apprehensive that some public affront, such as the Doctor's unpardonable folly, to use the mildest term, had richly deserved, would be put upon him. The medical men spoke out, and plainly told him that his daughter must resign or die.

At last paternal affection, medical authority, and the voice of all London crying shame, triumphed over Dr. Burney's love of courts. He determined that Frances should write a letter of resignation. It was with difficulty that, though her life was at stake, she mustered spirit to put the paper into the Queen's hands. "I could not," so runs the Diary, "summon courage to present my memorial: my heart always failed me from seeing the Queen's entire freedom from such an expectation. For though I was frequently so ill in her presence that I could hardly stand, I saw she concluded me, while life remained, inevitably hers."

At last with a trembling hand the paper was delivered. Then came the storm. Juno, as in the Æneid, delegated the work of vengeance to Alecto. The Queen was calm and gentle; but Madame Schwellenberg raved like a maniac in the incurable ward of Bedlam! Such insolence! Such ingratitude! Such folly! Would Miss Burney bring utter destruction on herself and her family? Would she throw away the inestimable advantage of royal protection? Would she part with privileges which, once relinquished, could never be regained? It was idle to talk of health and life. If people could not live in the palace, the best thing that could befall them was to die in it. The resignation was not accepted. The language of the medical men became stronger and stronger. Dr. Burney's parental fears were fully roused; and he explicitly declared, in a letter meant to be shown to the Queen, that his daughter must retire. The Schwellenberg raged like a wild cat. "A scene almost horrible ensued," says Miss Burney. "She was too much enraged for disguise, and uttered the most furious expressions of indignant contempt at our proceedings. I am sure she would gladly have confined us both in the Bastille, had England such a misery, as a fit place to bring us to ourselves, from a daring so outrageous, against imperial wishes." This passage deserves notice, as being the only one in the Diary, so far as we have observed, which shows Miss Burney to have been aware that she was a native of a free country, that she could not be pressed for a waiting-maid against her will, and that she had just as good a right to live, if she chose, in Saint Martin's Street, as Queen Charlotte had to live at Saint James's.

The Queen promised that, after the next birthday, Miss Burney should be set at liberty. But the promise was ill kept; and her Majesty showed displeasure at being reminded of it. At length Frances was informed that in a fortnight her attendance should cease. "I heard this," she says, "with a fearful presentiment I should surely never go through another fortnight, in so weak and languishing and painful a state of health. . . . As the time of separation approached, the Queen's cordiality rather diminished, and traces of internal displeasure appeared sometimes, arising from an opinion I ought rather to have struggled on, live or die, than to quit her. Yet I am sure she *saw* how poor was my own chance, except by a change in the mode of life, and at least ceased to wonder, though she could not approve." Sweet Queen! What noble candour, to admit that the undutifulness of people, who did not think the honour of adjusting her tuckers worth the sacrifice of their own lives, was, though highly criminal, not altogether unnatural.

We perfectly understand her Majesty's contempt for the lives of others where her own pleasure was concerned. But what pleasure she can have found in having Miss Burney about her, it is not so easy to comprehend. That Miss Burney was an eminently skilful keeper of the robes is not very probable. Few women, indeed, had paid less attention to dress. Now and then, in the course of five years, she had been asked to read aloud or to write a copy of verses. But better readers might easily have been found; and her verses were worse than even the Poet Laureate's Birthday Odes. Perhaps that economy, which was among her Majesty's most conspicuous virtues, had something to do with her conduct on this occasion. Miss Burney had never hinted that she expected a retiring pension; and indeed would gladly have given the little that she had for freedom. But her Majesty knew what the public thought, and what became her own dignity. She could not for very shame suffer a woman of distinguished genius, who had quitted a lucrative career to wait on her, who had served her faithfully for a pittance during five years, and whose constitution had been impaired by labour and watching to leave the court without some mark of royal liberality. George the Third, who, on all occasions where Miss Burney was concerned, seems to have behaved like an honest, good-natured gentleman, felt this, and said plainly that she was entitled to a provision. At length, in return for all the misery which she had undergone, and for the health which she had sacrificed, an annuity of one hundred pounds was granted to her, dependent on the Queen's pleasure.

Then the prison was opened, and Frances was free once more. Johnson, as Burke observed, might have added a striking page to his poem on the Vanity of Human Wishes, if he had lived to see his little Burney as she went into the palace and as she came out of it.

The pleasures, so long untasted, of liberty, of friendship, of domestic affection, were almost too acute for her shattered frame. But happy days and tranquil nights soon restored the health which the Queen's toilette and Madame Schwellenberg's card table had impaired. Kind and anxious faces surrounded the invalid. Conversation the most polished and brilliant revived her spirits. Travelling was recommended to her; and she rambled by easy journeys from cathedral to cathedral, and from watering place to watering place. She crossed the New Forest, and visited Stonehenge and Wilton, the cliffs of Lyme, and the beautiful valley of Sidmouth. Thence she journeyed by Powderham Castle, and by the ruins of Glastonbury Abbey to Bath, and from Bath, when the winter was approaching, returned well and cheerful to London. There she visited her old dungeon, and found her successor already far on the way to the grave, and kept to strict duty, from morning till midnight, with a sprained ankle and a nervous fever.

At this time England swarmed with French exiles driven from their country by the Revolution. A colony of these refugees settled at Juniper Hall, in Surrey, not far from Norbury Park, where Mr. Lock, an intimate friend of the Burney family, resided. Frances visited Norbury, and was introduced to the strangers. She had strong prejudices against them; for her Toryism was far beyond, we do not say that of Mr. Pitt, *but that of Mr. Reeves*; and the inmates of Juniper

Hall were all attached to the constitution of 1791, and were therefore more detested by the royalists of the first emigration than Petion or Marat. But such a woman as Miss Burney could not long resist the fascination of that remarkable society. She had lived with Johnson and Windham, with Mrs. Montagu and Mrs. Thrale. Yet she was forced to own that she had never heard conversation before. The most animated eloquence, the keenest observation, the most sparkling wit, the most courtly grace, were united to charm her. For Madame de Staël was there, and M. de Talleyrand. There too was M. de Narbonne, a noble representative of French aristocracy; and with M. de Narbonne was his friend and follower General D'Arblay, an honourable and amiable man, with a handsome person, frank soldierlike manners, and some taste for letters.

The prejudices which Frances had conceived against the constitutional royalists of France rapidly vanished. She listened with rapture to Talleyrand and Madame de Staël, joined with M. D'Arblay in execrating the Jacobins and in weeping for the unhappy Bourbons, took French lessons from him, fell in love with him, and married him on no better provision than a precarious annuity of one hundred pounds.

Here the Diary stops for the present. We will, therefore, bring our narrative to a speedy close, by rapidly recounting the most important events which we know to have befallen Madame D'Arblay during the latter part of her life.

M. D'Arblay's fortune had perished in the general wreck of the French Revolution; and in a foreign country his talents, whatever they may have been, could scarcely make him rich. The task of providing for the family devolved on his wife. In the year 1796, she published by subscription her third novel, Camilla. It was impatiently expected by the public; and the sum which she obtained for it was, we believe, greater than had ever at that time been received for a novel. We have heard that she cleared more than three thousand guineas. But we give this merely as a rumour. Camilla, however, never attained popularity like that which Evelina and Cecilia had enjoyed; and it must be allowed that there was a perceptible falling off, not indeed in humour or in power of portraying character, but in grace and in purity of style.

We have heard that, about this time, a tragedy by Madame D'Arblay was performed without success. We do not know whether it was ever printed; nor indeed have we had time to make any researches into its history or merits.

During the short truce which followed the treaty of Amiens, M. D'Arblay visited France. Lauriston and La Fayette represented his claims to the French government, and obtained a promise that he should be reinstated in his military rank. M. D'Arblay, however, insisted that he should never be required to serve against the countrymen of his wife. The First Consul, of course, would not hear of such a condition, and ordered the General's commission to be instantly revoked.

Madame D'Arblay joined her husband at Paris, a short time before the war of 1803 broke out, and remained in France ten years, cut off from almost all intercourse with the land of her birth. At length, when Napoleon was on his march to Moscow, she with great difficulty obtained from his ministers permission to visit her own country, in company with her son, who was a native of England. She returned in time to receive the last blessing of her father, who died in his eighty-seventh year. In 1814 she published her last novel, the Wanderer, a book which no judicious friend to her memory will attempt to draw from the oblivion into which it has justly fallen. In the same year her son Alexander was sent to Cambridge. He obtained *an honourable* place among the wranglers of his year, and was elected a fellow of Christ's College. But his reputation at the University was higher than might be inferred from his success in academical contests. His French education had not fitted him for the examinations of the Senate House; but, in pure mathematics, we have been assured by some of his competitors that he had very few equals. He went into the church, and it was thought likely that he would attain high eminence as a preacher; but he died before his mother. All that we have heard of him leads us to believe that he was such a son as such a mother deserved to have. In 1832, Madame D'Arblay published the memoirs of her father; and on the 6th of January, 1840, she died in her eighty-eighth year.

We now turn from the life of Madame D'Arblay to her writings. There can, we apprehend, be little difference of opinion as to the nature of her merit, whatever differences may exist as to its degree. She was emphatically what Johnson called her, a charactermonger. It was in the exhibition of human passions and whims that her strength lay; and in this department of art she had, we think, very distinguished skill.

But in order that we may, according to our duty as kings at arms, versed in the laws of literary precedence, marshal her to the exact seat to which she is entitled, we must carry our examination somewhat further.

There is, in one respect, a remarkable analogy between the faces and the minds of men. No two faces are alike; and yet very few faces deviate very widely from the common standard. Among the eighteen hundred thousand human beings who inhabit London, there is not one who could be taken by his acquaintance for another; yet we may walk from Paddington to Mile End without seeing one person in whom any feature is so overcharged that we turn round to stare at it. An infinite number of varieties lies between limits which are not very far asunder. The specimens which pass those limits on either side, form a very small minority.

It is the same with the characters of men. Here, too, the variety passes all enumeration. But the cases in which the deviation from the common standard is striking and grotesque, are very few. In one mind avarice predominates; in another, pride; in a third, love of pleasure; just as in one countenance the nose is the most marked feature, while in others the chief expression lies in the brow, or in the lines of the mouth. But there are very few countenances in which nose, brow, and mouth do not contribute, though in unequal degrees, to the general effect; and so there are very few characters in which one overgrown propensity makes all others utterly insignificant.

It is evident that a portrait painter, who was able only to represent faces and figures such as those which we pay money to see at fairs, would not, however spirited his execution might be, take rank among the highest artists. He must always be placed below those who have skill to seize peculiarities which do not amount to deformity. The slighter those peculiarities, the greater is the merit of the limner who can catch them and transfer them to his canvass. To paint Daniel Lambert or the living skeleton, the pig faced lady or the Siamese twins, so that nobody can mistake them, is an exploit within the reach of a sign-painter. A third-rate artist might give us the squint of Wilkes, and the depressed nose and protuberant cheeks of Gibbon. It would require a much higher degree of skill to paint two such men as Mr. Canning and Sir Thomas Lawrence, so that nobody who had ever seen them could for a moment hesitate to assign each picture to its original. Here the mere caricaturist would be quite at fault. He would find in neither face any thing on which he could lay hold for *the purpose of* making a distinction. Two ample bald

... two regular profiles, two full faces of the same ... would baffle his art; and he would be reduced to ... ...ble shift of writing their names at the foot of his ... Yet there was a great difference; and a person who ... seen them once would no more have mistaken one of ... for the other than he would have mistaken Mr. Pitt for Mr. Fox. But the difference lay in delicate lineaments and shades, reserved for pencils of a rare order.

This distinction runs through all the imitative arts. Foote's mimicry was exquisitely ludicrous, but it was all caricature. He could take off only some strange peculiarity, a stammer or a lisp, a Northumbrian burr or an Irish brogue, a stoop or a shuffle. "If a man," said Johnson, "hops on one leg, Foote can hop on one leg." Garrick, on the other hand, could seize those differences of manner and pronunciation, which, though highly characteristic, are yet too slight to be described. Foote, we have no doubt, could have made the Haymarket theatre shake with laughter by imitating a conversation between a Scotchman and a Somersetshireman. But Garrick could have imitated a conversation between two fashionable men, both models of the best breeding, Lord Chesterfield, for example, and Lord Albemarle, so that no person could doubt which was which, although no person could say that, in any point, either Lord Chesterfield or Lord Albemarle spoke or moved otherwise than in conformity with the usages of the best society.

The same distinction is found in the drama and in fictitious narrative. Highest among those who have exhibited human nature by means of dialogue, stands Shakspeare. His variety is like the variety of nature, endless diversity, scarcely any monstrosity. The characters of which he has given us an ...pression, as vivid as that which we receive from the charac... of our own associates, are to be reckoned by scores. Yet in all these scores hardly one character is to be found which deviates widely from the common standard, and which we should call very eccentric if we met it in real life. The silly notion that every man has one ruling passion, and that this clue, once known, unravels all the mysteries of his conduct, finds no countenance in the plays of Shakspeare. There man appears as he is, made up of a crowd of passions, which contend for the mastery over him, and govern him in turn. What is Hamlet's ruling passion? Or Othello's? Or Harry the Fifth's? Or Wolsey's? Or Lear's? Or Shylock's? Or Benedick's? Or Macbeth's? Or that of Cassius? Or that of Falconbridge? But we might go on for ever. Take a single example, Shylock. Is he so eager for money as to be indifferent to revenge? Or so eager for revenge as to be indifferent to money? Or so bent on both together as to be indifferent to the honour of his nation and the law of Moses? All his propensities are mingled with each other, so that, in trying to apportion to each its proper part, we find the same difficulty which constantly meets us in real life. A superficial critic may say, that hatred is Shylock's ruling passion. But how many passions have amalgamated to form that hatred? It is partly the result of wounded pride: Antonio has called him dog. It is partly the result of covetousness: Antonio has hindered him of half a million; and, when Antonio is gone, there will be no limit to the gains of usury. It is partly the result of national and religious feeling: Antonio has spit on the Jewish gabardine; and the oath of revenge has been sworn by the Jewish Sabbath. We might go through all the characters which we have mentioned, and through fifty more in the same way; for it is the constant manner of Shakspeare to represent the human mind as lying, not under the absolute dominion of one despotic propensity, but under a mixed government, in which a hundred powers balance each other.

Admirable as he was in all parts of his art, we most admire him for this, that while he has left us a greater number of striking portraits than all other dramatists put together, he has scarcely left us a single caricature.

Shakspeare has had neither equal nor second. But among the writers who, in the point which we have noticed, have approached nearest to the manner of the great master, we have no hesitation in placing Jane Austen, a woman of whom England is justly proud. She has given us a multitude of characters, all, in a certain sense, commonplace, all such as we meet every day. Yet they are all as perfectly discriminated from each other as if they were the most eccentric of human beings. There are, for example, four clergymen, none of whom we should be surprised to find in any parsonage in the kingdom, Mr. Edward Ferrars, Mr. Henry Tilney, Mr. Edmund Bertram, and Mr. Elton. They are all specimens of the upper part of the middle class. They have all been liberally educated. They all lie under the restraints of the same sacred profession. They are all young. They are all in love. Not one of them has any hobby-horse, to use the phrase of Sterne. Not one has a ruling passion, such as we read of in Pope. Who would not have expected them to be insipid likenesses of each other? No such thing. Harpagon is not more unlike to Jourdain, Joseph Surface is not more unlike to Sir Lucius O'Trigger, than every one of Miss Austen's young divines to all his reverend brethren. And almost all this is done by touches so delicate, that they elude analysis, that they defy the powers of description, and that we know them to exist only by the general effect to which they have contributed.

A line must be drawn, we conceive, between artists of this class, and those poets and novelists whose skill lies *in the exhibiting* of what Ben Jonson called humours. The words of Ben are so much to the purpose that we will quote them:

> "When some one peculiar quality
> Doth so possess a man, that it doth draw
> All his affects, his spirits, and his powers,
> In their confluxions all to run one way,
> This may be truly said to be a humour."

There are undoubtedly persons, in whom humours such as Ben describes have attained a complete ascendency. The avarice of Elwes, the insane desire of Sir Egerton Brydges for a barony to which he had no more right than to the crown of Spain, the malevolence which long meditation on imaginary wrongs generated in the gloomy mind of Bellingham, are instances. The feeling which animated Clarkson and other virtuous men against the slave-trade and slavery, is an instance of a more honourable kind.

Seeing that such humours exist, we cannot deny that they are proper subjects for the imitations of art. But we conceive that the imitation of such humours, however skilful and amusing, is not an achievement of the highest order; and, as such humours are rare in real life, they ought, we conceive, to be sparingly introduced into works which profess to be pictures of real life. Nevertheless, a writer may show so much genius in the exhibition of these humours as to be fairly entitled to a distinguished and permanent rank among classics. The chief seats of all, however, the places on the dais and under the canopy, are reserved for the few who have excelled in the difficult art of portraying characters in which no single feature is extravagantly overcharged.

If we have expounded the law soundly, we can have no difficulty in applying it to the particular case before us. Madame D'Arblay has left us scarcely any thing but humours. Almost every one of her men and women has some one propensity developed to a morbid degree. In Cecilia, for example, Mr. Delvile never opens his lips without some allusion to his own birth and station; or Mr. Briggs, without some allusion to the hoarding of money; or Mr. Hobson, without betraying the self-indulgence and self-importance of a purse-proud upstart; or Mr. Simkins, without uttering some sneaking remark for the purpose of currying favour with his customers; or Mr. Meadows, without expressing apathy and weariness of life; or Mr. Albany, without declaiming about the vices of the rich and the misery of the poor; or Mrs. Belfield, without some indelicate eulogy on her son; or Lady Margaret, without indicating jealousy of her husband. Morrice is all skipping, officious impertinence, Mr. Gosport all sarcasm, Lady Honoria all lively prattle, Miss Larolles all silly prattle. If ever Madame D'Arblay aimed at more, we do not think that she succeeded well.

We are, therefore, forced to refuse to Madame D'Arblay a place in the highest rank of art; but we cannot deny that, in the rank to which she belonged, she had few equals, and scarcely any superior. The variety of humours which is to be found in her novels is immense; and though the talk of each person separately is monotonous, the general effect is not monotony, but a very lively and agreeable diversity. Her plots are rudely constructed and improbable, if we consider them in themselves. But they are admirably framed for the purpose of exhibiting striking groups of eccentric characters, each governed by his own peculiar whim, each talking his own peculiar jargon, and each bringing out by opposition the oddities of all the rest. We will give one example out of many which occur to us. All probability is violated in order to bring Mr. Delvile, Mr. Briggs, Mr. Hobson, and Mr. Albany into a room together. But when we have them there, we soon forget probability in the exquisitely ludicrous effect which is pro-*duced by the* conflict of four old fools, each raging with a monomania of his own, each talking a dialect of his own, and each inflaming all the others anew every time he opens his mouth.

Madame D'Arblay was most successful in comedy, and indeed in comedy which bordered on farce. But we are inclined to infer from some passages, both in Cecilia and Camilla, that she might have attained equal distinction in the pathetic. We have formed this judgment, less from those ambitious scenes of distress which lie near the catastrophe of each of those novels, than from some exquisite strokes of natural tenderness which take us here and there by surprise. We would mention as examples, Mrs. Hill's account of her little boy's death in Cecilia, and the parting of Sir Hugh Tyrold and Camilla, when the honest baronet thinks himself dying.

It is melancholy to think that the whole fame of Madame D'Arblay rests on what she did during the earlier half of her life, and that every thing which she published during the forty-three years which preceded her death, lowered her reputation. Yet we have no reason to think that at the time when her faculties ought to have been in their maturity, they were smitten with any blight. In the Wanderer, we catch now and then a gleam of her genius. Even in the Memoirs of her father, there is no trace of dotage. They are very bad; but they are so, as it seems to us, not from a decay of power, but from a total perversion of power.

The truth is, that Madame D'Arblay's style underwent a gradual and most pernicious change, a change which, in degree at least, we believe to be unexampled in literary history, and of which it may be useful to trace the progress.

When she wrote her letters to Mr. Crisp, her early journals, and her first novel, her style was not indeed brilliant or energetic; but it was easy, clear, and free from all offensive faults. When she wrote Cecilia she aimed higher. She had then lived much in a circle of which Johnson was the centre; and she was herself one of his most submissive worshippers. It seems never to have crossed her mind that the style even of his best writings was by no means faultless, and that even had it been faultless, it might not be wise in her to imitate it. Phraseology which is proper in a disquisition on the Unities, or in a preface to a Dictionary, may be quite out of place in a tale of fashionable life. Old gentlemen do not criticize the reigning modes, nor do young gentlemen make love, with the balanced epithets and sonorous cadences which, on occasions of great dignity, a skilful writer may use with happy effect.

In an evil hour the author of Evelina took the Rambler for her model. This would not have been wise even if she could have imitated her pattern as well as Hawkesworth did. But such imitation was beyond her power. She had her own style. It was a tolerably good one; and might, without any violent change, have been improved into a very good one. She determined to throw it away, and to adopt a style in which she could attain excellence only by achieving an almost miraculous victory over nature and over habit. She could cease to be Fanny Burney; it was not so easy to become Samuel Johnson.

In Cecilia the change of manner began to appear. But in Cecilia the imitation of Johnson, though not always in the best taste, is sometimes eminently happy; and the passages which are so verbose as to be positively offensive, are few. There were people who whispered that Johnson had assisted his young friend, and that the novel owed all its finest passages to his hand. This was merely the fabrication of envy. Miss Burney's real excellences were as much beyond the reach of Johnson, as his real excellences were beyond her reach. He could no more have written the Masquerade scene, or the Vauxhall scene, than she could have written the Life of Cowley or the Review of Soame Jenyns. But we have not the smallest doubt that he revised Cecilia, and that he retouched the style of many passages. We know that he was in the habit of giving assistance of this kind most freely. Goldsmith, Hawkesworth, Boswell, Lord Hailes, Mrs. Williams, were among those who obtained his help. Nay, he even corrected the poetry of Mr. Crabbe, whom, we believe, he had never seen. When Miss Burney thought of writing a comedy, he promised to give her his best counsel, though he owned that he was not particularly well qualified to advise on matters relating to the stage. We therefore think it in the highest degree improbable that his little Fanny, when living in habits of the most affectionate intercourse with him, would have brought out an important work without consulting him; and, when we look into Cecilia, we see such traces of his hand in the grave and elevated passages as it is impossible to mistake. Before we conclude this article, we will give two or three examples.

When next Madame D'Arblay appeared before the world as a writer, she was in a very different situation. She would not content herself with the simple English in which Evelina had been written. She had no longer the friend, who, we are confident, had polished and strengthened the style of Cecilia. She had to write in Johnson's manner without Johnson's aid. The consequence was, that in Camilla every passage which she meant to be fine is detestable; and that the book has been saved from condemnation only by the admirable spirit and force of those scenes in which she was content to be familiar.

But there was to be a still deeper descent. After the publication of Camilla, Madame D'Arblay resided ten years at Paris. During those years there was scarcely any intercourse between France and England. It was with difficulty that a short letter *could* occasionally be transmitted. All Madame

D'Arblay's companions were French. She must have written, spoken, thought, in French. Ovid expressed his fear that a shorter exile might have affected the purity of his Latin. During a shorter exile, Gibbon unlearned his native English. Madame D'Arblay had carried a bad style to France. She brought back a style which we are really at a loss to describe. It is a sort of broken Johnsonese, a barbarous *patois*, bearing the same relation to the language of Rasselas, which the gibberish of the Negroes of Jamaica bears to the English of the House of Lords. Sometimes it reminds us of the finest, that is to say, the vilest parts, of Mr. Galt's novels; sometimes of the perorations of Exeter Hall; sometimes of the leading articles of the Morning Post. But it most resembles the puffs of Mr. Rowland and Dr. Goss. It matters not what ideas are clothed in such a style. The genius of Shakspeare and Bacon united, would not save a work so written from general derision.

It is only by means of specimens that we can enable our readers to judge how widely Madame D'Arblay's three styles differed from each other.

The following passage was written before she became intimate with Johnson. It is from Evelina.

"His son seems weaker in his understanding, and more gay in his temper; but his gaiety is that of a foolish overgrown schoolboy, whose mirth consists in noise and disturbance. He disdains his father for his close attention to business and love of money, though he seems himself to have no talents, spirit, or generosity to make him superior to either. His chief delight appears to be in tormenting and ridiculing his sisters, who in return most cordially despise him. Miss Branghton, the eldest daughter, is by no means ugly; but looks proud, ill-tempered, and conceited. She hates the city, though without knowing why; for it is easy to discover she has lived nowhere else. Miss Polly Branghton is rather pretty, very foolish, very ignorant, very giddy, and, I believe, very good-natured."

*This is* not a fine style, but simple, perspicuous, and agreeable. We now come to Cecilia, written during Miss

Burney's intimacy with Johnson; and we leave it to our readers to judge whether the following passage was not at least corrected by his hand.

"It is rather an imaginary than an actual evil, and though a deep wound to pride, no offence to morality. Thus have I laid open to you my whole heart, confessed my perplexities, acknowledged my vainglory, and exposed with equal sincerity the sources of my doubts and the motives of my decision. But now, indeed, how to proceed I know not. The difficulties which are yet to encounter I fear to enumerate, and the petition I have to urge I have scarce courage to mention. My family, mistaking ambition for honour, and rank for dignity, have long planned a splendid connection for me, to which, though my invariable repugnance has stopped any advances, their wishes and their views immoveably adhere. I am but too certain they will now listen to no other. I dread, therefore, to make a trial where I despair of success. I know not how to risk a prayer with those who may silence me by a command."

Take now a specimen of Madame D'Arblay's later style. This is the way in which she tells us that her father, on his journey back from the Continent, caught the rheumatism.

"He was assaulted, during his precipitated return, by the rudest fierceness of wintry elemental strife; through which, with bad accommodations and innumerable accidents, he became a prey to the merciless pangs of the acutest spasmodic rheumatism, which barely suffered him to reach his home, ere, long and piteously, it confined him, a tortured prisoner, to his bed. Such was the check that almost instantly curbed, though it could not subdue, the rising pleasure of his hopes of entering upon a new species of existence — that of an approved man of letters; for it was on the bed of sickness, exchanging the light wines of France, Italy, and Germany, for the black and loathsome potions of the Apothecaries' Hall, writhed by darting stitches, and burning with fiery fever, that he felt the full force of that sublunary equipoise that seems evermore to hang suspended over the attainment of long-sought and uncommon felicity, just as it is ripening to burst forth with enjoyment!"

Here is a second passage from Evelina.

"Mrs. Selwyn is very kind and attentive to me. She is extremely clever. Her understanding, indeed, may be called masculine; but unfortunately her manners deserve the same epithet; for, in studying to acquire the knowledge of the other sex, she has lost all the softness of her own. In regard to myself, however, as I have neither courage nor inclination to argue with her, I have never been personally hurt at her want of gentleness, a virtue which nevertheless seems so essential a part of the female character, that I find myself more awkward and less at ease with a woman who wants it than I do with a man."

This is a good style of its kind; and the following passage from Cecilia is also in a good style, though not in a faultless one. We say with confidence, either Sam Johnson or the Devil.

"Even the imperious Mr. Delvile was more supportable here than in London. Secure in his own castle, he looked round him with a pride of power and possession which softened while it swelled him. His superiority was undisputed: his will was without control. He was not, as in the great capital of the kingdom, surrounded by competitors. No rivalry disturbed his peace; no equality mortified his greatness. All he saw were either vassals of his power, or guests bending to his pleasure. He abated, therefore, considerably the stern gloom of his haughtiness, and soothed his proud mind by the courtesy of condescension."

We will stake our reputation for critical sagacity on this, that no such paragraph as that which we have last quoted, can be found in any of Madame D'Arblay's works except Cecilia. Compare with it the following example of her later style.

"If beneficence be judged by the happiness which it diffuses, whose claim, by that proof, shall stand higher than that of Mrs. Montagu, from the munificence with which she celebrated her annual festival for those hapless artificers who perform the most abject offices of any authorized calling, in being the active guardians of our blazing hearths? Not to vain glory, then, but to kindness of heart, should be adjudged the publicity of that superb charity which made its jetty objects, for one bright morning, cease to consider themselves as degraded outcasts from all society."

We add one or two shorter samples. Sheridan refused to permit his lovely wife to sing in public, and was warmly *praised* on this account by Johnson.

"*The last of* men," says Madame D'Arblay, "was Doctor

Johnson to have abetted squandering the delicacy of integrity by nullifying the labours of talents."

The Club, Johnson's Club, did itself no honour by rejecting on political grounds two distinguished men, one a Tory, the other a Whig. Madame D'Arblay tells the story thus: "A similar ebullition of political rancour with that which so difficultly had been conquered for Mr. Canning foamed over the ballot box to the exclusion of Mr. Rogers."

An offence punishable with imprisonment is, in this language, an offence "which produces incarceration." To be starved to death is "to sink from inanition into nonentity." Sir Isaac Newton is "the developer of the skies in their embodied movements;" and Mrs. Thrale, when a party of clever people sat silent, is said to have been "provoked by the dulness of a taciturnity that, in the midst of such renowned interlocutors, produced as narcotic a torpor as could have been caused by a dearth the most barren of all human faculties." In truth, it is impossible to look at any page of Madame D'Arblay's later works without finding flowers of rhetoric like these. Nothing in the language of those jargonists at whom Mr. Gosport laughed, nothing in the language of Sir Sedley Clarendel, approaches this new Euphuism.

It is from no unfriendly feeling to Madame D'Arblay's memory that we have expressed ourselves so strongly on the subject of her style. On the contrary, we conceive that we have really rendered a service to her reputation. That her later works were complete failures, is a fact too notorious to be dissembled: and some persons, we believe, have consequently taken up a notion that she was from the first an overrated writer, and that she had not the powers which were necessary to maintain her on the eminence on which good luck and fashion had placed her. We believe, on the contrary, that her early *popularity* was no more than the just reward of distinguished merit, and would never have undergone an eclipse, if she had only been content to go on writing in her mother tongue. If she failed when she quitted her own province, and attempted to occupy one in which she had neither part nor lot, this reproach is common to her with a crowd of distinguished men. Newton failed when he turned from the courses of the stars, and the ebb and flow of the ocean, to apocalyptic seals and vials. Bentley failed when he turned from Homer and Aristophanes, to edite the Paradise Lost. Inigo failed when he attempted to rival the Gothic churches of the fourteenth century. Wilkie failed when he took it into his head that the Blind Fiddler and the Rent Day were unworthy of his powers, and challenged competition with Lawrence as a portrait painter. Such failures should be noted for the instruction of posterity; but they detract little from the permanent reputation of those who have really done great things.

Yet one word more. It is not only on account of the intrinsic merit of Madame D'Arblay's early works that she is entitled to honourable mention. Her appearance is an important epoch in our literary history. Evelina was the first tale written by a woman, and purporting to be a picture of life and manners, that lived or deserved to live. The Female Quixote is no exception. That work has undoubtedly great merit, when considered as a wild satirical harlequinade; but, if we consider it as a picture of life and manners, we must pronounce it more absurd than any of the romances which it was designed to ridicule.

Indeed, most of the popular novels which preceded Evelina were such as no lady would have written; and many of them were such as no lady could without confusion own that she had read. The very name of novel was held in horror among religious people. In decent families, which did not profess ex*traordinary* sanctity, there was a strong feeling against all such works. Sir Anthony Absolute, two or three years before Evelina appeared, spoke the sense of the great body of sober fathers and husbands, when he pronounced the circulating library an evergreen tree of diabolical knowledge. This feeling, on the part of the grave and reflecting, increased the evil from which it had sprung. The novelist having little character to lose, and having few readers among serious people, took without scruple liberties which in our generation seem almost incredible.

Miss Burney did for the English novel what Jeremy Collier did for the English drama; and she did it in a better way. She first showed that a tale might be written in which both the fashionable and the vulgar life of London might be exhibited with great force, and with broad comic humour, and which yet should not contain a single line inconsistent with rigid morality, or even with virgin delicacy. She took away the reproach which lay on a most useful and delightful species of composition. She vindicated the right of her sex to an equal share in a fair and noble province of letters. Several accomplished women have followed in her track. At present, the novels which we owe to English ladies form no small part of the literary glory of our country. No class of works is more honourably distinguished by fine observation, by grace, by delicate wit, by pure moral feeling. Several among the successors of Madame D'Arblay have equalled her; two, we think, have surpassed her. But the fact that she has been surpassed gives her an additional claim to our respect and gratitude; for, in truth, we owe to her not only Evelina, Cecilia, and Camilla, but also Mansfield Park and the Absentee.

# THE LIFE AND WRITINGS OF ADDISON.
## (July, 1843.)

*The Life of Joseph Addison.* By Lucy Aikin. 2 vols. 8vo. London: 1843.

Some reviewers are of opinion that a lady who dares to publish a book renounces by that act the franchises appertaining to her sex, and can claim no exemption from the utmost rigour of critical procedure. From that opinion we dissent. We admit, indeed, that in a country which boasts of many female writers, eminently qualified by their talents and acquirements to influence the public mind, it would be of most pernicious consequence that inaccurate history or unsound philosophy should be suffered to pass uncensured, merely because the offender chanced to be a lady. But we conceive that, on such occasions, a critic would do well to imitate the courteous Knight who found himself compelled by duty to keep the lists against Bradamante. He, we are told, defended successfully the cause of which he was the champion; but, before the fight began, exchanged Balisarda for a less deadly sword, of which he carefully blunted the point and edge.[*]

Nor are the immunities of sex the only immunities which Miss Aikin may rightfully plead. Several of her works, and especially the very pleasing Memoirs of the Reign of James the First, have fully entitled her to the privileges enjoyed by good writers. One of those privileges we hold to be this, that such writers, when, either from the unlucky choice of a sub-

[*] Orlando Furioso, xlv. 68.

ject, or from the indolence too often produced by success, they happen to fail, shall not be subjected to the severe discipline which it is sometimes necessary to inflict upon dunces and impostors, but shall merely be reminded by a gentle touch, like that with which the Laputan flapper roused his dreaming lord, that it is high time to wake.

Our readers will probably infer from what we have said that Miss Aikin's book has disappointed us. The truth is, that she is not well acquainted with her subject. No person who is not familiar with the political and literary history of England during the reigns of William the Third, of Anne, and of George the First, can possibly write a good life of Addison. Now, we mean no reproach to Miss Aikin, and many will think that we pay her a compliment, when we say that her studies have taken a different direction. She is better acquainted with Shakspeare and Raleigh, than with Congreve and Prior; and is far more at home among the ruffs and peaked beards of Theobald's, than among the Steenkirks and flowing periwigs which surrounded Queen Anne's tea table at Hampton. She seems to have written about the Elizabethan age, because she had read much about it; she seems, on the other hand, to have read a little about the age of Addison, because she had determined to write about it. The consequence is that she has had to describe men and things without having either a correct or a vivid idea of them, and that she has often fallen into errors of a very serious kind. The reputation which Miss Aikin has justly earned stands so high, and the charm of Addison's letters is so great, that a second edition of this work may probably be required. If so, we hope that every paragraph will be revised, and that every date and fact about which there can be the smallest doubt will be carefully verified.

To Addison himself we are bound by a sentiment as much

like affection as any sentiment can be, which is inspired by one who has been sleeping a hundred and twenty years in Westminster Abbey. We trust, however, that this feeling will not betray us into that abject idolatry which we have often had occasion to reprehend in others, and which seldom fails to make both the idolater and the idol ridiculous. A man of genius and virtue is but a man. All his powers cannot be equally developed; nor can we expect from him perfect self-knowledge. We need not, therefore, hesitate to admit that Addison has left us some compositions which do not rise above mediocrity, some heroic poems hardly equal to Parnell's, some criticism as superficial as Dr. Blair's, and a tragedy not very much better than Dr. Johnson's. It is praise enough to say of a writer that, in a high department of literature, in which many eminent writers have distinguished themselves, he has had no equal; and this may with strict justice be said of Addison.

As a man, he may not have deserved the adoration which he received from those who, bewitched by his fascinating society, and indebted for all the comforts of life to his generous and delicate friendship, worshipped him nightly, in his favourite temple at Button's. But, after full inquiry and impartial reflection, we have long been convinced that he deserved as much love and esteem as can be justly claimed by any of our infirm and erring race. Some blemishes may undoubtedly be detected in his character; but the more carefully it is examined, the more will it appear, to use the phrase of the old anatomists, sound in the noble parts, free from all taint of perfidy, of cowardice, of cruelty, of ingratitude, of envy. Men may easily be named, in whom some particular good disposition has been more conspicuous than in Addison. But the just harmony of qualities, the exact temper between the stern and the humane virtues, the habitual observance of every law, not only of moral rectitude, but of moral grace and dignity, distinguish him from all men who have been tried by equally strong temptations, and about whose conduct we possess equally full information.

His father was the Reverend Lancelot Addison, who, though eclipsed by his more celebrated son, made some figure in the world, and occupies with credit two folio pages in the Biographia Britannica. Lancelot was sent up, as a poor scholar, from Westmoreland to Queen's College, Oxford, in the time of the Commonwealth; made some progress in learning, became, like most of his fellow students, a violent Royalist, lampooned the heads of the University, and was forced to ask pardon on his bended knees. When he had left college, he earned a humble subsistence by reading the liturgy of the fallen Church to the families of those sturdy squires whose manor houses were scattered over the Wild of Sussex. After the Restoration, his loyalty was rewarded with the post of chaplain to the garrison of Dunkirk. When Dunkirk was sold to France, he lost his employment. But Tangier had been ceded by Portugal to England as part of the marriage portion of the Infanta Catharine; and to Tangier Lancelot Addison was sent. A more miserable situation can hardly be conceived. It was difficult to say whether the unfortunate settlers were more tormented by the heats or by the rains, by the soldiers within the wall or by the Moors without it. One advantage the chaplain had. He enjoyed an excellent opportunity of studying the history and manners of Jews and Mahometans; and of this opportunity he appears to have made excellent use. On his return to England, after some years of banishment, he published an interesting volume on the Polity and Religion of Barbary, and another on the Hebrew Customs and the State of Rabbinical Learning. He rose to eminence *in his* profession, and became one of the royal chaplains, a Doctor of Divinity, Archdeacon of Salisbury, and Dean of Lichfield. It is said that he would have been made a bishop after the Revolution, if he had not given offence to the government by strenuously opposing, in the Convocation of 1689, the liberal policy of William and Tillotson.

In 1672, not long after Dr. Addison's return from Tangier, his son Joseph was born. Of Joseph's childhood we know little. He learned his rudiments at schools in his father's neighbourhood, and was then sent to the Charter House. The anecdotes which are popularly related about his boyish tricks do not harmonize very well with what we know of his riper years. There remains a tradition that he was the ringleader in a barring out, and another tradition that he ran away from school and hid himself in a wood, where he fed on berries and slept in a hollow tree, till after a long search he was discovered and brought home. If these stories be true, it would be curious to know by what moral discipline so mutinous and enterprising a lad was transformed into the gentlest and most modest of men.

We have abundant proof that, whatever Joseph's pranks may have been, he pursued his studies vigorously and successfully. At fifteen he was not only fit for the university, but carried thither a classical taste, and a stock of learning which would have done honour to a Master of Arts. He was entered at Queen's College, Oxford; but he had not been many months there, when some of his Latin verses fell by accident into the hands of Dr. Lancaster, Dean of Magdalene College. The young scholar's diction and versification were already such as veteran professors might envy. Dr. Lancaster was desirous to serve a boy of such promise; nor was an opportunity long wanting. The Revolution had just taken place; and nowhere had it been hailed with more delight than at *Magdalene College.* That great and opulent corporation had been treated by James, and by his Chancellor, with an insolence and injustice which, even in such a Prince and in such a Minister, may justly excite amazement; and which had done more than even the prosecution of the Bishops to alienate the Church of England from the throne. A president, duly elected, had been violently expelled from his dwelling: a Papist had been set over the society by a royal mandate: the Fellows who, in conformity with their oaths, had refused to submit to this usurper, had been driven forth from their quiet cloisters and gardens, to die of want or to live on charity. But the day of redress and retribution speedily came. The intruders were ejected: the venerable House was again inhabited by its old inmates: learning flourished under the rule of the wise and virtuous Hough; and with learning was united a mild and liberal spirit too often wanting in the princely colleges of Oxford. In consequence of the troubles through which the society had passed, there had been no valid election of new members during the year 1688. In 1689, therefore, there was twice the ordinary number of vacancies; and thus Dr. Lancaster found it easy to procure for his young friend admittance to the advantages of a foundation then generally esteemed the wealthiest in Europe.

At Magdalene, Addison resided during ten years. He was, at first, one of those scholars who are called Demies; but was subsequently elected a fellow. His college is still proud of his name; his portrait still hangs in the hall; and strangers are still told that his favourite walk was under the elms which fringe the meadow on the banks of the Cherwell. It is said, and is highly probable, that he was distinguished among his fellow students by the delicacy of his feelings, by the shyness of his manners, and by the assiduity with which he often prolonged his studies far into the night. It is certain that his reputation for ability and learning stood high. Many years later, the ancient Doctors of Magdalene continued to talk in their common room of his boyish compositions, and expressed their sorrow that no copy of exercises so remarkable had been preserved.

It is proper, however, to remark, that Miss Aikin has committed the error, very pardonable in a lady, of overrating Addison's classical attainments. In one department of learning, indeed, his proficiency was such as it is hardly possible to overrate. His knowledge of the Latin poets, from Lucretius and Catullus down to Claudian and Prudentius, was singularly exact and profound. He understood them thoroughly, entered into their spirit, and had the finest and most discriminating perception of all their peculiarities of style and melody; nay, he copied their manner with admirable skill, and surpassed, we think, all their British imitators who had preceded him, Buchanan and Milton alone excepted. This is high praise; and beyond this we cannot with justice go. It is clear that Addison's serious attention, during his residence at the university, was almost entirely concentrated on Latin poetry, and that, if he did not wholly neglect other provinces of ancient literature, he vouchsafed to them only a cursory glance. He does not appear to have attained more than an ordinary acquaintance with the political and moral writers of Rome; nor was his own Latin prose by any means equal to his Latin verse. His knowledge of Greek, though doubtless such as was, in his time, thought respectable at Oxford, was evidently less than that which many lads now carry away every year from Eton and Rugby. A minute examination of his works, if we had time to make such an examination, would fully bear out these remarks. We will briefly advert to a few of the facts on which our judgment is grounded.

Great praise is due to the Notes which Addison appended *to his version of* the second and third books of the Metamorphoses. Yet those notes, while they show him to have been, in his own domain, an accomplished scholar, show also how confined that domain was. They are rich in apposite references to Virgil, Statius, and Claudian; but they contain not a single illustration drawn from the Greek poets. Now, if, in the whole compass of Latin literature, there be a passage which stands in need of illustration drawn from the Greek poets, it is the story of Pentheus in the third book of the Metamorphoses. Ovid was indebted for that story to Euripides and Theocritus, both of whom he has sometimes followed minutely. But neither to Euripides nor to Theocritus does Addison make the faintest allusion; and we, therefore, believe that we do not wrong him by supposing that he had little or no knowledge of their works.

His travels in Italy, again, abound with classical quotations, happily introduced; but scarcely one of those quotations is in prose. He draws more illustrations from Ausonius and Manilius than from Cicero. Even his notions of the political and military affairs of the Romans seem to be derived from poets and poetasters. Spots made memorable by events which have changed the destinies of the world, and which have been worthily recorded by great historians, bring to his mind only scraps of some ancient versifier. In the gorge of the Apennines he naturally remembers the hardships which Hannibal's army endured, and proceeds to cite, not the authentic narrative of Polybius, not the picturesque narrative of Livy, but the languid hexameters of Silius Italicus. On the banks of the Rubicon he never thinks of Plutarch's lively description, or of the stern conciseness of the Commentaries, or of those letters to Atticus which so forcibly express the alternations of hope and fear in a sensitive mind at a great crisis. His only authority for the events of the civil war is Lucan.

All the best ancient works of art at Rome and Florence are

Greek. Addison saw them, however, without recalling one single verse of Pindar, of Callimachus, or of the Attic dramatists; but they brought to his recollection innumerable passages of Horace, Juvenal, Statius, and Ovid.

The same may be said of the Treatise on Medals. In that pleasing work we find about three hundred passages extracted with great judgment from the Roman poets: but we do not recollect a single passage taken from any Roman orator or historian; and we are confident that not a line is quoted from any Greek writer. No person, who had derived all his information on the subject of medals from Addison, would suspect that the Greek coins were in historical interest equal, and in beauty of execution far superior to those of Rome.

If it were necessary to find any further proof that Addison's classical knowledge was confined within narrow limits, that proof would be furnished by his Essay on the Evidences of Christianity. The Roman poets throw little or no light on the literary and historical questions which he is under the necessity of examining in that Essay. He is, therefore, left completely in the dark; and it is melancholy to see how helplessly he gropes his way from blunder to blunder. He assigns, as grounds for his religious belief, stories as absurd as that of the Cock-Lane ghost, and forgeries as rank as Ireland's Vortigern, puts faith in the lie about the Thundering Legion, is convinced that Tiberius moved the senate to admit Jesus among the gods, and pronounces the letter of Agbarus King of Edessa to be a record of great authority. Nor were these errors the effects of superstition; for to superstition Addison was by no means prone. The truth is that he was writing about what he did not understand.

Miss Aikin has discovered a letter, from which it appears that, while Addison resided at Oxford, he was one of several writers whom the booksellers engaged to make an English version of Herodotus; and she infers that he must have been a good Greek scholar. We can allow very little weight to this argument, when we consider that his fellow-labourers were to have been Boyle and Blackmore. Boyle is remembered chiefly as the nominal author of the worst book on Greek history and philology that ever was printed; and this book, bad as it is, Boyle was unable to produce without help. Of Blackmore's attainments in the ancient tongues, it may be sufficient to say that, in his prose, he has confounded an aphorism with an apophthegm, and that when, in his verse, he treats of classical subjects, his habit is to regale his readers with four false quantities to a page.

It is probable that the classical acquirements of Addison were of as much service to him as if they had been more extensive. The world generally gives its admiration, not to the man who does what nobody else even attempts to do, but to the man who does best what multitudes do well. Bentley was so immeasurably superior to all the other scholars of his time that very few among them could discover his superiority. But the accomplishment in which Addison excelled his contemporaries was then, as it is now, highly valued and assiduously cultivated at all English seats of learning. Every body who had been at a public school had written Latin verses; many had written such verses with tolerable success, and were quite able to appreciate, though by no means able to rival, the skill with which Addison imitated Virgil. His lines on the Barometer and the Bowling Green were applauded by hundreds, to whom the Dissertation on the Epistles of Phalaris was as unintelligible as the hieroglyphics on an obelisk.

Purity of style, and an easy flow of numbers, are common to all Addison's Latin poems. Our favourite piece is the Battle of the Cranes and Pygmies; for in that piece we discern a gleam of the fancy and humour which many years later enlivened thousands of breakfast tables. Swift boasted that he was never known to steal a hint; and he certainly owed as little to his predecessors as any modern writer. Yet we cannot help suspecting that he borrowed, perhaps unconsciously, one of the happiest touches in his Voyage to Lilliput from Addison's verses. Let our readers judge.

"The Emperor," says Gulliver, "is taller by about the breadth of my nail than any of his court, which alone is enough to strike an awe into the beholders."

About thirty years before Gulliver's travels appeared, Addison wrote these lines:

> "Jamque acies inter medias sese arduus infert
> Pygmeadum ductor, qui, majestate verendus,
> Incessuque gravis, reliquos supereminet omnes
> Mole gigantea, mediamque exsurgit in ulnam."

The Latin poems of Addison were greatly and justly admired both at Oxford and Cambridge, before his name had ever been heard by the wits who thronged the coffee-houses round Drury-Lane theatre. In his twenty-second year, he ventured to appear before the public as a writer of English verse. He addressed some complimentary lines to Dryden, who, after many triumphs and many reverses, had at length reached a secure and lonely eminence among the literary men of that age. Dryden appears to have been much gratified by the young scholar's praise; and an interchange of civilities and good offices followed. Addison was probably introduced by Dryden to Congreve, and was certainly presented by Congreve to Charles Montague, who was then Chancellor of the Exchequer, and leader of the Whig party in the House of Commons.

At this time Addison seemed inclined to devote himself to poetry. He published a translation of part of the fourth Georgic, Lines to King William, and other performances of equal value, that is to say, of no value at all. But in those days, the public was in the habit of receiving with applause pieces which would now have little chance of obtaining the Newdigate prize, or the Seatonian prize. And the reason is obvious. The heroic couplet was then the favourite measure. The art of arranging words in that measure, so that the lines may flow smoothly, that the accents may fall correctly, that the rhymes may strike the ear strongly, and that there may be a pause at the end of every distich, is an art as mechanical as that of mending a kettle, or shoeing a horse, and may be learned by any human being who has sense enough to learn any thing. But, like other mechanical arts, it was gradually improved by means of many experiments and many failures. It was reserved for Pope to discover the trick, to make himself complete master of it, and to teach it to every body else. From the time when his Pastorals appeared, heroic versification became matter of rule and compass; and, before long, all artists were on a level. Hundreds of dunces who never blundered on one happy thought or expression were able to write reams of couplets which, as far as euphony was concerned, could not be distinguished from those of Pope himself, and which very clever writers of the reign of Charles the Second, Rochester, for example, or Marvel, or Oldham, would have contemplated with admiring despair.

Ben Jonson was a great man, Hoole a very small man. But Hoole, coming after Pope, had learned how to manufacture decasyllable verses, and poured them forth by thousands and tens of thousands, all as well turned, as smooth, and as like each other as the blocks which have passed through Mr. Brunel's mill in the dockyard at Portsmouth. Ben's heroic couplets resemble blocks rudely hewn out by an unpractised hand, with a blunt hatchet. Take as a specimen his translation of a celebrated passage in the Æneid:

> "This child our parent earth, stirr'd up with spite
> Of all the gods, brought forth, and, as some write
> She was last sister of that giant race
> That sought to scale Jove's court, right swift of pace,
> And swifter far of wing, a monster vast
> And dreadful. Look, how many plumes are placed
> On her huge corpse, so many waking eyes
> Stick underneath, and, which may stranger rise
> In the report, as many tongues she wears."

Compare with these jagged misshapen distichs the neat fabric which Hoole's machine produces in unlimited abundance. We take the first lines on which we open in his version of Tasso. They are neither better nor worse than the rest:

> "O thou, whoe'er thou art, whose steps are led,
> By choice or fate, these lonely shores to tread,
> No greater wonders east or west can boast
> Than yon small island on the pleasing coast.
> If e'er thy sight would blissful scenes explore,
> The current pass, and seek the further shore."

Ever since the time of Pope there has been a glut of lines of this sort; and we are now as little disposed to admire a man for being able to write them, as for being able to write his name. But in the days of William the Third such versification was rare; and a rhymer who had any skill in it passed for a great poet, just as in the dark ages a person who could write his name passed for a great clerk. Accordingly, Duke, Stepney, Granville, Walsh, and others whose only title to fame was that they said in tolerable metre what might have been as well said in prose, or what was not worth saying at all, were honoured with marks of distinction which ought to be reserved for genius. With these Addison must have ranked, if he had not earned true and lasting glory by performances which very little resembled his juvenile poems.

Dryden was now busied with Virgil, and obtained from Addison a critical preface to the Georgics. In return for this service, and for other services of the same kind, the veteran poet, in the postscript to the translation of the Æneid, complimented his young friend with great liberality, and indeed with more liberality than sincerity. He affected to be afraid that his own performance would not sustain a comparison with the version of the fourth Georgic, by "the most ingenious Mr. Addison of Oxford." "After his bees," added Dryden, "my latter swarm is scarcely worth the hiving."

The time had now arrived when it was necessary for Addison to choose a calling. Every thing seemed to point his course towards the clerical profession. His habits were regular, his opinions orthodox. His college had large ecclesiastical preferment in its gift, and boasts that it has given at least one bishop to almost every see in England. Dr. Lancelot Addison held an honourable place in the Church, and had set his heart on seeing his son a clergyman. It is clear, from some expressions in the young man's rhymes, that his intention was to take orders. But Charles Montague interfered. Montague had first brought himself into notice by verses, well timed and not contemptibly written, but never, we think, rising above mediocrity. Fortunately for himself, and for his country, he early quitted poetry, in which he could never have attained a rank as high as that of Dorset or Rochester, and turned his mind to official and parliamentary business. It is written that the ingenious person, who undertook to instruct Rasselas, prince of Abyssinia, in the art of flying, ascended an eminence, waved his wings, sprang into the air, and instantly dropped into the lake. But it is added that the wings, which were unable to support him through the sky, bore him up effectually as soon as he was in the water. This is no bad type of the fate of Charles Montague, and of men like him. When he attempted to soar into the regions of poetical invention, he altogether failed; but, as soon as he had descended from his ethereal elevation into a lower and grosser element, his talents instantly raised him above the mass. He became a distinguished financier, debater, courtier, and party leader. He still retained his fondness for the pursuits of his early days; but he showed that fondness, not by wearying the public with his own feeble performances, but by discovering and encouraging literary excellence in others. A crowd of wits and poets, who would easily have vanquished him as competitor, revered him as a judge and a patron. In his plans for the encouragement of learning, he was cordially supported by the ablest and most virtuous of his colleagues, the Lord Chancellor Somers. Though both these great statesmen had a sincere love of letters, it was not solely from a love of letters that they were desirous to enlist youths of high intellectual qualifications in the public service. The Revolution had altered the whole system of government. Before that event, the press had been controlled by censors, and the Parliament had sat only two months in eight years. Now the press was free, and had begun to exercise unprecedented influence on the public mind. Parliament met annually and sat long. The chief power in the State had passed to the House of Commons. At such a conjuncture, it was natural that literary and oratorical talents should rise in value. There was danger that a Government which neglected such talents might be subverted by them. It was, therefore, a profound and enlightened policy which led Montague and Somers to attach such talents to the Whig party, by the strongest ties both of interest and of gratitude.

It is remarkable that, in a neighbouring country, we have recently seen similar effects follow from similar causes. The Revolution of July 1830 established representative government in France. The men of letters instantly rose to the highest importance in the state. At the present moment most of the persons whom we see at the head both of the Administration and of the Opposition have been Professors, Historians, Journalists, Poets. The influence of the literary class in England, during the generation which followed the Revolution, was great; but by no means so great as it has lately been in France. For, in England, the aristocracy of intellect had to contend with a powerful and deeply-rooted aristocracy of a very different kind. France has no Somersets and Shrewsburies to keep down her Addisons and Priors.

It was in the year 1699, when Addison had just completed his twenty-seventh year, that the course of his life was finally determined. Both the great chiefs of the Ministry were kindly disposed towards him. In political opinions he already was, what he continued to be through life, a firm, though a moderate Whig. He had addressed the most polished and vigorous of his early English lines to Somers, and had dedicated to Montague a Latin poem, truly Virgilian, both in style and rhythm, on the peace of Ryswick. The wish of the young poet's great friends was, it should seem, to employ him in the service of the crown abroad. But an intimate knowledge of the French language was a qualification indispensable to a diplomatist; and this qualification Addison had not acquired. It was, therefore, thought desirable that he should pass some time on the Continent in preparing himself for official employment. His own means were not such as would enable him to travel: but a pension of three hundred pounds a-year was procured for him by the interest of the Lord Chancellor. It seems to have been apprehended that some difficulty might be started by the rulers of Magdalene College. But the Chancellor of the Exchequer wrote in the strongest terms to Hough. The State — such was the purport of Montague's letter — could not, at that time, spare to the Church such a man as Addison. Too many high civil posts were already occupied by adventurers, who, destitute of every liberal art and sentiment, at once pillaged and disgraced the country which they pretended to serve. It had become necessary to recruit for the public service from a very different class, from that class of which Addison was the representative. The close of the Minister's letter was remarkable. "I am called," he said, "an enemy of the Church. But I will never do it any other injury than keeping Mr. Addison out of it."

This interference was successful; and, in the summer of 1699, Addison, made a rich man by his pension, and still retaining his fellowship, quitted his beloved Oxford, and set out on his travels. He crossed from Dover to Calais, proceeded to Paris, and was received there with great kindness and politeness by a kinsman of his friend Montague, Charles Earl of Manchester, who had just been appointed Ambassador to the Court of France. The Countess, a Whig and a toast, was probably as gracious as her lord; for Addison long retained an agreeable recollection of the impression which she at this time made on him, and, in some lively lines written on the glasses of the Kit Cat club, described the envy which her cheeks, glowing with the genuine bloom of England, had excited among the painted beauties of Versailles.

Lewis the Fourteenth was at this time expiating the vices of his youth by a devotion which had no root in reason, and bore no fruit of charity. The servile literature of France had changed its character to suit the changed character of the prince. No book appeared that had not an air of sanctity. Racine, who was just dead, had passed the close of his life in writing sacred dramas; and Dacier was seeking for the Athanasian mysteries in Plato. Addison described this state of things in a short but lively and graceful letter to Montague. Another letter, written about the same time to the Lord Chancellor, conveyed the strongest assurances of gratitude and attachment. "The only return I can make to your Lordship," said Addison, "will be to apply myself entirely to my business." With this view he quitted Paris and repaired to Blois, a place where it was supposed that the French language was spoken in its highest purity, and where not a single Englishman could be found. Here he passed some months pleasantly and profitably. Of his way of life at Blois, one of his associates, an Abbé named Philippeaux, gave an account to Joseph Spence. If this account is to be trusted, Addison studied much, mused much, talked little, had fits of absence, and either had no love affairs, or was too discreet to confide them to the Abbé. A man who, even when surrounded by fellow countrymen and fellow students, had always been remarkably shy and silent, was not likely to be loquacious in a foreign tongue, and among foreign companions. But it is clear from Addison's letters, some of which were long after published in the Guardian, that, while he appeared to be absorbed in his own meditations, he was really observing French society with that keen and sly, yet not ill-natured side glance, which was peculiarly his own.

From Blois he returned to Paris; and, having now mastered the French language, found great pleasure in the society of French philosophers and poets. He gave an account, in a letter to Bishop Hough, of two highly interesting conversations, one with Malbranche, the other with Boileau. Malbranche expressed great partiality for the English, and extolled the genius of Newton, but shook his head when Hobbes was mentioned, and was indeed so unjust as to call the author of the Leviathan a poor silly creature. Addison's modesty restrained him from fully relating, in his letter, the circumstances of his introduction to Boileau. Boileau, having survived the friends and rivals of his youth, old, deaf, and melancholy, lived in retirement, seldom went either to Court or to the Academy, and was almost inaccessible to strangers.

Of the English and of English literature he knew nothing. He had hardly heard the name of Dryden. Some of our countrymen, in the warmth of their patriotism, have asserted that this ignorance must have been affected. We own that we see no ground for such a supposition. English literature was to the French of the age of Lewis the Fourteenth what German literature was to our own grandfathers. Very few, we suspect, of the accomplished men who, sixty or seventy years ago, used to dine in Leicester Square with Sir Joshua, or at Streatham with Mrs. Thrale, had the slightest notion that Wieland was one of the first wits and poets, and Lessing, beyond all dispute, the first critic in Europe. Boileau knew just as little about the Paradise Lost, and about Absalom and Ahitophel; but he had read Addison's Latin poems, and admired them greatly. They had given him, he said, quite a new notion of the state of learning and taste among the English. Johnson will have it that these praises were insincere. "Nothing," says he, "is better known of Boileau than that he had an injudicious and peevish contempt of modern Latin; and therefore his profession of regard was probably the effect of his civility rather than approbation." Now, nothing is better known of Boileau than that he was singularly sparing of compliments. We do not remember that either friendship or fear ever induced him to bestow praise on any composition which he did not approve. On literary questions, his caustic, disdainful, and self-confident spirit rebelled against that authority to which every thing else in France bowed down. He had the spirit to tell Lewis the Fourteenth firmly, and even rudely, that his Majesty knew nothing about poetry, and admired verses which were detestable. What was there in Addison's position that could induce the satirist, whose stern and fastidious temper had been the dread of two generations, to turn sycophant for the first and last time? Nor was Boileau's contempt of modern Latin either injudicious or peevish. He thought, indeed, that no poem of the first order would ever be written in a dead language. And did he think amiss? Has not the experience of centuries confirmed his opinion? Boileau also thought it probable that, in the best modern Latin, a writer of the Augustan age would have detected ludicrous improprieties. And who can think otherwise? What modern scholar can honestly declare that he sees the smallest impurity in the style of Livy? Yet is it not certain that, in the style of Livy, Pollio, whose taste had been formed on the banks of the Tiber, detected the inelegant idiom of the Po? Has any modern scholar understood Latin better than Frederic the Great understood French? Yet is it not notorious that Frederic the Great, after reading, speaking, writing French, and nothing but French, during more than half a century, after unlearning his mother tongue in order to learn French, after living familiarly during many years with French associates, could not, to the last, compose in French, without imminent risk of committing some mistake which would have moved a smile in the literary circles of Paris? Do we believe that Erasmus and Fracastorius wrote Latin as well as Dr. Robertson and Sir Walter Scott wrote English? And are there not in the Dissertation on India, the last of Dr. Robertson's works, in Waverley, in Marmion, Scotticisms at which a London apprentice would laugh? But does it follow, because we think thus, that we can find nothing to admire in the noble alcaics of Gray, or in the playful elegiacs of Vincent Bourne? Surely not. Nor was Boileau so ignorant or tasteless as to be incapable of appreciating good modern Latin. In the very letter to which Johnson alludes, Boileau says — "Ne croyez pas pourtant que je veuille par là blâmer les vers Latins que vous m'avez envoyés d'un de vos illustres académiciens. Je les ai trouvés fort beaux, et dignes de Vida et de Sannazar, mais non pas d'Horace et de Virgile." Several poems, in modern Latin, have been praised by Boileau quite as liberally as it was his habit to praise any thing. He says, for example, of the Père Fraguier's epigrams, that Catullus seems to have come to life again. But the best proof that Boileau did not feel the undiscerning contempt for modern Latin verses which has been imputed to him, is, that he wrote and published Latin verses in several metres. Indeed it happens, curiously enough, that the most severe censure ever pronounced by him on modern Latin is conveyed in Latin hexameters. We allude to the fragment which begins —

"Quid numeris iterum me balbutire Latinis,
Longe Alpes citra natum de patre Sicambro,
Musa, jubes?"

For these reasons we feel assured that the praise which Boileau bestowed on the *Machinæ Gesticulantes*, and the *Gerano-Pygmæomachia*, was sincere. He certainly opened himself to Addison with a freedom which was a sure indication of esteem. Literature was the chief subject of conversation. The old man talked on his favourite theme much and well, indeed, as his young hearer thought, incomparably well. Boileau had undoubtedly some of the qualities of a great critic. He wanted imagination; but he had strong sense. His literary code was formed on narrow principles; but in applying it, he showed great judgment and penetration. In mere style, abstracted from the ideas of which style is the garb, his taste was excellent. He was well acquainted with the great Greek writers; and, though unable fully to appreciate their creative genius, admired the majestic simplicity of their manner, and had learned from them to despise bombast and tinsel. It is easy, we think, to discover, in the Spectator and the Guardian, traces of the influence, in part salutary and in part pernicious, which the mind of Boileau had on the mind of Addison.

While Addison was at Paris, an event took place which made that capital a disagreeable residence for an Englishman and a Whig. Charles, second of the name, King of Spain, died; and bequeathed his dominions to Philip, Duke of Anjou, a younger son of the Dauphin. The King of France, in direct violation of his engagements both with Great Britain and with the States General, accepted the bequest on behalf of his grandson. The house of Bourbon was at the summit of human grandeur. England had been outwitted, and found herself in a situation at once degrading and perilous. The people of France, not presaging the calamities by which they were destined to expiate the perfidy of their sovereign, went mad with pride and delight. Every man looked as if a great estate had just been left him. "The French conversation," said Addison, "begins to grow insupportable; that which was before the vainest nation in the world is now worse than ever." Sick of the arrogant exultation of the Parisians, and probably foreseeing that the peace between France and England could not be of long duration, he set off for Italy.

In December 1700* he embarked at Marseilles. As he glided along the Ligurian coast, he was delighted by the sight of myrtles and olive trees, which retained their verdure under the winter solstice. Soon, however, he encountered one of the black storms of the Mediterranean. The captain of the ship gave up all for lost, and confessed himself to a capuchin who happened to be on board. The English heretic, in the mean time, fortified himself against the terrors of death with

* It is strange that Addison should, in the first line of his travels, have misdated his departure from Marseilles by a whole year, and still more strange that this slip of the pen, which throws the whole narrative into inextricable confusion, should have been repeated in a succession of editions, *and never detected* by Tickell or by Hurd.

devotions of a very different kind. How strong an impression this perilous voyage made on him, appears from the ode, "How are thy servants blest, O Lord!" which was long after published in the Spectator. After some days of discomfort and danger, Addison was glad to land at Savona, and to make his way, over mountains where no road had yet been hewn out by art, to the city of Genoa.

At Genoa, still ruled by her own Doge, and by the nobles whose names were inscribed on her Book of Gold, Addison made a short stay. He admired the narrow streets overhung by long lines of towering palaces, the walls rich with frescoes, the gorgeous temple of the Annunciation, and the tapestries whereon were recorded the long glories of the house of Doria. Thence he hastened to Milan, where he contemplated the Gothic magnificence of the cathedral with more wonder than pleasure. He passed Lake Benacus while a gale was blowing, and saw the waves raging as they raged when Virgil looked upon them. At Venice, then the gayest spot in Europe, the traveller spent the Carnival, the gayest season of the year, in the midst of masques, dances, and serenades. Here he was at once diverted and provoked, by the absurd dramatic pieces which then disgraced the Italian stage. To one of those pieces, however, he was indebted for a valuable hint. He was present when a ridiculous play on the death of Cato was performed. Cato, it seems, was in love with a daughter of Scipio. The lady had given her heart to Cæsar. The rejected lover determined to destroy himself. He appeared seated in his library, a dagger in his hand, a Plutarch and a Tasso before him; and, in this position, he pronounced a soliloquy before he struck the blow. We are surprised that so remarkable a circumstance as this should have escaped the notice of all Addison's biographers. There cannot, we conceive, be the smallest doubt that this scene, in spite of its absurdities and anachronisms, struck the traveller's imagination, and suggested to him the thought of bringing Cato on the English stage. It is well known that about this time he began his tragedy, and that he finished the first four acts before he returned to England.

On his way from Venice to Rome, he was drawn some miles out of the beaten road, by a wish to see the smallest independent state in Europe. On a rock where the snow still lay, though the Italian spring was now far advanced, was perched the little fortress of San Marino. The roads which led to the secluded town were so bad that few travellers had ever visited it, and none had ever published an account of it. Addison could not suppress a goodnatured smile at the simple manners and institutions of this singular community. But he observed, with the exultation of a Whig, that the rude mountain tract which formed the territory of the republic swarmed with an honest, healthy, and contented peasantry, while the rich plain which surrounded the metropolis of civil and spiritual tyranny was scarcely less desolate than the uncleared wilds of America.

At Rome Addison remained on his first visit only long enough to catch a glimpse of St. Peter's and of the Pantheon. His haste is the more extraordinary because the Holy Week was close at hand. He has given no hint which can enable us to pronounce why he chose to fly from a spectacle which every year allures from distant regions persons of far less taste and sensibility than his. Possibly, travelling, as he did, at the charge of a Government distinguished by its enmity to the Church of Rome, he may have thought that it would be imprudent in him to assist at the most magnificent rite of that Church. Many eyes would be upon him; and he might find it difficult to behave in such a manner as to give offence neither to his patrons in England, nor to those among whom he resided. Whatever his motives may have been, he turned his back on the most august and affecting ceremony which is known among men, and posted along the Appian way to Naples.

Naples was then destitute of what are now, perhaps, its chief attractions. The lovely bay and the awful mountain were indeed there. But a farmhouse stood on the theatre of Herculaneum, and rows of vines grew over the streets of Pompeii. The temples of Pæstum had not indeed been hidden from the eye of man by any great convulsion of nature; but strange to say, their existence was a secret even to artists and antiquaries. Though situated within a few hours' journey of a great capital, where Salvator had not long before painted, and where Vico was then lecturing, those noble remains were as little known to Europe as the ruined cities overgrown by the forests of Yucatan. What was to be seen at Naples Addison saw. He climbed Vesuvius, explored the tunnel of Posilipo, and wandered among the vines and almond trees of Capreæ. But neither the wonders of nature, nor those of art, could so occupy his attention as to prevent him from noticing, though cursorily, the abuses of the government and the misery of the people. The great kingdom which had just descended to Philip the Fifth, was in a state of paralytic dotage. Even Castile and Aragon were sunk in wretchedness. Yet, compared with the Italian dependencies of the Spanish crown, Castile and Aragon might be called prosperous. It is clear that all the observations which Addison made in Italy tended to confirm him in the political opinions which he had adopted at home. To the last, he always spoke of foreign travel as the best cure for Jacobitism. In his Freeholder, the Tory foxhunter asks what travelling is good for, except to teach a man to jabber French, and to talk against passive obedience.

*Naples,* Addison returned to Rome by sea, along

the coast which his favourite Virgil had celebrated. The felucca passed the headland where the oar and trumpet were placed by the Trojan adventurers on the tomb of Misenus, and anchored at night under the shelter of the fabled promontory of Circe. The voyage ended in the Tiber, still overhung with dark verdure, and still turbid with yellow sand, as when it met the eyes of Æneas. From the ruined port of Ostia, the stranger hurried to Rome; and at Rome he remained during those hot and sickly months when, even in the Augustan age, all who could make their escape fled from mad dogs and from streets black with funerals, to gather the first figs of the season in the country. It is probable that, when he, long after, poured forth in verse his gratitude to the Providence which had enabled him to breathe unhurt in tainted air, he was thinking of the August and September which he passed at Rome.

It was not till the latter end of October that he tore himself away from the masterpieces of ancient and modern art which are collected in the city so long the mistress of the world. He then journeyed northward, passed through Sienna, and for a moment forgot his prejudices in favour of classic architecture as he looked on the magnificent cathedral. At Florence he spent some days with the Duke of Shrewsbury, who, cloyed with the pleasures of ambition, and impatient of its pains, fearing both parties, and loving neither, had determined to hide in an Italian retreat talents and accomplishments which, if they had been united with fixed principles and civil courage, might have made him the foremost man of his age. These days, we are told, passed pleasantly; and we can easily believe it. For Addison was a delightful companion when he was at his ease; and the Duke, though he seldom forgot that he was a Talbot, had the invaluable art of putting at ease all who came near him.

Addison gave some time to Florence, and especially to the sculptures in the Museum, which he preferred even to those of the Vatican. He then pursued his journey through a country in which the ravages of the last war were still discernible, and in which all men were looking forward with dread to a still fiercer conflict. Eugene had already descended from the Rhætian Alps, to dispute with Catinat the rich plain of Lombardy. The faithless ruler of Savoy was still reckoned among the allies of Lewis. England had not yet actually declared war against France: but Manchester had left Paris; and the negotiations which produced the Grand Alliance against the House of Bourbon were in progress. Under such circumstances, it was desirable for an English traveller to reach neutral ground without delay. Addison resolved to cross Mont Cenis. It was December; and the road was very different from that which now reminds the stranger of the power and genius of Napoleon. The winter, however, was mild; and the passage was, for those times, easy. To this journey Addison alluded when, in the ode which we have already quoted, he said that for him the Divine goodness had warmed the hoary Alpine hills.

It was in the midst of the eternal snow that he composed his Epistle to his friend Montague, now Lord Halifax. That Epistle, once widely renowned, is now known only to curious readers, and will hardly be considered by those to whom it is known as in any perceptible degree heightening Addison's fame. It is, however, decidedly superior to any English composition which he had previously published. Nay, we think it quite as good as any poem in heroic metre which appeared during the interval between the death of Dryden and the publication of the Essay on Criticism. It contains passages as good as the second-rate passages of Pope, and would have added to the reputation of Parnell or Prior.

But, whatever be the literary merits or defects of the Epistle, it undoubtedly does honour to the principles and spirit of the author. Halifax had now nothing to give. He had fallen from power, had been held up to obloquy, had been impeached by the House of Commons, and, though his Peers had dismissed the impeachment, had, as it seemed, little chance of ever again filling high office. The Epistle, written at such a time, is one among many proofs that there was no mixture of cowardice or meanness in the suavity and moderation which distinguished Addison from all the other public men of those stormy times.

At Geneva, the traveller learned that a partial change of ministry had taken place in England, and that the Earl of Manchester had become Secretary of State. Manchester exerted himself to serve his young friend. It was thought advisable that an English agent should be near the person of Eugene in Italy; and Addison, whose diplomatic education was now finished, was the man selected. He was preparing to enter on his honourable functions, when all his prospects were for a time darkened by the death of William the Third.

Anne had long felt a strong aversion, personal, political, and religious, to the Whig party. That aversion appeared in the first measures of her reign. Manchester was deprived of the seals, after he had held them only a few weeks. Neither Somers nor Halifax was sworn of the Privy Council. Addison shared the fate of his three patrons. His hopes of employment in the public service were at an end; his pension was stopped; and it was necessary for him to support himself by his own exertions. He became tutor to a young English traveller, and appears to have rambled with his pupil over great part of Switzerland and Germany. At this time he wrote his pleasing treatise on Medals. It was not published till after his death; but several *distinguished* scholars saw the manuscript, and gave just praise to the grace of the style, and to the learning and ingenuity evinced by the quotations.

From Germany Addison repaired to Holland, where he learned the melancholy news of his father's death. After passing some months in the United Provinces, he returned about the close of the year 1703 to England. He was there cordially received by his friends, and introduced by them into the Kit Cat Club, a society in which were collected all the various talents and accomplishments which then gave lustre to the Whig party.

Addison was, during some months after his return from the Continent, hard pressed by pecuniary difficulties. But it was soon in the power of his noble patrons to serve him effectually. A political change, silent and gradual, but of the highest importance, was in daily progress. The accession of Anne had been hailed by the Tories with transports of joy and hope; and for a time it seemed that the Whigs had fallen never to rise again. The throne was surrounded by men supposed to be attached to the prerogative and to the Church; and among these none stood so high in the favour of the sovereign as the Lord Treasurer Godolphin and the Captain General Marlborough.

The country gentlemen and country clergymen had fully expected that the policy of these ministers would be directly opposed to that which had been almost constantly followed by William; that the landed interest would be favoured at the expense of trade; that no addition would be made to the funded debt; that the privileges conceded to Dissenters by the late King would be curtailed, if not withdrawn; that the war with France, if there must be such a war, would, on our part, be almost entirely naval; and that the Government would avoid close connections with foreign powers, and, above all, *with Holland.*

But the country gentlemen and country clergymen were fated to be deceived, not for the last time. The prejudices and passions which raged without control in vicarages, in cathedral closes, and in the manor-houses of foxhunting squires, were not shared by the chiefs of the ministry. Those statesmen saw that it was both for the public interest, and for their own interest, to adopt a Whig policy, at least as respected the alliances of the country and the conduct of the war. But, if the foreign policy of the Whigs were adopted, it was impossible to abstain from adopting also their financial policy. The natural consequences followed. The rigid Tories were alienated from the Government. The votes of the Whigs became necessary to it. The votes of the Whigs could be secured only by further concessions; and further concessions the Queen was induced to make.

At the beginning of the year 1704, the state of parties bore a close analogy to the state of parties in 1826. In 1826, as in 1704, there was a Tory ministry divided into two hostile sections. The position of Mr. Canning and his friends in 1826 corresponded to that which Marlborough and Godolphin occupied in 1704. Nottingham and Jersey were, in 1704, what Lord Eldon and Lord Westmoreland were in 1826. The Whigs of 1704 were in a situation resembling that in which the Whigs of 1826 stood. In 1704, Somers, Halifax, Sunderland, Cowper, were not in office. There was no avowed coalition between them and the moderate Tories. It is probable that no direct communication tending to such a coalition had yet taken place; yet all men saw that such a coalition was inevitable, nay, that it was already half formed. Such, or nearly such, was the state of things when tidings arrived of the great battle fought at Blenheim on the 13th August, 1704. By the Whigs the news was hailed with transports of joy and pride. *No fault, no cause of quarrel, could be remembered* by them against the Commander whose genius had, in one day, changed the face of Europe, saved the Imperial throne, humbled the House of Bourbon, and secured the Act of Settlement against foreign hostility. The feeling of the Tories was very different. They could not indeed, without imprudence, openly express regret at an event so glorious to their country; but their congratulations were so cold and sullen as to give deep disgust to the victorious general and his friends.

Godolphin was not a reading man. Whatever time he could spare from business he was in the habit of spending at Newmarket or at the card table. But he was not absolutely indifferent to poetry; and he was too intelligent an observer not to perceive that literature was a formidable engine of political warfare, and that the great Whig leaders had strengthened their party, and raised their character, by extending a liberal and judicious patronage to good writers. He was mortified, and not without reason, by the exceeding badness of the poems which appeared in honour of the battle of Blenheim. One of these poems has been rescued from oblivion by the exquisite absurdity of three lines.

> "Think of two thousand gentlemen at least,
> And each man mounted on his capering beast;
> Into the Danube they were pushed by shoals."

Where to procure better verses the Treasurer did not know. He understood how to negotiate a loan, or remit a subsidy: he was also well-versed in the history of running horses and fighting cocks; but his acquaintance among the poets was very small. He consulted Halifax; but Halifax affected to decline the office of adviser. He had, he said, done his best, when he had power, to encourage men whose abilities and acquirements might do honour to their country. Those times were over. Other maxims had prevailed. Merit was suffered to pine in obscurity; and the public money was squandered on the undeserving. "I do know," he added, "a gentleman who would celebrate the battle in a manner worthy of the subject: but I will not name him." Godolphin, who was expert at the soft answer which turneth away wrath, and who was under the necessity of paying court to the Whigs, gently replied that there was too much ground for Halifax's complaints, but that what was amiss should in time be rectified, and that in the mean time the services of a man such as Halifax had described should be liberally rewarded. Halifax then mentioned Addison, but, mindful of the dignity as well as of the pecuniary interest of his friend, insisted that the Minister should apply in the most courteous manner to Addison himself; and this Godolphin promised to do.

Addison then occupied a garret up three pair of stairs, over a small shop in the Haymarket. In this humble lodging he was surprised, on the morning which followed the conversation between Godolphin and Halifax, by a visit from no less a person than the Right Honourable Henry Boyle, then Chancellor of the Exchequer, and afterwards Lord Carleton. This highborn minister had been sent by the Lord Treasurer as ambassador to the needy poet. Addison readily undertook the proposed task, a task which, to so good a Whig, was probably a pleasure. When the poem was little more than half finished, he showed it to Godolphin, who was delighted with it, and particularly with the famous similitude of the Angel. Addison was instantly appointed to a Commissionership with about two hundred pounds a-year, and was assured that this appointment was only an earnest of greater favours.

The Campaign came forth, and was as much admired by the public as by the Minister. It pleases us less on the whole than the Epistle to Halifax. Yet it undoubtedly ranks high among the *poems* which appeared during the interval between the death of Dryden and the dawn of Pope's genius. The chief merit of the Campaign, we think, is that which was noticed by Johnson, the manly and rational rejection of fiction. The first great poet whose works have come down to us sang of war long before war became a science or a trade. If, in his time, there was enmity between two little Greek towns, each poured forth its crowd of citizens, ignorant of discipline, and armed with implements of labour rudely turned into weapons. On each side appeared conspicuous a few chiefs, whose wealth had enabled them to procure good armour, horses, and chariots, and whose leisure had enabled them to practise military exercises. One such chief, if he were a man of great strength, agility, and courage, would probably be more formidable than twenty common men; and the force and dexterity with which he hurled his spear might have no inconsiderable share in deciding the event of the day. Such were probably the battles with which Homer was familiar. But Homer related the actions of men of a former generation, of men who sprang from the Gods, and communed with the Gods face to face, of men, one of whom could with ease hurl rocks which two sturdy hinds of a later period would be unable even to lift. He therefore naturally represented their martial exploits as resembling in kind, but far surpassing in magnitude, those of the stoutest and most expert combatants of his own age. Achilles, clad in celestial armour, drawn by celestial coursers, grasping the spear which none but himself could raise, driving all Troy and Lycia before him, and choking Scamander with dead, was only a magnificent exaggeration of the real hero, who, strong, fearless, accustomed to the use of weapons, guarded by a shield and helmet of the best Sidonian fabric, and whirled along by horses of Thessalian breed, struck down with his own right after foe. In all rude societies similar notions are found. There are at this day countries where the Lifeguardsman Shaw would be considered as a much greater warrior than the Duke of Wellington. Buonaparte loved to describe the astonishment with which the Mamelukes looked at his diminutive figure. Mourad Bey, distinguished above all his fellows by his bodily strength, and by the skill with which he managed his horse and his sabre, could not believe that a man who was scarcely five feet high, and rode like a butcher, was the greatest soldier in Europe.

Homer's descriptions of war had therefore as much truth as poetry requires. But truth was altogether wanting to the performances of those who, writing about battles which had scarcely any thing in common with the battles of his times, servilely imitated his manner. The folly of Silius Italicus, in particular, is positively nauseous. He undertook to record in verse the vicissitudes of a great struggle between generals of the first order: and his narrative is made up of the hideous wounds which these generals inflicted with their own hands. Asdrubal flings a spear which grazes the shoulder of the consul Nero; but Nero sends his spear into Asdrubal's side. Fabius slays Thuris and Butes and Maris and Arses, and the long-haired Adherbes, and the gigantic Thylis, and Sapharus and Monæsus, and the trumpeter Morinus. Hannibal runs Perusinus through the groin with a stake, and breaks the backbone of Telesinus with a huge stone. This detestable fashion was copied in modern times, and continued to prevail down to the age of Addison. Several versifiers had described William turning thousands to flight by his single prowess, and dyeing the Boyne with Irish blood. Nay, so estimable a writer as John Philips, the author of the Splendid Shilling, represented Marlborough as having won the battle of Blenheim merely by strength of muscle and skill in fence. The following lines may serve as an example:

"Churchill, viewing where
The violence of Tallard most prevailed,
Came to oppose his slaughtering arm. With speed
Precipitate he rode, urging his way
O'er hills of gasping heroes, and fallen steeds
Rolling in death. Destruction, grim with blood,
Attends his furious course. Around his head
The glowing balls play innocent, while he
With dire impetuous sway deals fatal blows
Among the flying Gauls. In Gallic blood
He dyes his reeking sword, and strews the ground
With headless ranks. What can they do? Or how
Withstand his wide-destroying sword?"

Addison, with excellent sense and taste, departed from this ridiculous fashion. He reserved his praise for the qualities which made Marlborough truly great, energy, sagacity, military science. But, above all, the poet extolled the firmness of that mind which, in the midst of confusion, uproar, and slaughter, examined and disposed every thing with the serene wisdom of a higher intelligence.

Here it was that he introduced the famous comparison of Marlborough to an Angel guiding the whirlwind. We will not dispute the general justice of Johnson's remarks on this passage. But we must point out one circumstance which appears to have escaped all the critics. The extraordinary effect which this simile produced when it first appeared, and which to the following generation seemed inexplicable, is doubtless to be chiefly attributed to a line which most readers now regard as a feeble parenthesis,

"Such as, of late, o'er pale Britannia pass'd."

Addison spoke, not of a storm, but of the storm. The great tempest of November 1703, the only tempest which in our latitude has equalled the rage of a tropical hurricane, had a dreadful recollection in the minds of all men. No other t was ever in this country the occasion of a parliamentary address or of a public fast. Whole fleets had been cast away. Large mansions had been blown down. One Prelate had been buried beneath the ruins of his Palace. London and Bristol had presented the appearance of cities just sacked. Hundreds of families were still in mourning. The prostrate trunks of large trees, and the ruins of houses, still attested, in all the southern counties, the fury of the blast. The popularity which the simile of the angel enjoyed among Addison's contemporaries, has always seemed to us to be a remarkable instance of the advantage which, in rhetoric and poetry, the particular has over the general.

Soon after the Campaign, was published Addison's Narrative of his Travels in Italy. The first effect produced by this Narrative was disappointment. The crowd of readers who expected politics and scandal, speculations on the projects of Victor Amadeus, and anecdotes about the jollities of convents and the amours of cardinals and nuns, were confounded by finding that the writer's mind was much more occupied by the war between the Trojans and Rutulians than by the war between France and Austria; and that he seemed to have heard no scandal of later date than the gallantries of the Empress Faustina. In time, however, the judgment of the many was overruled by that of the few; and, before the book was reprinted, it was so eagerly sought that it sold for five times the original price. It is still read with pleasure: the style is pure and flowing; the classical quotations and allusions are numerous and happy; and we are now and then charmed by that singularly humane and delicate humour in which Addison excelled all men. Yet this agreeable work, even when considered merely as the history of a literary tour, may justly be censured on account of its faults of omission. We have already said that, though rich in extracts from the Latin poets, it contains scarcely any references to the Latin orators and historians. We must add that it contains little, or rather no information, respecting the history and literature of modern Italy. To the best of our remembrance, Addison does not mention Dante, Petrarch, Boccaccio, Boiardo, Berni, Lorenzo de' Medici, or Machiavelli. He coldly tells us, that at Ferrara he saw the tomb of Ariosto, and that at Venice he heard the gondoliers sing verses of Tasso. But for Tasso and Ariosto he cared far less than for Valerius Flaccus and Sidonius Apollinaris. The gentle flow of the Ticin brings a line of Silius to his mind. The sulphurous steam of Albula suggests to him several passages of Martial. But he has not a word to say of the illustrious dead of Santa Croce; he crosses the wood of Ravenna without recollecting the Spectre Huntsman, and wanders up and down Rimini without one thought of Francesca. At Paris, he had eagerly sought an introduction to Boileau; but he seems not to have been at all aware that at Florence he was in the vicinity of a poet with whom Boileau could not sustain a comparison, of the greatest lyric poet of modern times, of Vincenzio Filicaja. This is the more remarkable, because Filicaja was the favourite poet of the accomplished Somers, under whose protection Addison travelled, and to whom the account of the Travels is dedicated. The truth is, that Addison knew little, and cared less, about the literature of modern Italy. His favourite models were Latin. His favourite critics were French. Half the Tuscan poetry that he had read seemed to him monstrous, and the other half tawdry.

His Travels were followed by the lively Opera of Rosamond. This piece was ill set to music, and therefore failed on the stage; but it completely succeeded in print, and is indeed excellent in its kind. The smoothness with which the verses glide, and the elasticity with which they bound, is, to y pleasing. We are inclined to think that if Addison had left heroic couplets to Pope, and blank verse to Rowe, and had employed himself in writing airy and spirited songs, his reputation as a poet would have stood far higher than it now does. Some years after his death, Rosamond was set to new music by Doctor Arne; and was performed with complete success. Several passages long retained their popularity, and were daily sung, during the latter part of George the Second's reign, at all the harpsichords in England.

While Addison thus amused himself, his prospects, and the prospects of his party, were constantly becoming brighter and brighter. In the spring of 1705, the ministers were freed from the restraint imposed by a House of Commons, in which Tories of the most perverse class had the ascendency. The elections were favourable to the Whigs. The coalition which had been tacitly and gradually formed was now openly avowed. The Great Seal was given to Cowper. Somers and Halifax were sworn of the Council. Halifax was sent in the following year to carry the decorations of the order of the garter to the Electoral Prince of Hanover, and was accompanied on this honourable mission by Addison, who had just been made Undersecretary of State. The Secretary of State under whom Addison first served was Sir Charles Hedges, a Tory. But Hedges was soon dismissed to make room for the most vehement of Whigs, Charles, Earl of Sunderland. In every department of the state, indeed, the High Churchmen were compelled to give place to their opponents. At the close of 1707, the Tories who still remained in office strove to rally, with Harley at their head. But the attempt, though favoured by the Queen, who had always been a Tory at heart, and who had now quarrelled with the Duchess of Marlborough, was unsuccessful. The time was not yet. The Captain General was at the *height of* popularity and glory. The Low Church party had a majority in Parliament. The country squires and rectors, though occasionally uttering a savage growl, were for the most part in a state of torpor, which lasted till they were roused into activity, and indeed into madness, by the prosecution of Sacheverell. Harley and his adherents were compelled to retire. The victory of the Whigs was complete. At the general election of 1708, their strength in the House of Commons became irresistible; and, before the end of that year, Somers was made Lord President of the Council, and Wharton Lord Lieutenant of Ireland.

Addison sat for Malmsbury in the House of Commons which was elected in 1708. But the House of Commons was not the field for him. The bashfulness of his nature made his wit and eloquence useless in debate. He once rose, but could not overcome his diffidence, and ever after remained silent. Nobody can think it strange that a great writer should fail as a speaker. But many, probably, will think it strange that Addison's failure as a speaker should have had no unfavourable effect on his success as a politician. In our time, a man of high rank and great fortune might, though speaking very little and very ill, hold a considerable post. But it would now be inconceivable that a mere adventurer, a man who, when out of office, must live by his pen, should in a few years become successively Undersecretary of State, chief Secretary for Ireland, and Secretary of State, without some oratorical talent. Addison, without high birth, and with little property, rose to a post which Dukes, the heads of the great houses of Talbot, Russell, and Bentinck, have thought it an honour to fill. Without opening his lips in debate, he rose to a post, the highest that Chatham or Fox ever reached. And this he did before he had been nine years in Parliament. We must look for the explanation of this seeming miracle to the peculiar circumstances in which that generation was placed.

During the interval which elapsed between the time when the Censorship of the Press ceased, and the time when parliamentary proceedings began to be freely reported, literary talents were, to a public man, of much more importance, and oratorical talents of much less importance, than in our time. At present, the best way of giving rapid and wide publicity to a fact or an argument is to introduce that fact or argument into a speech made in Parliament. If a political tract were to appear superior to the Conduct of the Allies, or to the best numbers of the Freeholder, the circulation of such a tract would be languid indeed when compared with the circulation of every remarkable word uttered in the deliberations of the legislature. A speech made in the House of Commons at four in the morning is on thirty thousand tables before ten. A speech made on the Monday is read on the Wednesday by multitudes in Antrim and Aberdeenshire. The orator, by the help of the shorthand writer, has to a great extent superseded the pamphleteer. It was not so in the reign of Anne. The best speech could then produce no effect except on those who heard it. It was only by means of the press that the opinion of the public without doors could be influenced; and the opinion of the public without doors could not but be of the highest importance in a country governed by parliaments, and indeed at that time governed by triennial parliaments. The pen was therefore a more formidable political engine than the tongue. Mr. Pitt and Mr. Fox contended only in Parliament. But Walpole and Pulteney, the Pitt and Fox of an earlier period, had not done half of what was necessary, when they sat down amidst the acclamations of the House of Commons. They had still to plead their cause before the country, and this they could do only by means of the press. Their works are now forgotten. But it is certain that there were in Grub Street few more assiduous scribblers of

Thoughts, Letters, Answers, Remarks, than these two great chiefs of parties. Pulteney, when leader of the Opposition, and possessed of thirty thousand a-year, edited the Craftsman. Walpole, though not a man of literary habits, was the author of at least ten pamphlets, and retouched and corrected many more. These facts sufficiently show of how great importance literary assistance then was to the contending parties. St. John was, certainly, in Anne's reign, the best Tory speaker; Cowper was probably the best Whig speaker. But it may well be doubted whether St. John did so much for the Tories as Swift, and whether Cowper did so much for the Whigs as Addison. When these things are duly considered, it will not be thought strange that Addison should have climbed higher in the state than any other Englishman has ever, by means merely of literary talents, been able to climb. Swift would, in all probability, have climbed as high, if he had not been encumbered by his cassock and his pudding sleeves. As far as the homage of the great went, Swift had as much of it as if he had been Lord Treasurer.

To the influence which Addison derived from his literary talents was added all the influence which arises from character. The world, always ready to think the worst of needy political adventurers, was forced to make one exception. Restlessness, violence, audacity, laxity of principle, are the vices ordinarily attributed to that class of men. But faction itself could not deny that Addison had, through all changes of fortune, been strictly faithful to his early opinions, and to his early friends; that his integrity was without stain; that his whole deportment indicated a fine sense of the becoming; that, in the utmost heat of controversy, his zeal was tempered by a regard for truth, humanity, and social decorum; that no outrage could ever provoke him to retaliation unworthy of a Christian and a gentleman; and that his only faults were a too sensitive delicacy, and a modesty which amounted to bashfulness.

He was undoubtedly one of the most popular men of his ime; and much of his popularity he owed, we believe, to that very timidity which his friends lamented. That timidity often prevented him from exhibiting his talents to the best advantage. But it propitiated Nemesis. It averted that envy which would otherwise have been excited by fame so splendid, and by so rapid an elevation. No man is so great a favourite with the public as he who is at once an object of admiration, of respect, and of pity; and such were the feelings which Addison inspired. Those who enjoyed the privilege of hearing his familiar conversation, declared with one voice that it was superior even to his writings. The brilliant Mary Montague said, that she had known all the wits, and that Addison was the best company in the world. The malignant Pope was forced to own, that there was a charm in Addison's talk, which could be found nowhere else. Swift, when burning with animosity against the Whigs, could not but confess to Stella that, after all, he had never known any associate so agreeable as Addison. Steele, an excellent judge of lively conversation, said, that the conversation of Addison was at once the most polite, and the most mirthful, that could be imagined; that it was Terence and Catullus in one, heightened by an exquisite something which was neither Terence nor Catullus, but Addison alone. Young, an excellent judge of serious conversation, said, that when Addison was at his ease, he went on in a noble strain of thought and language, so as to chain the attention of every hearer. Nor were Addison's great colloquial powers more admirable than the courtesy and softness of heart which appeared in his conversation. At the same time, it would be too much to say that he was wholly devoid of the malice which is, perhaps, inseparable from a keen sense of the ludicrous. He had one habit which both Swift and Stella applauded, and which we hardly know how to blame. If his first attempts to set a presuming dunce right were ill received, he changed his tone "assented with civil leer," and lured the flattered coxcomb deeper and deeper into absurdity. That such was his practice we should, we think, have guessed from his works. The Tatler's criticisms on Mr. Softly's sonnet, and the Spectator's dialogue with the politician who is so zealous for the honour of Lady Q—p—t—s, are excellent specimens of this innocent mischief.

Such were Addison's talents for conversation. But his rare gifts were not exhibited to crowds or to strangers. As soon as he entered a large company, as soon as he saw an unknown face, his lips were sealed, and his manners became constrained. None who met him only in great assemblies would have been able to believe that he was the same man who had often kept a few friends listening and laughing round a table, from the time when the play ended, till the clock of St. Paul's in Covent Garden struck four. Yet, even at such a table, he was not seen to the best advantage. To enjoy his conversation in the highest perfection, it was necessary to be alone with him, and to hear him, in his own phrase, think aloud. "There is no such thing," he used to say, "as real conversation, but between two persons."

This timidity, a timidity surely neither ungraceful nor unamiable, led Addison into the two most serious faults which can with justice be imputed to him. He found that wine broke the spell which lay on his fine intellect, and was therefore too easily seduced into convivial excess. Such excess was in that age regarded, even by grave men, as the most venial of all peccadilloes, and was so far from being a mark of ill-breeding that it was almost essential to the character of a fine gentleman. But the smallest speck is seen on a white ground; and almost all the biographers of Addison have said something about this failing. Of any other statesman or writer of Queen Anne's reign, we should no more think of saying that he sometimes took too much wine, than that he wore a long wig and a sword.

To the excessive modesty of Addison's nature, we must ascribe another fault which generally arises from a very different cause. He became a little too fond of seeing himself surrounded by a small circle of admirers, to whom he was as a King or rather as a God. All these men were far inferior to him in ability, and some of them had very serious faults. Nor did those faults escape his observation; for, if ever there was an eye which saw through and through men, it was the eye of Addison. But, with the keenest observation, and the finest sense of the ridiculous, he had a large charity. The feeling with which he looked on most of his humble companions was one of benevolence, slightly tinctured with contempt. He was at perfect ease in their company; he was grateful for their devoted attachment; and he loaded them with benefits. Their veneration for him appears to have exceeded that with which Johnson was regarded by Boswell, or Warburton by Hurd. It was not in the power of adulation to turn such a head, or deprave such a heart, as Addison's. But it must in candour be admitted that he contracted some of the faults which can scarcely be avoided by any person who is so unfortunate as to be the oracle of a small literary coterie.

One member of this little society was Eustace Budgell, a young Templar of some literature, and a distant relation of Addison. There was at this time no stain on the character of Budgell, and it is not improbable that his career would have been prosperous and honourable, if the life of his cousin had been prolonged. But, when the master was laid in the grave, the disciple broke loose from all restraint, descended rapidly from one degree of vice and misery to another, ruined his fortune by follies, attempted to repair it by crimes, and at length closed a wicked and unhappy life by self-murder. Yet, to the last, the wretched man, gambler, lampooner, cheat, forger, as he was, retained his affection and veneration for Addison, and recorded those feelings in the last lines which he traced before he hid himself from infamy under London Bridge.

Another of Addison's favourite companions was Ambrose Phillipps, a good Whig and a middling poet, who had the honour of bringing into fashion a species of composition which has been called, after his name, Namby Pamby. But the most remarkable members of the little senate, as Pope long afterwards called it, were Richard Steele and Thomas Tickell.

Steele had known Addison from childhood. They had been together at the Charter House and at Oxford; but circumstances had then, for a time, separated them widely. Steele had left college without taking a degree, had been disinherited by a rich relation, had led a vagrant life, had served in the army, had tried to find the philosopher's stone, and had written a religious treatise and several comedies. He was one of those people whom it is impossible either to hate or to respect. His temper was sweet, his affections warm, his spirits lively, his passions strong, and his principles weak. His life was spent in sinning and repenting; in inculcating what was right, and doing what was wrong. In speculation, he was a man of piety and honour; in practice he was much of the rake and a little of the swindler. He was, however, so goodnatured that it was not easy to be seriously angry with him, and that even rigid moralists felt more inclined to pity than to blame him, when he diced himself into a spunging house or drank himself into a fever. Addison regarded Steele

with kindness not unmingled with scorn, tried, with little
success, to keep him out of scrapes, introduced him to the
great, procured a good place for him, corrected his plays,
and, though by no means rich, lent him large sums of money.
One of these loans appears, from a letter dated in August
1708, to have amounted to a thousand pounds. These
pecuniary transactions probably led to frequent bickerings.
It is said that, on one occasion, Steele's negligence, or
dishonesty, provoked Addison to repay himself by the help
of a bailiff. We cannot join with Miss Aikin in rejecting this
story. Johnson heard it from Savage, who heard it from
Steele. Few private transactions which took place a hundred
and twenty years ago, are proved by stronger evidence than
this. But we can by no means agree with those who condemn
Addison's severity. The most amiable of mankind may well
be moved to indignation, when what he has earned hardly,
and lent with great inconvenience to himself, for the purpose
of relieving a friend in distress, is squandered with insane
profusion. We will illustrate our meaning by an example,
which is not the less striking because it is taken from fiction.
Dr. Harrison, in Fielding's Amelia, is represented as the
most benevolent of human beings; yet he takes in execution,
not only the goods, but the person of his friend Booth.
Dr. Harrison resorts to this strong measure because he has
been informed that Booth, while pleading poverty as an excuse for not paying just debts, has been buying fine jewellery,
and setting up a coach. No person who is well acquainted
with Steele's life and correspondence can doubt that he
behaved quite as ill to Addison as Booth was accused of
behaving to Dr. Harrison. The real history, we have little
doubt, was something like this: — A letter comes to Addison,
imploring help in pathetic terms, and promising reformation
and speedy repayment. Poor Dick declares that he has not

an inch of candle, or a bushel of coals, or credit with the butcher for a shoulder of mutton. Addison is moved. He determines to deny himself some medals which are wanting to his series of the Twelve Cæsars; to put off buying the new edition of Bayle's Dictionary; and to wear his old sword and buckles another year. In this way he manages to send a hundred pounds to his friend. The next day he calls on Steele, and finds scores of gentlemen and ladies assembled. The fiddles are playing. The table is groaning under Champagne, Burgundy, and pyramids of sweetmeats. Is it strange that a man whose kindness is thus abused, should send sheriff's officers to reclaim what is due to him?

Tickell was a young man, fresh from Oxford, who had introduced himself to public notice by writing a most ingenious and graceful little poem in praise of the opera of Rosamond. He deserved, and at length attained, the first place in Addison's friendship. For a time Steele and Tickell were on good terms. But they loved Addison too much to love each other, and at length became as bitter enemies as the rival bulls in Virgil.

At the close of 1708 Wharton became Lord Lieutenant of Ireland, and appointed Addison Chief Secretary. Addison was consequently under the necessity of quitting London for Dublin. Besides the chief secretaryship, which was then worth about two thousand pounds a-year, he obtained a patent appointing him keeper of the Irish Records for life, with a salary of three or four hundred a-year. Budgell accompanied his cousin in the capacity of private Secretary.

Wharton and Addison had nothing in common but Whiggism. The Lord Lieutenant was not only licentious and corrupt, but was distinguished from other libertines and jobbers by a callous impudence which presented the strongest contrast to the Secretary's gentleness and delicacy. Many parts of the Irish administration at this time appear to have deserved serious blame. But against Addison there was not a murmur. He long afterwards asserted, what all the evidence which we have ever seen tends to prove, that his diligence and integrity gained the friendship of all the most considerable persons in Ireland.

The parliamentary career of Addison in Ireland has, we think, wholly escaped the notice of all his biographers. He was elected member for the borough of Cavan in the summer of 1709; and in the journals of two sessions his name frequently occurs. Some of the entries appear to indicate that he so far overcame his timidity as to make speeches. Nor is this by any means improbable; for the Irish House of Commons was a far less formidable audience than the English House; and many tongues which were tied by fear in the greater assembly became fluent in the smaller. Gerard Hamilton, for example, who, from fear of losing the fame gained by his single speech, sat mute at Westminster during forty years, spoke with great effect at Dublin when he was Secretary to Lord Halifax.

While Addison was in Ireland, an event occurred to which he owes his high and permanent rank among British writers. As yet his fame rested on performances which, though highly respectable, were not built for duration, and which would, if he had produced nothing else, have now been almost forgotten, on some excellent Latin verses, on some English verses which occasionally rose above mediocrity, and on a book of travels, agreeably written, but not indicating any extraordinary powers of mind. These works showed him to be a man of taste, sense, and learning. The time had come when he was to prove himself a man of genius, and to enrich our literature with compositions which will live as long as the English language.

[illegible]

[illegible] project, [illegible]
[illegible] consequences.
[illegible] published in
[illegible] in some of them
[illegible] casuistry had been
[illegible] works was small in-
[illegible] known only to the
[illegible]

[illegible] Sunderland, at
[illegible] and thus had access to
[illegible] authentic than was in
[illegible] newswriter. This
[illegible] to him the scheme of
[illegible] plan. It was to appear
[illegible] London for the country,
[illegible] the Tuesdays, Thursdays,
[illegible] the foreign news, accounts
[illegible] and the literary gossip of Will's
[illegible] to contain remarks on the
[illegible] compliments to beauties, pas-
[illegible] criticisms on popular preach-
[illegible] not appear to have been at
[illegible] ill qualified to conduct the
[illegible] public intelligence he drew
[illegible] the town, and had paid dear
[illegible] read much more than the dissi-
[illegible] habit of reading. He was a
[illegible] among rakes. His style
[illegible] though his wit and humour
[illegible] spirits imparted to his
[illegible] ordinary readers could
[illegible] His writings have been
[illegible] though deficient in

body and flavour, are yet a pleasant small drink, if not kept too long, or carried too far.

Isaac Bickerstaff, Esquire, Astrologer, was an imaginary person, almost as well known in that age as Mr. Paul Pry or Mr. Samuel Pickwick in ours. Swift had assumed the name of Bickerstaff in a satirical pamphlet against Partridge, the maker of almanacks. Partridge had been fool enough to publish a furious reply. Bickerstaff had rejoined in a second pamphlet still more diverting than the first. All the wits had combined to keep up the joke, and the town was long in convulsions of laughter. Steele determined to employ the name which this controversy had made popular; and, in 1709, it was announced that Isaac Bickerstaff, Esquire, Astrologer, was about to publish a paper called the Tatler.

Addison had not been consulted about this scheme: but as soon as he heard of it, he determined to give his assistance. The effect of that assistance cannot be better described than in Steele's own words. "I fared," he said, "like a distressed prince who calls in a powerful neighbour to his aid. I was undone by my auxiliary. When I had once called him in, I could not subsist without dependence on him." "The paper," he says elsewhere, "was advanced indeed. It was raised to a greater thing than I intended it."

It is probable that Addison, when he sent across St. George's Channel his first contributions to the Tatler, had no notion of the extent and variety of his own powers. He was the possessor of a vast mine, rich with a hundred ores. But he had been acquainted only with the least precious part of his treasures, and had hitherto contented himself with producing sometimes copper and sometimes lead, intermingled with a silver. All at once, and by mere accident, he had lighted inexhaustible vein of the finest gold.

he mere *choice* and arrangement of his words would

have sufficed to make his essays classical. For never, not even by Dryden, not even by Temple, had the English language been written with such sweetness, grace, and facility. But this was the smallest part of Addison's praise. Had he clothed his thoughts in the half French style of Horace Walpole, or in the half Latin style of Dr. Johnson, or in the half German jargon of the present day, his genius would have triumphed over all faults of manner. As a moral satirist he stands unrivalled. If ever the best Tatlers and Spectators were equalled in their own kind, we should be inclined to guess that it must have been by the lost comedies of Menander.

In wit, properly so called, Addison was not inferior to Cowley or Butler. No single ode of Cowley contains so many happy analogies as are crowded into the lines to Sir Godfrey Kneller; and we would undertake to collect from the Spectators as great a number of ingenious illustrations as can be found in Hudibras. The still higher faculty of invention Addison possessed in still larger measure. The numerous fictions, generally original, often wild and grotesque, but always singularly graceful and happy, which are found in his essays, fully entitle him to the rank of a great poet, a rank to which his metrical compositions give him no claim. As an observer of life, of manners, of all the shades of human character, he stands in the first class. And what he observed he had the art of communicating in two widely different ways. He could describe virtues, vices, habits, whims, as well as Clarendon. But he could do something better. He could call human beings into existence, and make them exhibit themselves. If we wish to find anything more vivid than Addison's best portraits, we must go either to Shakspeare or to Cervantes.

But what shall we say of Addison's humour, of his sense *of the ludicrous*, of his power of awakening that sense in others, and of drawing mirth from incidents which occur every day, and from little peculiarities of temper and manner, such as may be found in every man? We feel the charm: we give ourselves up to it: but we strive in vain to analyse it.

Perhaps the best way of describing Addison's peculiar pleasantry is to compare it with the pleasantry of some other great satirists. The three most eminent masters of the art of ridicule, during the eighteenth century, were, we conceive, Addison, Swift, and Voltaire. Which of the three had the greatest power of moving laughter may be questioned. But each of them, within his own domain, was supreme.

Voltaire is the prince of buffoons. His merriment is without disguise or restraint. He gambols; he grins; he shakes his sides; he points the finger; he turns up the nose; he shoots out the tongue. The manner of Swift is the very opposite to this. He moves laughter, but never joins in it. He appears in his works such as he appeared in society. All the company are convulsed with merriment, while the Dean, the author of all the mirth, preserves an invincible gravity, and even sourness of aspect, and gives utterance to the most eccentric and ludicrous fancies, with the air of a man reading the commination service.

The manner of Addison is as remote from that of Swift as from that of Voltaire. He neither laughs out like the French wit, nor, like the Irish wit, throws a double portion of severity into his countenance while laughing inwardly; but preserves a look peculiarly his own, a look of demure serenity, disturbed only by an arch sparkle of the eye, an almost imperceptible elevation of the brow, an almost imperceptible curl of the lip. His tone is never that either of a Jack Pudding or of a Cynic. It is that of a gentleman, in whom the quickest sense of the ridiculous is constantly tempered by good nature and good breeding.

We own that the humour of Addison is, in our opinion, of a more delicious flavour than the humour of either Swift or Voltaire. Thus much, at least, is certain, that both Swift and Voltaire have been successfully mimicked, and that no man has yet been able to mimic Addison. The letter of the Abbé Coyer to Pansophe is Voltaire all over, and imposed, during a long time, on the Academicians of Paris. There are passages in Arbuthnot's satirical works which we, at least, cannot distinguish from Swift's best writing. But of the many eminent men who have made Addison their model, though several have copied his mere diction with happy effect, none has been able to catch the tone of his pleasantry. In the World, in the Connoisseur, in the Mirror, in the Lounger, there are numerous papers written in obvious imitation of his Tatlers and Spectators. Most of those papers have some merit; many are very lively and amusing; but there is not a single one which could be passed off as Addison's on a critic of the smallest perspicacity.

But that which chiefly distinguishes Addison from Swift, from Voltaire, from almost all the other great masters of ridicule, is the grace, the nobleness, the moral purity, which we find even in his merriment. Severity, gradually hardening and darkening into misanthropy, characterizes the works of Swift. The nature of Voltaire was, indeed, not inhuman; but he venerated nothing. Neither in the masterpieces of art nor in the purest examples of virtue, neither in the Great First Cause nor in the awful enigma of the grave, could he see any thing but subjects for drollery. The more solemn and august the theme, the more monkeylike was his grimacing and chattering. The mirth of Swift is the mirth of Mephistophiles; *the mirth of* Voltaire is the mirth of Puck. If, as Soame

Jenyns oddly imagined, a portion of the happiness of Seraphim and just men made perfect be derived from an exquisite perception of the ludicrous, their mirth must surely be none other than the mirth of Addison; a mirth consistent with tender compassion for all that is frail, and with profound reverence for all that is sublime. Nothing great, nothing amiable, no moral duty, no doctrine of natural or revealed religion, has ever been associated by Addison with any degrading idea. His humanity is without a parallel in literary history. The highest proof of virtue is to possess boundless power without abusing it. No kind of power is more formidable than the power of making men ridiculous; and that power Addison possessed in boundless measure. How grossly that power was abused by Swift and by Voltaire is well known. But of Addison it may be confidently affirmed that he has blackened no man's character, nay, that it would be difficult, if not impossible, to find in all the volumes which he has left us a single taunt which can be called ungenerous or unkind. Yet he had detractors, whose malignity might have seemed to justify as terrible a revenge as that which men, not superior to him in genius, wreaked on Bettesworth and on Franc de Pompignan. He was a politician; he was the best writer of his party; he lived in times of fierce excitement, in times when persons of high character and station stooped to scurrility such as is now practised only by the basest of mankind. Yet no provocation and no example could induce him to return railing for railing.

Of the service which his Essays rendered to morality it is difficult to speak too highly. It is true that, when the Tatler appeared, that age of outrageous profaneness and licentiousness which followed the Restoration had passed away. Jeremy Collier had shamed the theatres into something which, compared with the excesses of Etherege and Wycherley, might be called decency. Yet there still lingered in the public mind a pernicious notion that there was some connection between genius and profligacy, between the domestic virtues and the sullen formality of the Puritans. That error it is the glory of Addison to have dispelled. He taught the nation that the faith and the morality of Hale and Tillotson might be found in company with wit more sparkling than the wit of Congreve, and with humour richer than the humour of Vanbrugh. So effectually, indeed, did he retort on vice the mockery which had recently been directed against virtue, that, since his time, the open violation of decency has always been considered among us as the mark of a fool. And this revolution, the greatest and most salutary ever effected by any satirist, he accomplished, be it remembered, without writing one personal lampoon.

In the early contributions of Addison to the Tatler his peculiar powers were not fully exhibited. Yet from the first, his superiority to all his coadjutors was evident. Some of his later Tatlers are fully equal to any thing that he ever wrote. Among the portraits, we most admire Tom Folio, Ned Softly, and the Political Upholsterer. The proceedings of the Court of Honour, the Thermometer of Zeal, the story of the Frozen Words, the Memoirs of the Shilling, are excellent specimens of that ingenious and lively species of fiction in which Addison excelled all men. There is one still better paper of the same class. But though that paper, a hundred and thirty-three years ago, was probably thought as edifying as one of Smalridge's sermons, we dare not indicate it to the squeamish readers of the nineteenth century.

During the session of Parliament which commenced in November 1709, and which the impeachment of Sacheverell has made memorable, Addison appears to have resided in *London*. The Tatler was now more popular than any periodical paper had ever been; and his connection with it was generally known. It was not known, however, that almost every thing good in the Tatler was his. The truth is that the fifty or sixty numbers which we owe to him were not merely the best, but so decidedly the best that any five of them are more valuable than all the two hundred numbers in which he had no share.

He required, at this time, all the solace which he could derive from literary success. The Queen had always disliked the Whigs. She had during some years disliked the Marlborough family. But, reigning by a disputed title, she could not venture directly to oppose herself to a majority of both Houses of Parliament; and, engaged as she was in a war on the event of which her own Crown was staked, she could not venture to disgrace a great and successful general. But at length, in the year 1710, the causes which had restrained her from showing her aversion to the Low Church party ceased to operate. The trial of Sacheverell produced an outbreak of public feeling scarcely less violent than the outbreaks which we can ourselves remember in 1820, and in 1831. The country gentlemen, the country clergymen, the rabble of the towns, were all, for once, on the same side. It was clear that, if a general election took place before the excitement abated, the Tories would have a majority. The services of Marlborough had been so splendid that they were no longer necessary. The Queen's throne was secure from all attack on the part of Lewis. Indeed, it seemed much more likely that the English and German armies would divide the spoils of Versailles and Marli than that a Marshal of France would bring back the Pretender to St. James's. The Queen, acting by the advice of Harley, determined to dismiss her servants. In June the change commenced. Sunderland was the first who fell. *The Tories* exulted over his fall. The Whigs tried, during a few weeks, to persuade themselves that her Majesty had acted only from personal dislike to the Secretary, and that she meditated no further alteration. But, early in August, Godolphin was surprised by a letter from Anne, which directed him to break his white staff. Even after this event, the irresolution or dissimulation of Harley kept up the hopes of the Whigs during another month; and then the ruin became rapid and violent. The Parliament was dissolved. The Ministers were turned out. The Tories were called to office. The tide of popularity ran violently in favour of the High Church party. That party, feeble in the late House of Commons, was now irresistible. The power which the Tories had thus suddenly acquired, they used with blind and stupid ferocity. The howl which the whole pack set up for prey and for blood appalled even him who had roused and unchained them. When, at this distance of time, we calmly review the conduct of the discarded ministers, we cannot but feel a movement of indignation at the injustice with which they were treated. No body of men had ever administered the government with more energy, ability, and moderation; and their success had been proportioned to their wisdom. They had saved Holland and Germany. They had humbled France. They had, as it seemed, all but torn Spain from the House of Bourbon. They had made England the first power in Europe. At home they had united England and Scotland. They had respected the rights of conscience and the liberty of the subject. They retired, leaving their country at the height of prosperity and glory. And yet they were pursued to their retreat by such a roar of obloquy as was never raised against the government which threw away thirteen colonies, or against the government which sent a gallant army to perish in the ditches of Walcheren.

*None of the Whigs suffered more in the general wreck than*

Addison. He had just sustained some heavy pecuniary losses, of the nature of which we are imperfectly informed, when his Secretaryship was taken from him. He had reason to believe that he should also be deprived of the small Irish office which he held by patent. He had just resigned his Fellowship. It seems probable that he had already ventured to raise his eyes to a great lady, and that, while his political friends were in power, and while his own fortunes were rising, he had been, in the phrase of the romances which were then fashionable, permitted to hope. But Mr. Addison the ingenious writer, and Mr. Addison the chief Secretary, were, in her ladyship's opinion, two very different persons. All these calamities united, however, could not disturb the serene cheerfulness of a mind conscious of innocence, and rich in its own wealth. He told his friends, with smiling resignation, that they ought to admire his philosophy, that he had lost at once his fortune, his place, his fellowship, and his mistress, that he must think of turning tutor again, and yet that his spirits were as good as ever.

He had one consolation. Of the unpopularity which his friends had incurred, he had no share. Such was the esteem with which he was regarded that, while the most violent measures were taken for the purpose of forcing Tory members on Whig corporations, he was returned to Parliament without even a contest. Swift, who was now in London, and who had already determined on quitting the Whigs, wrote to Stella in these remarkable words: "The Tories carry it among the new members six to one. Mr. Addison's election has passed easy and undisputed; and I believe if he had a mind to be king, he would hardly be refused."

The good will with which the Tories regarded Addison is the more honourable to him, because it had not been purchased by any concession on his part. During the general election he published a political Journal, entitled the Whig Examiner. Of that Journal it may be sufficient to say that Johnson, in spite of his strong political prejudices, pronounced it to be superior in wit to any of Swift's writings on the other side. When it ceased to appear, Swift, in a letter to Stella, expressed his exultation at the death of so formidable an antagonist. "He might well rejoice," says Johnson, "at the death of that which he could not have killed." "On no occasion," he adds, "was the genius of Addison more vigorously exerted, and in none did the superiority of his powers more evidently appear."

The only use which Addison appears to have made of the favour with which he was regarded by the Tories was to save some of his friends from the general ruin of the Whig party. He felt himself to be in a situation which made it his duty to take a decided part in politics. But the case of Steele and of Ambrose Phillipps was different. For Phillipps, Addison even condescended to solicit, with what success we have not ascertained. Steele held two places. He was Gazetteer, and he was also a Commissioner of Stamps. The Gazette was taken from him. But he was suffered to retain his place in the Stamp Office, on an implied understanding that he should not be active against the new government; and he was, during more than two years, induced by Addison to observe this armistice with tolerable fidelity.

Isaac Bickerstaff accordingly became silent upon politics, and the article of news, which had once formed about one third of his paper, altogether disappeared. The Tatler had completely changed its character. It was now nothing but a series of essays on books, morals, and manners. Steele therefore resolved to bring it to a close, and to commence a new work on an improved plan. It was announced that this *new work* would be published daily. The undertaking was generally regarded as bold, or rather rash; but the event amply justified the confidence with which Steele relied on the fertility of Addison's genius. On the second of January 1711, appeared the last Tatler. At the beginning of March following, appeared the first of an incomparable series of papers, containing observations on life and literature by an imaginary Spectator.

The Spectator himself was conceived and drawn by Addison; and it is not easy to doubt that the portrait was meant to be in some features a likeness of the painter. The Spectator is a gentleman who, after passing a studious youth at the university, has travelled on classic ground, and has bestowed much attention on curious points of antiquity. He has, on his return, fixed his residence in London, and has observed all the forms of life which are to be found in that great city, has daily listened to the wits of Will's, has smoked with the philosophers of the Grecian, and has mingled with the parsons at Child's, and with the politicians at the St. James's. In the morning, he often listens to the hum of Exchange; in the evening, his face is constantly to be seen in the pit of Drury Lane theatre. But an insurmountable bashfulness prevents him from opening his mouth, except in a small circle of intimate friends.

These friends were first sketched by Steele. Four of the club, the templar, the clergyman, the soldier, and the merchant, were uninteresting figures, fit only for a background. But the other two, on old country baronet and an old town rake, though not delineated with a very delicate pencil, had some good strokes. Addison took the rude outlines into his own hands, retouched them, coloured them, and is in truth the creator of the Sir Roger de Coverley and the Will Honeycomb with whom we are all familiar.

The plan of the Spectator must be allowed to be both original and eminently happy. Every valuable essay in the series may be read with pleasure separately; yet the five or six hundred essays form a whole, and a whole which has the interest of a novel. It must be remembered, too, that at that time no novel, giving a lively and powerful picture of the common life and manners of England, had appeared. Richardson was working as a compositor. Fielding was robbing birds' nests. Smollett was not yet born. The narrative, therefore, which connects together the Spectator's Essays, gave to our ancestors their first taste of an exquisite and untried pleasure That narrative was indeed constructed with no art or labour. The events were such events as occur every day. Sir Roger comes up to town to see Eugenio, as the worthy baronet always calls Prince Eugene, goes with the Spectator on the water to Spring Gardens, walks among the tombs in the Abbey, and is frightened by the Mohawks, but conquers his apprehension so far as to go to the theatre, when the Distressed Mother is acted. The Spectator pays a visit in the summer to Coverley Hall, is charmed with the old house, the old butler, and the old chaplain, eats a jack caught by Will Wimble, rides to the assizes, and hears a point of law discussed by Tom Touchy. At last a letter from the honest butler brings to the club the news that Sir Roger is dead. Will Honeycomb marries and reforms at sixty. The club breaks up; and the Spectator resigns his functions. Such events can hardly be said to form a plot; yet they are related with such truth, such grace, such wit, such humour, such pathos, such knowledge of the human heart, such knowledge of the ways of the world, that they charm us on the hundredth perusal. We have not the least doubt that, if Addison had written a novel, on an extensive plan, it would have been superior to any that we *possess*. *As it is*, he is entitled to be considered not only as the greatest of the English essayists, but as the forerunner of the great English novelists.

We say this of Addison alone; for Addison is the Spectator. About three sevenths of the work are his; and it is no exaggeration to say, that his worst essay is as good as the best essay of any of his coadjutors. His best essays approach near to absolute perfection; nor is their excellence more wonderful than their variety. His invention never seems to flag; nor is he ever under the necessity of repeating himself, or of wearing out a subject. There are no dregs in his wine. He regales us after the fashion of that prodigal nabob who held that there was only one good glass in a bottle. As soon as we have tasted the first sparkling foam of a jest, it is withdrawn, and a fresh draught of nectar is at our lips. On the Monday we have an allegory as lively and ingenious as Lucian's Auction of Lives; on the Tuesday an Eastern apologue, as richly coloured as the Tales of Scherezade; on the Wednesday, a character described with the skill of La Bruyère; on the Thursday, a scene from common life, equal to the best chapters in the Vicar of Wakefield; on the Friday, some sly Horatian pleasantry on fashionable follies, on hoops, patches, or puppet shows; and on the Saturday a religious meditation, which will bear a comparison with the finest passages in Massillon.

It is dangerous to select where there is so much that deserves the highest praise. We will venture, however, to say, that any person who wishes to form a just notion of the extent and variety of Addison's powers, will do well to read at one sitting the following papers, the two Visits to the Abbey, the Visit to the Exchange, the Journal of the Retired Citizen, the Vision of Mirza, the Transmigrations of Pug the Monkey, and the Death of Sir Roger de Coverley.*

* . Nos. 26, 329, 69, 317, 159, 343, 517. These papers are all in the first seven volumes. The eighth must be considered as a separate work.

The least valuable of Addison's contributions to the Spectator are, in the judgment of our age, his critical papers. Yet his critical papers are always luminous, and often ingenious. The very worst of them must be regarded as creditable to him, when the character of the school in which he had been trained is fairly considered. The best of them were much too good for his readers. In truth, he was not so far behind our generation as he was before his own. No essays in the Spectator were more censured and derided than those in which he raised his voice against the contempt with which our fine old ballads were regarded, and showed the scoffers that the same gold which, burnished and polished, gives lustre to the Æneid and the Odes of Horace, is mingled with the rude dross of Chevy Chace.

It is not strange that the success of the Spectator should have been such as no similar work has ever obtained. The number of copies daily distributed was at first three thousand. It subsequently increased, and had risen to near four thousand when the stamp tax was imposed. That tax was fatal to a crowd of journals. The Spectator, however, stood its ground, doubled its price, and, though its circulation fell off, still yielded a large revenue both to the state and to the authors. For particular papers, the demand was immense; of some, it is said, twenty thousand copies were required. But this was not all. To have the Spectator served up every morning with the bohea and rolls, was a luxury for the few. The majority were content to wait till essays enough had appeared to form a volume. Ten thousand copies of each volume were immediately taken off, and new editions were called for. It must be remembered, that the population of England was then hardly a third of what it now is. The number of Englishmen who were in the habit of reading, was not a sixth of what it now is. A shopkeeper or a farmer who found any pleasure in literature, was a rarity. Nay, there was doubtless more than one knight of the shire whose country seat did not contain ten books, receipt books and books on farriery included. In these circumstances, the sale of the Spectator must be considered as indicating a popularity quite as great as that of the most successful works of Sir Walter Scott and Mr. Dickens in our own time.

At the close of 1712 the Spectator ceased to appear. It was probably felt that the shortfaced gentleman and his club had been long enough before the town; and that it was time to withdraw them, and to replace them by a new set of characters. In a few weeks the first number of the Guardian was published. But the Guardian was unfortunate both in its birth and in its death. It began in dulness, and disappeared in a tempest of faction. The original plan was bad. Addison contributed nothing till sixty-six numbers had appeared; and it was then impossible to make the Guardian what the Spectator had been. Nestor Ironsides and the Miss Lizards were people to whom even he could impart no interest. He could only furnish some excellent little essays, both serious and comic; and this he did.

Why Addison gave no assistance to the Guardian, during the first two months of its existence, is a question which has puzzled the editors and biographers, but which seems to us to admit of a very easy solution. He was then engaged in bringing his Cato on the stage.

The first four acts of this drama had been lying in his desk since his return from Italy. His modest and sensitive nature shrank from the risk of a public and shameful failure; and, though all who saw the manuscript were loud in praise, some thought it possible that an audience might become impatient even of very good rhetoric, and advised Addison to print the play without hazarding a representation. At length, after many fits of apprehension, the poet yielded to the urgency of his political friends, who hoped that the public would discover some analogy between the followers of Cæsar and the Tories, between Sempronius and the apostate Whigs, between Cato struggling to the last for the liberties of Rome, and the band of patriots who still stood firm round Halifax and Wharton.

Addison gave the play to the managers of Drury Lane theatre, without stipulating for any advantage to himself. They, therefore, thought themselves bound to spare no cost in scenery and dresses. The decorations, it is true, would not have pleased the skilful eye of Mr. Macready. Juba's waistcoat blazed with gold lace; Marcia's hoop was worthy of a Duchess on the birthday; and Cato wore a wig worth fifty guineas. The prologue was written by Pope, and is undoubtedly a dignified and spirited composition. The part of the hero was excellently played by Booth. Steele undertook to pack a house. The boxes were in a blaze with the stars of the Peers in Opposition. The Pit was crowded with attentive and friendly listeners from the Inns of Court and the literary coffee-houses. Sir Gilbert Heathcote, Governor of the Bank of England, was at the head of a powerful body of auxiliaries from the city, warm men and true Whigs, but better known at Jonathan's and Garraway's than in the haunts of wits and critics.

These precautions were quite superfluous. The Tories, as a body, regarded Addison with no unkind feelings. Nor was it for their interest, professing, as they did, profound reverence for law and prescription, and abhorrence both of popular insurrections and of standing armies, to appropriate to themselves reflections thrown on the great military chief and demagogue, who, with the support of the legions and of the common people, subverted all the ancient institutions of *his* country. Accordingly, every shout that was raised by the members of the Kit Cat was echoed by the High Churchmen of the October; and the curtain at length fell amidst thunders of unanimous applause.

The delight and admiration of the town were described by the Guardian in terms which we might attribute to partiality, were it not that the Examiner, the organ of the Ministry, held similar language. The Tories, indeed, found much to sneer at in the conduct of their opponents. Steele had on this, as on other occasions, shown more zeal than taste or judgment. The honest citizens who marched under the orders of Sir Gibby, as he was facetiously called, probably knew better when to buy and when to sell stock than when to clap and when to hiss at a play, and incurred some ridicule by making the hypocritical Sempronius their favourite, and by giving to his insincere rants louder plaudits than they bestowed on the temperate eloquence of Cato. Wharton, too, who had the incredible effrontery to applaud the lines about flying from prosperous vice and from the power of impious men to a private station, did not escape the sarcasms of those who justly thought that he could fly from nothing more vicious or impious than himself. The epilogue, which was written by Garth, a zealous Whig, was severely and not unreasonably censured as ignoble and out of place. But Addison was described, even by the bitterest Tory writers, as a gentleman of wit and virtue, in whose friendship many persons of both parties were happy, and whose name ought not to be mixed up with factious squabbles.

Of the jests by which the triumph of the Whig party was disturbed, the most severe and happy was Bolingbroke's. Between two acts, he sent for Booth to his box, and presented him, before the whole theatre, with a purse of fifty guineas for defending the cause of liberty so well against a perpetual Dictator. This was a pungent allusion to the attempt which

Marlborough had made, not long before his fall, to obtain a patent creating him Captain General for life.

It was April; and in April, a hundred and thirty years ago, the London season was thought to be far advanced. During a whole month, however, Cato was performed to overflowing houses, and brought into the treasury of the theatre twice the gains of an ordinary spring. In the summer the Drury Lane company went down to the Act at Oxford, and there, before an audience which retained an affectionate remembrance of Addison's accomplishments and virtues, his tragedy was acted during several days. The gownsmen began to besiege the theatre in the forenoon, and by one in the afternoon all the seats were filled.

About the merits of the piece which had so extraordinary an effect, the public, we suppose, has made up its mind. To compare it with the masterpieces of the Attic stage, with the great English dramas of the time of Elizabeth, or even with the productions of Schiller's manhood, would be absurd indeed. Yet it contains excellent dialogue and declamation, and, among plays fashioned on the French model, must be allowed to rank high; not indeed with Athalie, or Saul; but, we think, not below Cinna, and certainly above any other English tragedy of the same school, above many of the plays of Corneille, above many of the plays of Voltaire and Alfieri, and above some plays of Racine. Be this as it may, we have little doubt that Cato did as much as the Tatlers, Spectators, and Freeholders united, to raise Addison's fame among his contemporaries.

The modesty and good nature of the successful dramatist d tamed even the malignity of faction. But literary envy, should seem, is a fiercer passion than party spirit. It was alous Whig that the fiercest attack on the Whig tragedy de. John Dennis published Remarks on Cato, which were written with some acuteness and with much coarseness and asperity. Addison neither defended himself nor retaliated. On many points he had an excellent defence; and nothing would have been easier than to retaliate; for Dennis had written bad odes, bad tragedies, bad comedies: he had, moreover, a larger share than most men of those infirmities and eccentricities which excite laughter; and Addison's power of turning either an absurd book or an absurd man into ridicule was unrivalled. Addison, however, serenely conscious of his superiority, looked with pity on his assailant, whose temper, naturally irritable and gloomy, had been soured by want, by controversy, and by literary failures.

But among the young candidates for Addison's favour there was one distinguished by talents above the rest, and distinguished, we fear, not less by malignity and insincerity. Pope was only twenty-five. But his powers had expanded to their full maturity; and his best poem, the Rape of the Lock, had recently been published. Of his genius, Addison had always expressed high admiration. But Addison had early discerned, what might indeed have been discerned by an eye less penetrating than his, that the diminutive, crooked, sickly boy was eager to revenge himself on society for the unkindness of nature. In the Spectator, the Essay on Criticism had been praised with cordial warmth; but a gentle hint had been added, that the writer of so excellent a poem would have done well to avoid ill natured personalities. Pope, though evidently more galled by the censure than gratified by the praise, returned thanks for the admonition, and promised to profit by it. The two writers continued to exchange civilities, counsel, and small good offices. Addison publicly extolled Pope's miscellaneous pieces; and Pope furnished Addison with a prologue. This did not last long. Pope hated Dennis, *whom he had injured* without provocation. The appearance of the Remarks on Cato gave the irritable poet an opportunity of venting his malice under the show of friendship; and such an opportunity could not but be welcome to a nature which was implacable in enmity, and which always preferred the tortuous to the straight path. He published, accordingly, the Narrative of the Frenzy of John Dennis. But Pope had mistaken his powers. He was a great master of invective and sarcasm: he could dissect a character in terse and sonorous couplets, brilliant with antithesis: but of dramatic talent he was altogether destitute. If he had written a lampoon on Dennis, such as that on Atticus, or that on Sporus, the old grumbler would have been crushed. But Pope writing dialogue resembled — to borrow Horace's imagery and his own — a wolf, which, instead of biting, should take to kicking, or a monkey which should try to sting. The Narrative is utterly contemptible. Of argument there is not even the show; and the jests are such as, if they were introduced into a farce, would call forth the hisses of the shilling gallery. Dennis raves about the drama; and the nurse thinks that he is calling for a dram. "There is," he cries, "no peripetia in the tragedy, no change of fortune, no change at all." "Pray, good Sir, be not angry," says the old woman; "I'll fetch change." This is not exactly the pleasantry of Addison.

There can be no doubt that Addison saw through this officious zeal, and felt himself deeply aggrieved by it. So foolish and spiteful a pamphlet could do him no good, and, if he were thought to have any hand in it, must do him harm. Gifted with incomparable powers of ridicule, he had never, even in self-defence, used those powers inhumanly or uncourteously; and he was not disposed to let others make his fame and his interests a pretext under which they might commit outrages from which he had himself constantly abstained. He accordingly declared that he had no concern in the narrative, that he disapproved of it, and that, if he answered the remarks, he would answer them like a gentleman; and he took care to communicate this to Dennis. Pope was bitterly mortified; and to this transaction we are inclined to ascribe the hatred with which he ever after regarded Addison.

In September 1713 the Guardian ceased to appear. Steele had gone mad about politics. A general election had just taken place: he had been chosen member for Stockbridge; and he fully expected to play a first part in Parliament. The immense success of the Tatler and Spectator had turned his head. He had been the editor of both those papers; and was not aware how entirely they owed their influence and popularity to the genius of his friend. His spirits, always violent, were now excited by vanity, ambition, and faction, to such a pitch that he every day committed some offence against good sense and good taste. All the discreet and moderate members of his own party regretted and condemned his folly. "I am in a thousand troubles," Addison wrote, "about poor Dick, and wish that his zeal for the public may not be ruinous to himself. But he has sent me word that he is determined to go on, and that any advice I may give him in this particular will have no weight with him."

Steele set up a political paper called the Englishman, which, as it was not supported by contributions from Addison, completely failed. By this work, by some other writings of the same kind, and by the airs which he gave himself at the first meeting of the new Parliament, he made the Tories so angry that they determined to expel him. The Whigs stood by him gallantly, but were unable to save him. The vote of expulsion was regarded by all dispassionate men as a tyrannical exercise of the power of the majority. But Steele's violence and folly, though they by no means justified the steps which his enemies took, had completely disgusted his friends; no did he ever regain the place which he had held in the public estimation.

Addison about this time conceived the design of adding an eighth volume to the Spectator. In June 1714 the first number of the new series appeared, and during about six months three papers were published weekly. Nothing can be more striking than the contrast between the Englishman and the eighth volume of the Spectator, between Steele without Addison and Addison without Steele. The Englishman is forgotten; the eighth volume of the Spectator contains, perhaps, the finest essays, both serious and playful, in the English language.

Before this volume was completed, the death of Anne produced an entire change in the administration of public affairs. The blow fell suddenly. It found the Tory party distracted by internal feuds, and unprepared for any great effort. Harley had just been disgraced. Bolingbroke, it was supposed, would be the chief minister. But the Queen was on her deathbed before the white staff had been given, and her last public act was to deliver it with a feeble hand to the Duke of Shrewsbury. The emergency produced a coalition between all sections of public men who were attached to the Protestant succession. George the First was proclaimed without opposition. A Council, in which the leading Whigs had seats, took the direction of affairs till the new King should arrive. The first act of the Lords Justices was to appoint Addison their secretary.

There is an idle tradition that he was directed to prepare a letter to the King, that he could not satisfy himself as to the style of this composition, and that the Lords Justices called in a clerk who at once did what was wanted. It is not strange that a story so flattering to mediocrity should be popular; and we are sorry to deprive dunces of their consolation. But the truth must be told. It was well observed by Sir James Mackintosh, whose knowledge of these times was unequalled, that Addison never, in any official document, affected wit or eloquence, and that his despatches are, without exception, remarkable for unpretending simplicity. Every body who knows with what ease Addison's finest essays were produced must be convinced that, if well turned phrases had been wanted, he would have had no difficulty in finding them. We are, however, inclined to believe, that the story is not absolutely without a foundation. It may well be that Addison did not know, till he had consulted experienced clerks, who remembered the times when William the Third was absent on the Continent, in what form a letter from the Council of Regency to the King ought to be drawn. We think it very likely that the ablest statesmen of our time, Lord John Russell, Sir Robert Peel, Lord Palmerston, for example, would, in similar circumstances, be found quite as ignorant. Every office has some little mysteries which the dullest man may learn with a little attention, and which the greatest man cannot possibly know by intuition. One paper must be signed by the chief of the department, another by his deputy. To a third the royal sign manual is necessary. One communication is to be registered, and another is not. One sentence must be in black ink and another in red ink. If the ablest Secretary for Ireland were moved to the India Board, if the ablest President of the India Board were moved to the War Office, he would require instruction on points like these; and we do not doubt that Addison required such instruction when he became, for the first time, Secretary to the Lords Justices.

George the First took possession of his kingdom without opposition. A new ministry was formed, and a new Parliament favourable to the Whigs chosen. Sunderland was appointed Lord Lieutenant of Ireland; and Addison again went to Dublin as Chief Secretary.

At Dublin Swift resided; and there was much speculation

about the way in which the Dean and the Secretary would behave towards each other. The relations which existed between these remarkable men form an interesting and pleasing portion of literary history. They had early attached themselves to the same political party and to the same patrons. While Anne's Whig ministry was in power, the visits of Swift to London and the official residence of Addison in Ireland had given them opportunities of knowing each other. They were the two shrewdest observers of their age. But their observations on each other had led them to favourable conclusions. Swift did full justice to the rare powers of conversation which were latent under the bashful deportment of Addison. Addison, on the other hand, discerned much good nature under the severe look and manner of Swift; and, indeed, the Swift of 1708 and the Swift of 1738 were two very different men.

But the paths of the two friends diverged widely. The Whig statesmen loaded Addison with solid benefits. They praised Swift, asked him to dinner, and did nothing more for him. His profession laid them under a difficulty. In the state they could not promote him; and they had reason to fear that, by bestowing preferment in the church on the author of the Tale of a Tub, they might give scandal to the public, which had no high opinion of their orthodoxy. He did not make fair allowance for the difficulties which prevented Halifax and Somers from serving him, thought himself an ill used man, sacrificed honour and consistency to revenge, joined the Tories, and became their most formidable champion. He soon found, however, that his old friends were less to blame than he had supposed. The dislike with which the Queen and the heads of the Church regarded him was insurmountable; and it was with the greatest difficulty that he obtained an ecclesiastical dignity of no great value, on condition of fixing his residence in a country which he detested.

Difference of political opinion had produced, not indeed a quarrel, but a coolness between Swift and Addison. They at length ceased altogether to see each other. Yet there was between them a tacit compact like that between the hereditary guests in the Iliad.

> Ἔγχεα δ' ἀλλήλων ἀλεώμεθα καὶ δι' ὁμίλου·
> Πολλοὶ μὲν γὰρ ἐμοὶ Τρῶες κλειτοί τ' ἐπίκουροι,
> Κτείνειν, ὅν κε θεός γε πόρῃ καὶ ποσσὶ κιχείω,
> Πολλοὶ δ' αὖ σοὶ Ἀχαιοί, ἐναιρέμεν, ὅν κε δύνηαι.

It is not strange that Addison, who calumniated and insulted nobody, should not have calumniated or insulted Swift. But it is remarkable that Swift, to whom neither genius nor virtue was sacred, and who generally seemed to find, like most other renegades, a peculiar pleasure in attacking old friends, should have shown so much respect and tenderness to Addison.

Fortune had now changed. The accession of the House of Hanover had secured in England the liberties of the people, and in Ireland the dominion of the Protestant caste. To that caste Swift was more odious than any other man. He was hooted and even pelted in the streets of Dublin; and could not venture to ride along the strand for his health without the attendance of armed servants. Many whom he had formerly served now libelled and insulted him. At this time Addison arrived. He had been advised not to show the smallest civility to the Dean of St. Patrick's. He had answered, with admirable spirit, that it might be necessary for men whose fidelity to their party was suspected, to hold no intercourse with political opponents; but that one who had been a steady Whig in the worst times might venture, when the good cause was triumphant, to shake hands with an old friend who was one of the vanquished Tories. His kindness was soothing to the proud and cruelly wounded spirit of Swift; and the two great satirists resumed their habits of friendly intercourse.

Those associates of Addison whose political opinions agreed with his shared his good fortune. He took Tickel with him to Ireland. He procured for Budgell a lucrative place in the same kingdom. Ambrose Phillips was provided for in England. Steele had injured himself so much by his eccentricity and perverseness that he obtained but a very small part of what he thought his due. He was, however, knighted: he had a place in the household; and he subsequently received other marks of favour from the court.

Addison did not remain long in Ireland. In 1715 he quitted his secretaryship for a seat at the Board of Trade. In the same year his comedy of the Drummer was brought on the stage. The name of the author was not announced; the piece was coldly received; and some critics have expressed a doubt whether it were really Addison's. To us the evidence, both external and internal, seems decisive. It is not in Addison's best manner; but it contains numerous passages which no other writer known to us could have produced. It was again performed after Addison's death, and, being known to be his, was loudly applauded.

Towards the close of the year 1715, while the Rebellion was still raging in Scotland, Addison published the first number of a paper called the Freeholder. Among his political works the Freeholder is entitled to the first place. Even in the Spectator there are few serious papers nobler than the character of his friend Lord Somers, and certainly no satirical papers superior to those in which the Tory foxhunter is introduced. This character is the original of Squire Western, and is drawn with all Fielding's force, and with a delicacy of which Fielding was altogether destitute. As none of Addison's works exhibits stronger marks of his genius than the Freeholder, so none does more honour to his moral character. It is difficult to extol too highly the candour and humanity of a political writer, whom even the excitement of civil war cannot hurry into unseemly violence. Oxford, it is well known, was then the stronghold of Toryism. The High Street had been repeatedly lined with bayonets in order to keep down the disaffected gownsmen; and traitors pursued by the messengers of the Government had been concealed in the garrets of several colleges. Yet the admonition which, even under such circumstances, Addison addressed to the University, is singularly gentle, respectful, and even affectionate. Indeed, he could not find it in his heart to deal harshly even with imaginary persons. His foxhunter, though ignorant, stupid, and violent, is at heart a good fellow, and is at last reclaimed by the clemency of the King. Steele was dissatisfied with his friend's moderation, and, though he acknowledged that the Freeholder was excellently written, complained that the ministry played on a lute when it was necessary to blow the trumpet. He accordingly determined to execute a flourish after his own fashion, and tried to rouse the public spirit of the nation by means of a paper called the Town Talk, which is now as utterly forgotten as his Englishman, as his Crisis, as his Letter to the Bailiff of Stockbridge, as his Reader, in short, as everything that he wrote without the help of Addison.

In the same year in which the Drummer was acted, and in which the first numbers of the Freeholder appeared, the estrangement of Pope and Addison became complete. Addison had from the first seen that Pope was false and malevolent. Pope had discovered that Addison was jealous. The breach was made in a strange manner. Pope had written the Rape of the Lock, in two cantos, without supernatural machinery. These two cantos had been loudly applauded, and by none more loudly than by Addison. Then Pope thought of the Sylphs and Gnomes, Ariel, Momentilla, Crispissa, and Umbriel, and resolved to interweave the Rosicrucian mythology with the original fabric. He asked Addison's advice. Addison said that the poem as it stood was a delicious little thing, and entreated Pope not to run the risk of marring what was so excellent in trying to mend it. Pope afterwards declared that this insidious counsel first opened his eyes to the baseness of him who gave it.

Now there can be no doubt that Pope's plan was most ingenious, and that he afterwards executed it with great skill and success. But does it necessarily follow that Addison's advice was bad? And if Addison's advice was bad, does it necessarily follow that it was given from bad motives? If a friend were to ask us whether we would advise him to risk his all in a lottery of which the chances were ten to one against him, we should do our best to dissuade him from running such a risk. Even if he were so lucky as to get the thirty thousand pound prize, we should not admit that we had counselled him ill; and we should certainly think it the height of injustice in him to accuse us of having been actuated by malice. We think Addison's advice good advice. It rested on a sound principle, the result of long and wide experience. The general rule undoubtedly is that, when a successful work of imagination has been produced, it should not be recast. We cannot at this moment call to mind a single instance in which this rule has been transgressed with happy effect, except the instance of the Rape of the Lock. Tasso recast his Jerusalem. Akenside recast his Pleasures of the Imagination, and his Epistle to Curio. Pope himself, emboldened no doubt by the success with which he had expanded and remodelled of the Lock, made the same experiment on the Du*these attempts* failed. Who was to foresee that P once in his life, be able to do what he could not himself do twice, and what nobody else has ever done?

Addison's advice was good. But had it been bad, why should we pronounce it dishonest? Scott tells us that one of his best friends predicted the failure of Waverley. Herder adjured Goethe not to take so unpromising a subject as Faust. Hume tried to dissuade Robertson from writing the History of Charles the Fifth. Nay, Pope himself was one of those who prophesied that Cato would never succeed on the stage, and advised Addison to print it without risking a representation. But Scott, Goethe, Robertson, Addison, had the good sense and generosity to give their advisers credit for the best intentions. Pope's heart was not of the same kind with theirs.

In 1715, while he was engaged in translating the Iliad, he met Addison at a coffee-house. Phillipps and Budgell were there; but their sovereign got rid of them, and asked Pope to dine with him alone. After dinner, Addison said that he lay under a difficulty which he wished to explain. "Tickell," he said, "translated some time ago the first book of the Iliad. I have promised to look it over and correct it. I cannot therefore ask to see yours; for that would be double dealing." Pope made a civil reply, and begged that his second book might have the advantage of Addison's revision. Addison readily agreed, looked over the second book, and sent it back with warm commendations.

Tickell's version of the first book appeared soon after this conversation. In the preface, all rivalry was earnestly disclaimed. Tickell declared that he should not go on with the Iliad. That enterprise he should leave to powers which he admitted to be superior to his own. His only view, he said, in publishing this specimen was to bespeak the favour of the public to a translation of the Odyssey, in which he had made some progress.

Addison, and Addison's devoted followers, pronounced both the versions good, but maintained that Tickell's had more of the original. The town gave a decided preference to Pope's. We do not think it worth while to settle such a question of precedence. Neither of the rivals can be said to have translated the Iliad, unless, indeed, the word translation be used in the sense which it bears in the Midsummer Night's Dream. When Bottom makes his appearance with an ass's head instead of his own, Peter Quince exclaims, "Bless thee! Bottom, bless thee! thou art translated." In this sense, undoubtedly, the readers of either Pope or Tickell may very properly exclaim, "Bless thee! Homer; thou art translated indeed."

Our readers will, we hope, agree with us in thinking that no man in Addison's situation could have acted more fairly and kindly, both towards Pope, and towards Tickell, than he appears to have done. But an odious suspicion had sprung up in the mind of Pope. He fancied, and he soon firmly believed, that there was a deep conspiracy against his fame and his fortunes. The work on which he had staked his reputation was to be depreciated. The subscription, on which rested his hopes of a competence, was to be defeated. With this view Addison had made a rival translation: Tickell had consented to father it; and the wits of Button's had united to puff it.

Is there any external evidence to support this grave accusation? The answer is short. There is absolutely none.

Was there any internal evidence which proved Addison to be the author of this version? Was it a work which Tickell was incapable of producing? Surely not. Tickell was a fellow of a College at Oxford, and must be supposed to have been able to construe the Iliad; and he was a better versifier than his friend. We are not aware that Pope pretended to have discovered any turns of expression peculiar to Addison. Had such turns of expression been discovered, they would be suffiently accounted for by supposing Addison to have corrected his friend's lines, as he owned that he had done.

Is there any thing in the character of the accused persons which makes the accusation probable? We answer confidently — nothing. Tickell was long after this time described by Pope himself as a very fair and worthy man. Addison had been, during many years, before the public. Literary rivals, political opponents, had kept their eyes on him. But neither envy nor faction, in their utmost rage, had ever imputed to him a single deviation from the laws of honour and of social morality. Had he been indeed a man meanly jealous of fame, and capable of stooping to base and wicked arts for the purpose of injuring his competitors, would his vices have remained latent so long? He was a writer of tragedy: had he ever injured Rowe? He was a writer of comedy: had he not done ample justice to Congreve, and given valuable help to Steele? He was a pamphleteer: have not his good nature and generosity been acknowledged by Swift, his rival in fame and his adversary in politics?

That Tickell should have been guilty of a villany seems to us highly improbable. That Addison should have been guilty of a villany seems to us highly improbable. But that these two men should have conspired together to commit a villany seems to us improbable in a tenfold degree. All that is known to us of their intercourse tends to prove, that it was not the intercourse of two accomplices in crime. These are some of the lines in which Tickell poured forth his sorrow over the coffin of Addison:

> "Or dost thou warn poor mortals left behind,
> A task well suited to thy gentle mind?
> Oh, if sometimes thy spotless form descend,
> To me thine aid, thou guardian genius, lend.
> When rage misguides me, or when fear alarms,
> When pain distresses, or when pleasure charms,
> In silent whisperings purer thoughts impart,
> And turn from ill a frail and feeble heart;
> Lead through the paths thy virtue trod before,
> Till bliss shall join, nor death can part us more."

In what words, we should like to know, did this guardian genius invite his pupil to join in a plan such as the Editor of the Satirist would hardly dare to propose to the Editor of the Age?

We do not accuse Pope of bringing an accusation which he knew to be false. We have not the smallest doubt that he believed it to be true; and the evidence on which he believed it he found in his own bad heart. His own life was one long series of tricks, as mean and as malicious as that of which he suspected Addison and Tickell. He was all stiletto and mask. To injure, to insult, and to save himself from the consequences of injury and insult by lying and equivocating, was the habit of his life. He published a lampoon on the Duke of Chandos; he was taxed with it; and he lied and equivocated. He published a lampoon on Aaron Hill; he was taxed with it; and he lied and equivocated. He published a still fouler lampoon on Lady Mary Wortley Montague; he was taxed with it; and he lied with more than usual effrontery and vehemence. He puffed himself and abused his enemies under feigned names. He robbed himself of his own letters, and then raised the hue and cry after them. Besides his frauds of malignity, of fear, of interest, and of vanity, there were frauds which he seems to have committed from love of fraud alone. He *had a habit of stratagem*, a pleasure in outwitting all who came *near him*. Whatever his object might be, the indirect road to it was that which he preferred. For Bolingbroke, Pope undoubtedly felt as much love and veneration as it was in his nature to feel for any human being. Yet Pope was scarcely dead when it was discovered that, from no motive except the mere love of artifice, he had been guilty of an act of gross perfidy to Bolingbroke.

Nothing was more natural than that such a man as this should attribute to others that which he felt within himself. A plain, probable, coherent explanation is frankly given to him. He is certain that it is all a romance. A line of conduct scrupulously fair, and even friendly, is pursued towards him. He is convinced that it is merely a cover for a vile intrigue by which he is to be disgraced and ruined. It is vain to ask him for proofs. He has none, and wants none, except those which he carries in his own bosom.

Whether Pope's malignity at length provoked Addison to retaliate for the first and last time, cannot now be known with certainty. We have only Pope's story, which runs thus. A pamphlet appeared containing some reflections which stung Pope to the quick. What those reflections were, and whether they were reflections of which he had a right to complain, we have now no means of deciding. The Earl of Warwick, a foolish and vicious lad, who regarded Addison with the feelings with which such lads generally regard their best friends, told Pope, truly or falsely, that this pamphlet had been written by Addison's direction. When we consider what a tendency stories have to grow, in passing even from one honest man to another honest man, and when we consider that to the name of honest man neither Pope nor the Earl of Warwick had a claim, we are not disposed to attach much importance to this anecdote.

It is certain, however, that Pope was furious. He had already sketched the character of Atticus in prose. In his anger he turned this prose into the brilliant and energetic lines which every body knows by heart, or ought to know by heart, and sent them to Addison. One charge which Pope has enforced with great skill is probably not without foundation. Addison was, we are inclined to believe, too fond of presiding over a circle of humble friends. Of the other imputations which these famous lines are intended to convey, scarcely one has ever been proved to be just, and some are certainly false. That Addison was not in the habit of "damning with faint praise" appears from innumerable passages in his writings, and from none more than from those in which he mentions Pope. And it is not merely unjust, but ridiculous, to describe a man who made the fortune of almost every one of his intimate friends, as "so obliging that he ne'er obliged."

That Addison felt the sting of Pope's satire keenly, we cannot doubt. That he was conscious of one of the weaknesses with which he was reproached, is highly probable. But his heart, we firmly believe, acquitted him of the gravest part of the accusation. He acted like himself. As a satirist he was, at his own weapons, more than Pope's match; and he would have been at no loss for topics. A distorted and diseased body, tenanted by a yet more distorted and diseased mind; spite and envy thinly disguised by sentiments as benevolent and noble as those which Sir Peter Teazle admired in Mr. Joseph Surface; a feeble sickly licentiousness; an odious love of filthy and noisome images; these were things which a genius less powerful than that to which we owe the Spectator could easily have held up to the mirth and hatred of mankind. Addison had, moreover, at his command other means of vengeance which a bad man would not have scrupled to use. *He was* powerful in the state. Pope was a Catholic; and, in *those times*, a minister would have found it easy to harrass the most innocent Catholic by innumerable petty vexations. Pope, near twenty years later, said that "through the lenity of the government alone he could live with comfort." "Consider," he exclaimed, "the injury that a man of high rank and credit may do to a private person, under penal laws and many other disadvantages." It is pleasing to reflect that the only revenge which Addison took was to insert in the Freeholder a warm encomium on the translation of the Iliad, and to exhort all lovers of learning to put down their names as subscribers. There could be no doubt, he said, from the specimens already published, that the masterly hand of Pope would do as much for Homer as Dryden had done for Virgil. From that time to the end of his life, he always treated Pope, by Pope's own acknowledgment, with justice. Friendship was, of course, at an end.

One reason which induced the Earl of Warwick to play the ignominious part of talebearer on this occasion, may have been his dislike of the marriage which was about to take place between his mother and Addison. The Countess Dowager, a daughter of the old and honourable family of the Myddletons of Chirk, a family which, in any country but ours, would be called noble, resided at Holland House. Addison had, during some years, occupied at Chelsea a small dwelling, once the abode of Nell Gwynn. Chelsea is now a district of London, and Holland House may be called a town residence. But, in the days of Anne and George the First, milkmaids and sportsmen wandered between green hedges and over fields bright with daisies, from Kensington almost to the shore of the Thames. Addison and Lady Warwick were country neighbours, and became intimate friends. The great wit and scholar tried to allure the young Lord from the fashionable amusements of beating watchmen, breaking windows, and rolling women in hogsheads down Holborn Hill, to the study of letters and the practice of virtue. These well meant exertions did little good, however, either to the disciple or to the master. Lord Warwick grew up a rake; and Addison fell in love. The mature beauty of the Countess has been celebrated by poets in language which, after a very large allowance has been made for flattery, would lead us to believe that she was a fine woman; and her rank doubtless heightened her attractions. The courtship was long. The hopes of the lover appear to have risen and fallen with the fortunes of his party. His attachment was at length matter of such notoriety that, when he visited Ireland for the last time, Rowe addressed some consolatory verses to the Chloe of Holland House. It strikes us as a little strange that, in these verses, Addison should be called Lycidas, a name of singularly evil omen for a swain just about to cross St. George's Channel.

At length Chloe capitulated. Addison was indeed able to treat with her on equal terms. He had reason to expect preferment even higher than that which he had attained. He had inherited the fortune of a brother who died Governor of Madras. He had purchased an estate in Warwickshire, and had been welcomed to his domain in very tolerable verse by one of the neighbouring squires, the poetical foxhunter, William Somervile. In August 1716, the newspapers announced that Joseph Addison, Esquire, famous for many excellent works both in verse and prose, had espoused the Countess Dowager of Warwick.

He now fixed his abode at Holland House, a house which can boast of a greater number of inmates distinguished in political and literary history than any other private dwelling in England. His portrait still hangs there. The features are pleasing; the complexion is remarkably fair; but, in the *expression*, we trace rather the gentleness of his disposition than *the force* and keenness of his intellect.

Not long after his marriage he reached the height of civil greatness. The Whig Government had, during some time, been torn by internal dissensions. Lord Townshend led one section of the Cabinet, Lord Sunderland the other. At length, in the spring of 1717, Sunderland triumphed. Townshend retired from office, and was accompanied by Walpole and Cowper. Sunderland proceeded to reconstruct the Ministry; and Addison was appointed Secretary of State. It is certain that the Seals were pressed upon him, and were at first declined by him. Men equally versed in official business might easily have been found; and his colleagues knew that they could not expect assistance from him in debate. He owed his elevation to his popularity, to his stainless probity, and to his literary fame.

But scarcely had Addison entered the Cabinet when his health began to fail. From one serious attack he recovered in the autumn; and his recovery was celebrated in Latin verses, worthy of his own pen, by Vincent Bourne, who was then at Trinity College, Cambridge. A relapse soon took place; and, in the following spring, Addison was prevented by a severe asthma from discharging the duties of his post. He resigned it, and was succeeded by his friend Craggs, a young man whose natural parts, though little improved by cultivation, were quick and showy, whose graceful person and winning manners had made him generally acceptable in society, and who, if he had lived, would probably have been the most formidable of all the rivals of Walpole.

As yet there was no Joseph Hume. The Ministers, therefore, were able to bestow on Addison a retiring pension of fifteen hundred pounds a-year. In what form this pension was given we are not told by the biographers, and have not time to inquire. But it is certain that Addison did not vacate his seat in the *House of* Commons.

Rest of mind and body seemed to have re-established his health; and he thanked God, with cheerful piety, for having set him free both from his office and from his asthma. Many years seemed to be before him, and he meditated many works, a tragedy on the death of Socrates, a translation of the Psalms, a treatise on the evidences of Christianity. Of this last performance, a part, which we could well spare, has come down to us.

But the fatal complaint soon returned, and gradually prevailed against all the resources of medicine. It is melancholy to think that the last months of such a life should have been overclouded both by domestic and by political vexations. A tradition which began early, which has been generally received, and to which we have nothing to oppose, has represented his wife as an arrogant and imperious woman. It is said that, till his health failed him, he was glad to escape from the Countess Dowager and her magnificent dining room, blazing with the gilded devices of the House of Rich, to some tavern where he could enjoy a laugh, a talk about Virgil and Boileau, and a bottle of claret, with the friends of his happier days. All those friends, however, were not left to him. Sir Richard Steele had been gradually estranged by various causes. He considered himself as one who, in evil times, had braved martyrdom for his political principles, and demanded, when the Whig party was triumphant, a large compensation for what he had suffered when it was militant. The Whig leaders took a very different view of his claims. They thought that he had, by his own petulance and folly, brought them as well as himself into trouble, and though they did not absolutely neglect him, doled out favours to him with a sparing hand. It was natural that he should be angry with *them,* and especially angry with Addison. But what above *all seems* to have disturbed Sir Richard, was the elevation of Tickell, who, at thirty, was made by Addison Undersecretary of State; while the Editor of the Tatler and Spectator, the author of the Crisis, the member for Stockbridge who had been persecuted for firm adherence to the House of Hanover, was, at near fifty, forced, after many solicitations and complaints, to content himself with a share in the patent of Drury Lane theatre. Steele himself says in his celebrated letter to Congreve, that Addison, by his preference of Tickell, "incurred the warmest resentment of other gentlemen;" and every thing seems to indicate that, of those resentful gentlemen, Steele was himself one.

While poor Sir Richard was brooding over what he considered as Addison's unkindness, a new cause of quarrel arose. The Whig party, already divided against itself, was rent by a new schism. The celebrated Bill for limiting the number of Peers had been brought in. The proud Duke of Somerset, first in rank of all the nobles whose religion permitted them to sit in Parliament, was the ostensible author of the measure. But it was supported, and, in truth, devised by the Prime Minister.

We are satisfied that the Bill was most pernicious; and we fear that the motives which induced Sunderland to frame it were not honourable to him. But we cannot deny that it was supported by many of the best and wisest men of that age. Nor was this strange. The royal prerogative had, within the memory of the generation then in the vigour of life, been so grossly abused, that it was still regarded with a jealousy which, when the peculiar situation of the House of Brunswick is considered, may perhaps be called immoderate. The particular prerogative of creating peers had, in the opinion of the Whigs, been grossly abused by Queen Anne's last ministry; and even the Tories admitted that her Majesty, in swamping, as it has since been called, the Upper House, had done what only an extreme case could justify. The theory of the English constitution, according to many high authorities, was that three independent powers, the sovereign, the nobility, and the commons, ought constantly to act as checks on each other. If this theory were sound, it seemed to follow that to put one of these powers under the absolute control of the other two, was absurd. But if the number of peers were unlimited, it could not well be denied that the Upper House was under the absolute control of the Crown and the Commons, and was indebted only to their moderation for any power which it might be suffered to retain.

Steele took part with the Opposition, Addison with the Ministers. Steele, in a paper called the Plebeian, vehemently attacked the bill. Sunderland called for help on Addison, and Addison obeyed the call. In a paper called the Old Whig, he answered, and indeed refuted, Steele's arguments. It seems to us that the premises of both the controversialists were unsound, that, on those premises, Addison reasoned well and Steele ill, and that consequently Addison brought out a false conclusion, while Steele blundered upon the truth. In style, in wit, and in politeness, Addison maintained his superiority, though the Old Whig is by no means one of his happiest performances.

At first, both the anonymous opponents observed the laws of propriety. But at length Steele so far forgot himself as to throw an odious imputation on the morals of the chiefs of the administration. Addison replied with severity, but, in our opinion, with less severity than was due to so grave an offence against morality and decorum; nor did he, in his just anger, forget for a moment the laws of good taste and good breeding. One calumny which has been often repeated, and never yet *contradicted*, it is our duty to expose. It is asserted in the *Biographia Britannica*, that Addison designated Steele as "little Dicky." This assertion was repeated by Johnson, who had never seen the Old Whig, and was therefore excusable. It has also been repeated by Miss Aikin, who has seen the Old Whig, and for whom therefore there is less excuse. Now, it is true that the words "little Dicky" occur in the Old Whig, and that Steele's name was Richard. It is equally true that the words "little Isaac" occur in the Duenna, and that Newton's name was Isaac. But we confidently affirm that Addison's little Dicky had no more to do with Steele, than Sheridan's little Isaac with Newton. If we apply the words "little Dicky" to Steele, we deprive a very lively and ingenious passage, not only of all its wit, but of all its meaning. Little Dicky was the nickname of Henry Norris, an actor of remarkably small stature, but of great humour, who played the usurer Gomez, then a most popular part, in Dryden's Spanish Friar.*

The merited reproof which Steele had received, though softened by some kind and courteous expressions, galled him bitterly. He replied with little force and great acrimony; but no rejoinder appeared. Addison was fast hastening to his grave; and had, we may well suppose, little disposition to prosecute a quarrel with an old friend. His complaint had

* We will transcribe the whole paragraph. How it can ever have been misunderstood is unintelligible to us.

"But our author's chief concern is for the poor House of Commons, whom he represents as naked and defenceless, when the Crown, by losing this prerogative, would be less able to protect them against the power of a House of Lords. Who forbears laughing when the Spanish Friar represents little Dicky, under the person of Gomez, insulting the Colonel that was able to fright him out of his wits with a single frown? This Gomez, says he, flew upon him like a dragon, got him down, the Devil being strong in him, and gave him bastinado on bastinado, and buffet on buffet, which the poor Colonel, being prostrate, suffered with a most Christian patience. The improbability of the fact never fails to raise mirth in the audience; and one may venture to answer for a British House of Commons, if we may guess from its conduct hitherto, that it will scarce be either so tame or so weak as our author supposes."

terminated in dropsy. He bore up long and manfully. But at length he abandoned all hope, dismissed his physicians, and calmly prepared himself to die.

His works he intrusted to the care of Tickell, and dedicated them a very few days before his death to Craggs, in a letter written with the sweet and graceful eloquence of a Saturday's Spectator. In this his last composition, he alluded to his approaching end in words so manly, so cheerful, and so tender, that it is difficult to read them without tears. At the same time he earnestly recommended the interests of Tickell to the care of Craggs.

Within a few hours of the time at which this dedication was written, Addison sent to beg Gay, who was then living by his wits about town, to come to Holland House. Gay went and was received with great kindness. To his amazement his forgiveness was implored by the dying man. Poor Gay, the most good natured and simple of mankind, could not imagine what he had to forgive. There was, however, some wrong, the remembrance of which weighed on Addison's mind, and which he declared himself anxious to repair. He was in a state of extreme exhaustion; and the parting was doubtless a friendly one on both sides. Gay supposed that some plan to serve him had been in agitation at Court, and had been frustrated by Addison's influence. Nor is this improbable. Gay had paid assiduous court to the royal family. But in the Queen's days he had been the eulogist of Bolingbroke, and was still connected with many Tories. It is not strange that Addison, while heated by conflict, should have thought himself justified in obstructing the preferment of one whom he might regard as a political enemy. Neither is it strange that, when reviewing his whole life, and earnestly scrutinising all his motives, he should think that he had acted an unkind and ungenerous part, in using his power against a distressed man of letters, who was as harmless and as helpless as a child.

One inference may be drawn from this anecdote. It appears that Addison, on his deathbed, called himself to a strict account; and was not at ease till he had asked pardon for an injury which it was not even suspected that he had committed, for an injury which would have caused disquiet only to a very tender conscience. Is it not then reasonable to infer that, if he had really been guilty of forming a base conspiracy against the fame and fortunes of a rival, he would have expressed some remorse for so serious a crime? But it is unnecessary to multiply arguments and evidence for the defence, when there is neither argument nor evidence for the accusation.

The last moments of Addison were perfectly serene. His interview with his son-in-law is universally known. "See," he said, "how a Christian can die." The piety of Addison was, in truth, of a singularly cheerful character. The feeling which predominates in all his devotional writings is gratitude. God was to him the allwise and allpowerful friend who had watched over his cradle with more than maternal tenderness; who had listened to his cries before they could form themselves in prayer; who had preserved his youth from the snares of vice; who had made his cup run over with worldly blessings; who had doubled the value of those blessings, by bestowing a thankful heart to enjoy them, and dear friends to partake them; who had rebuked the waves of the Ligurian gulf, had purified the autumnal air of the Campagna, and had restrained the avalanches of Mont Cenis. Of the Psalms, his favourite was that which represents the Ruler of all things under the endearing image of a shepherd, whose crook guides the flock safe, through gloomy and desolate glens, to meadows well watered and rich with herbage. On that goodness to which he ascribed all the happiness of his life, he relied in the hour of death with the love which casteth out fear. He died on the seventeenth of June 1719. He had just entered on his forty-eighth year.

His body lay in state in the Jerusalem Chamber, and was borne thence to the Abbey at dead of night. The choir sang a funeral hymn. Bishop Atterbury, one of those Tories who had loved and honoured the most accomplished of the Whigs, met the corpse, and led the procession by torch-light, round the shrine of Saint Edward and the graves of the Plantagenets, to the Chapel of Henry the Seventh. On the north side of that Chapel, in the vault of the House of Albemarle, the coffin of Addison lies next to the coffin of Montague. Yet a few months; and the same mourners passed again along the same aisle. The same sad anthem was again chanted. The same vault was again opened; and the coffin of Craggs was placed close to the coffin of Addison.

Many tributes were paid to the memory of Addison; but one alone is now remembered. Tickell bewailed his friend in an elegy which would do honour to the greatest name in our literature, and which unites the energy and magnificence of Dryden to the tenderness and purity of Cowper. This fine poem was prefixed to a superb edition of Addison's works, which was published, in 1721, by subscription. The names of the subscribers proved how widely his fame had been spread. That his countrymen should be eager to possess his writings, even in a costly form, is not wonderful. But it is wonderful that, though English literature was then little studied on the continent, Spanish Grandees, Italian Prelates, Marshals of France, should be found in the list. Among the most remarkable names are those of the Queen of Sweden, of Prince Eugene, of the Grand Duke of Tuscany, of the *Dukes* of Parma, Modena, and Guastalla, of the Doge of *Genoa*, of the Regent Orleans, and of Cardinal Dubois. We ought to add that this edition, though eminently beautiful, is in some important points defective; nor, indeed, do we yet possess a complete collection of Addison's writings.

It is strange that neither his opulent and noble widow, nor any of his powerful and attached friends, should have thought of placing even a simple tablet, inscribed with his name, on the walls of the Abbey. It was not till three generations had laughed and wept over his pages that the omission was supplied by the public veneration. At length, in our own time, his image, skilfully graven, appeared in Poet's Corner. It represents him, as we can conceive him, clad in his dressing gown, and freed from his wig, stepping from his parlour at Chelsea into his trim little garden, with the account of the Everlasting Club, or the Loves of Hilpa and Shalum, just finished for the next day's Spectator, in his hand. Such a mark of national respect was due to the unsullied statesman, to the accomplished scholar, to the master of pure English eloquence, to the consummate painter of life and manners. It was due, above all, to the great satirist, who alone knew how to use ridicule without abusing it, who, without inflicting a wound, effected a great social reform, and who reconciled wit and virtue, after a long and disastrous separation, during which wit had been led astray by profligacy, and virtue by fanaticism.

# THE EARL OF CHATHAM. (October, 1844.)

1. *Correspondence of William Pitt, Earl of Chatham.* 4 vols. 8vo. London: 1840.

2. *Letters of Horace Walpole, Earl of Orford, to Horace Mann.* 4 vols. 8vo. London: 1843-4.

More than ten years ago we commenced a sketch of the political life of the great Lord Chatham. We then stopped at the death of George the Second, with the intention of speedily resuming our task. Circumstances, which it would be tedious to explain, long prevented us from carrying this intention into effect. Nor can we regret the delay. For the materials which were within our reach in 1834 were scanty and unsatisfactory, when compared with those which we at present possess. Even now, though we have had access to some valuable sources of information which have not yet been opened to the public, we cannot but feel that the history of the first ten years of the reign of George the Third is but imperfectly known to us. Nevertheless, we are inclined to think that we are in a condition to lay before our readers a narrative neither uninstructive nor uninteresting. We therefore return with pleasure to our long interrupted labour.

We left Pitt in the zenith of prosperity and glory, the idol of England, the terror of France, the admiration of the whole civilised world. The wind, from whatever quarter it blew, carried to England tidings of battles won, fortresses taken, *provinces* added to the empire. At home, factions had sunk *into a lethargy,* such as had never been known since the great religious schism of the sixteenth century had roused the public mind from repose.

In order that the events which we have to relate may be clearly understood, it may be desirable that we should advert to the causes which had for a time suspended the animation of both the great English parties.

If, rejecting all that is merely accidental, we look at the essential characteristics of the Whig and the Tory, we may consider each of them as the representative of a great principle, essential to the welfare of nations. One is, in an especial manner, the guardian of liberty, and the other, of order. One is the moving power, and the other the steadying power of the state. One is the sail, without which society would make no progress, the other the ballast, without which there would be small safety in a tempest. But, during the forty-six years which followed the accession of the House of Hanover, these distinctive peculiarities seemed to be effaced. The Whig conceived that he could not better serve the cause of civil and religious freedom than by strenuously supporting the Protestant dynasty. The Tory conceived that he could not better prove his hatred of revolutions than by attacking a government to which a revolution had given birth. Both came by degrees to attach more importance to the means than to the end. Both were thrown into unnatural situations; and both, like animals transported to an uncongenial climate, languished and degenerated. The Tory, removed from the sunshine of the court, was as a camel in the snows of Lapland. The Whig, basking in the rays of royal favour, was as a reindeer in the sands of Arabia.

Dante tells us that he saw, in Malebolge, a strange encounter between a human form and a serpent. The enemies, after cruel wounds inflicted, stood for a time glaring on each other. A great cloud surrounded them, and then a wonderful metamorphosis began. Each creature was transfigured into the likeness of its antagonist. The serpent's tail divided itself into two legs; the man's legs intertwined themselves into a tail. The body of the serpent put forth arms; the arms of the man shrank into his body. At length the serpent stood up a man, and spake; the man sank down a serpent, and glided hissing away. Something like this was the transformation which, during the reign of George the First, befell the two English parties. Each gradually took the shape and colour of its foe, till at length the Tory rose up erect the zealot of freedom, and the Whig crawled and licked the dust at the feet of power.

It is true that, when these degenerate politicians discussed questions merely speculative, and, above all, when they discussed questions relating to the conduct of their own grandfathers, they still seemed to differ as their grandfathers had differed. The Whig, who, during three Parliaments, had never given one vote against the court, and who was ready to sell his soul for the Comptroller's staff or for the Great Wardrobe, still professed to draw his political doctrines from Locke and Milton, still worshipped the memory of Pym and Hampden, and would still, on the thirtieth of January, take his glass, first to the man in the mask, and then to the man who would do it without a mask. The Tory, on the other hand, while he reviled the mild and temperate Walpole as a deadly enemy of liberty, could see nothing to reprobate in the iron tyranny of Strafford and Laud. But, whatever judgment the Whig or the Tory of that age might pronounce on transactions long past, there can be no doubt that, as respected the practical questions then pending, the Tory was a reformer, and indeed an intemperate and indiscreet reformer, *while the* Whig was conservative even to bigotry. We have *ourselves* seen similar effects produced in a neighbouring country by similar causes. Who would have believed, fifteen years ago, that M. Guizot and M. Villemain would have to defend property and social order against the attacks of such enemies as M. Genoude and M. de La Roche Jaquelin?

Thus the successors of the old Cavaliers had turned demagogues; the successors of the old Roundheads had turned courtiers. Yet was it long before their mutual animosity began to abate; for it is the nature of parties to retain their original enmities far more firmly than their original principles. During many years, a generation of Whigs, whom Sidney would have spurned as slaves, continued to wage deadly war with a generation of Tories whom Jeffreys would have hanged for republicans.

Through the whole reign of George the First, and through nearly half of the reign of George the Second, a Tory was regarded as an enemy of the reigning house, and was excluded from all the favours of the crown. Though most of the country gentlemen were Tories, none but Whigs were created peers and baronets. Though most of the clergy were Tories, none but Whigs were appointed deans and bishops. In every county, opulent and well descended Tory squires complained that their names were left out of the commission of the peace, while men of small estate and mean birth, who were for toleration and excise, septennial parliaments and standing armies, presided at quarter sessions, and became deputy lieutenants.

By degrees some approaches were made towards a reconciliation. While Walpole was at the head of affairs, enmity to his power induced a large and powerful body of Whigs, headed by the heir apparent of the throne, to make an alliance with the Tories, and a truce even with the Jacobites. After Sir Robert's fall, the ban which lay on the Tory party was taken off. The chief places in the administration continued to be filled by Whigs, and, indeed, could scarcely have been filled otherwise; for the Tory nobility and gentry, though strong in numbers and in property, had among them scarcely a single man distinguished by talents, either for business or for debate. A few of them, however, were admitted to subordinate offices; and this indulgence produced a softening effect on the temper of the whole body. The first levee of George the Second after Walpole's resignation was a remarkable spectacle. Mingled with the constant supporters of the House of Brunswick, with the Russells, the Cavendishes, and the Pelhams, appeared a crowd of faces utterly unknown to the pages and gentlemen ushers, lords of rural manors, whose ale and foxhounds were renowned in the neighbourhood of the Mendip hills, or round the Wrekin, but who had never crossed the threshold of the palace since the days when Oxford, with the white staff in his hand, stood behind Queen Anne.

During the eighteen years which followed this day, both factions were gradually sinking deeper and deeper into repose. The apathy of the public mind is partly to be ascribed to the unjust violence with which the administration of Walpole had been assailed. In the body politic, as in the natural body, morbid languor generally succeeds morbid excitement. The people had been maddened by sophistry, by calumny, by rhetoric, by stimulants applied to the national pride. In the fulness of bread, they had raved as if famine had been in the land. While enjoying such a measure of civil and religious freedom as, till then, no great society had ever known, they had cried out for a Timoleon or a Brutus to stab their oppressor to the heart. They were in this frame of mind when the change of administration took place; and they soon found that there was to be no change whatever in the system of *government*. The natural consequences followed. To frantic zeal succeeded sullen indifference. The cant of patriotism had not merely ceased to charm the public ear, but had become as nauseous as the cant of Puritanism after the downfall of the Rump. The hot fit was over: the cold fit had begun: and it was long before seditious arts, or even real grievances, could bring back the fiery paroxysm which had run its course and reached its termination.

Two attempts were made to disturb this tranquillity. The banished heir of the House of Stuart headed a rebellion; the discontented heir of the House of Brunswick headed an opposition. Both the rebellion and the opposition came to nothing. The battle of Culloden annihilated the Jacobite party. The death of Prince Frederic dissolved the faction which, under his guidance, had feebly striven to annoy his father's government. His chief followers hastened to make their peace with the ministry; and the political torpor became complete.

Five years after the death of Prince Frederic, the public mind was for a time violently excited. But this excitement had nothing to do with the old disputes between Whigs and Tories. England was at war with France. The war had been feebly conducted. Minorca had been torn from us. Our fleet had retired before the white flag of the House of Bourbon. A bitter sense of humiliation, new to the proudest and bravest of nations, superseded every other feeling. The cry of all the counties and great towns of the realm was for a government which would retrieve the honour of the English arms. The two most powerful men in the country were the Duke of Newcastle and Pitt. Alternate victories and defeats had made them sensible that neither of them could stand alone. The interest of the state, and the interest of their own ambition impelled them to coalesce. By their coalition was formed the ministry which was in power when George the Third ascended the throne.

The more carefully the structure of this celebrated ministry is examined, the more shall we see reason to marvel at the skill or the luck which had combined in one harmonious whole such various and, as it seemed, incompatible elements of force. The influence which is derived from stainless integrity, the influence which is derived from the vilest arts of corruption, the strength of aristocratical connection, the strength of democratical enthusiasm, all these things were for the first time found together. Newcastle brought to the coalition a vast mass of power, which had descended to him from Walpole and Pelham. The public offices, the church, the courts of law, the army, the navy, the diplomatic service, swarmed with his creatures. The boroughs, which long afterwards made up the memorable schedules A and B, were represented by his nominees. The great Whig families, which, during several generations, had been trained in the discipline of party warfare, and were accustomed to stand together in a firm phalanx, acknowledged him as their captain. Pitt, on the other hand, had what Newcastle wanted, an eloquence which stirred the passions and charmed the imagination, a high reputation for purity, and the confidence and ardent love of millions.

The partition which the two ministers made of the powers of government was singularly happy. Each occupied a province for which he was well qualified; and neither had any inclination to intrude himself into the province of the other. Newcastle took the treasury, the civil and ecclesiastical patronage, and the disposal of that part of the secret service money which was then employed in bribing members of Parliament. Pitt was Secretary of State, with the direction of the war and of foreign affairs. Thus the filth of all the noisome and pestilential sewers of government was poured into *one channel*. Through the other passed only what was bright and stainless. Mean and selfish politicians, pining for commissionerships, gold sticks, and ribands, flocked to the great house at the corner of Lincoln's Inn Fields. There, at every levee, appeared eighteen or twenty pair of lawn sleeves; for there was not, it was said, a single Prelate who had not owed either his first elevation or some subsequent translation to Newcastle. There appeared those members of the House of Commons in whose silent votes the main strength of the government lay. One wanted a place in the excise for his butler. Another came about a prebend for his son. A third whispered that he had always stood by his Grace and the Protestant succession; that his last election had been very expensive; that potwallopers had now no conscience; that he had been forced to take up money on mortgage; and that he hardly knew where to turn for five hundred pounds. The Duke pressed all their hands, passed his arms round all their shoulders, patted all their backs, and sent away some with wages, and some with promises. From this traffic Pitt stood haughtily aloof. Not only was he himself incorruptible, but he shrank from the loathsome drudgery of corrupting others. He had not, however, been twenty years in Parliament, and ten in office, without discovering how the government was carried on. He was perfectly aware that bribery was practised on a large scale by his colleagues. Hating the practice, yet despairing of putting it down, and doubting whether, in those times, any ministry could stand without it, he determined to be blind to it. He would see nothing, know nothing, believe nothing. People who came to talk to him about shares in lucrative contracts, or about the means of securing a Cornish corporation, were soon put out of countenance by his arrogant humility. They did him too much honour. Such matters were beyond his capacity. It was true that his poor advice about expeditions and treaties was listened to with indulgence by a gracious sovereign. If the question were, who should command in North America, or who should be ambassador at Berlin, his colleagues would probably condescend to take his opinion. But he had not, the smallest influence with the Secretary of the Treasury, and could not venture to ask even for a tidewaiter's place.

It may be doubted whether he did not owe as much of his popularity to his ostentatious purity as to his eloquence, or to his talents for the administration of war. It was every where said with delight and admiration that the great Commoner, without any advantages of birth or fortune, had, in spite of the dislike of the Court and of the aristocracy, made himself the first man in England, and made England the first country in the world; that his name was mentioned with awe in every palace from Lisbon to Moscow; that his trophies were in all the four quarters of the globe; yet that he was still plain William Pitt, without title or riband, without pension or sinecure place. Whenever he should retire, after saving the state, he must sell his coach horses and his silver candlesticks. Widely as the taint of corruption had spread, his hands were clean. They had never received, they had never given, the price of infamy. Thus the coalition gathered to itself support from all the high and all the low parts of human nature, and was strong with the whole united strength of virtue and of Mammon.

Pitt and Newcastle were coordinate chief ministers. The subordinate places had been filled on the principle of including in the government every party and shade of party, the avowed Jacobites alone excepted, nay, every public man who, from his abilities or from his situation, seemed likely to be either useful in office or formidable in opposition.

The Whigs, according to what was then considered as their prescriptive right, held by far the largest share of power. The main support of the administration was what may be called the great Whig connection, a connection which, during near half a century, had generally had the chief sway in the country and which derived an immense authority from rank, wealth, borough interest, and firm union. To this connection, of which Newcastle was the head, belonged the houses of Cavendish, Lennox, Fitzroy, Bentinck, Manners, Conway, Wentworth, and many others of high note.

There were two other powerful Whig connections, either of which might have been a nucleus for a strong opposition. But room had been found in the government for both. They were known as the Grenvilles and the Bedfords.

The head of the Grenvilles was Richard Earl Temple. His talents for administration and debate were of no high order. But his great possessions, his turbulent and unscrupulous character, his restless activity, and his skill in the most ignoble tactics of faction, made him one of the most formidable enemies that a ministry could have. He was keeper of the privy seal. His brother George was treasurer of the navy. They were supposed to be on terms of close friendship with Pitt, who had married their sister, and was the most uxorious of husbands.

The Bedfords, or, as they were called by their enemies, the Bloomsbury gang, professed to be led by John Duke of Bedford, but in truth led him wherever they chose, and very often led him where he never would have gone of his own accord. He had many good qualities of head and heart, and would have been certainly a respectable, and possibly a distinguished man, if he had been less under the influence of his friends, or more fortunate in choosing them. Some of them were indeed, to do them justice, men of parts. But here, we are afraid, eulogy must end. Sandwich and Rigby were able debaters, pleasant boon companions, dexterous intriguers, masters of all the arts of jobbing and electioneering, and, both in public and private life, shamelessly immoral. Weymouth had a natural eloquence, which sometimes astonished those who knew how little he owed to study. But he was indolent and dissolute, and had early impaired a fine estate with the dicebox, and a fine constitution with the bottle. The wealth and power of the Duke, and the talents and audacity of some of his retainers, might have seriously annoyed the strongest ministry. But his assistance had been secured. He was Lord Lieutenant of Ireland; Rigby was his secretary; and the whole party dutifully supported the measures of the government.

Two men had, a short time before, been thought likely to contest with Pitt the lead of the House of Commons, William Murray and Henry Fox. But Murray had been removed to the Lords, and was Chief Justice of the King's Bench. Fox was indeed still in the Commons: but means had been found to secure, if not his strenuous support, at least his silent acquiescence. He was a poor man; he was a doting father. The office of Paymaster-General during an expensive war was, in that age, perhaps the most lucrative situation in the gift of the government. This office was bestowed on Fox. The prospect of making a noble fortune in a few years, and of providing amply for his darling boy Charles, was irresistibly tempting. To hold a subordinate place, however profitable, after having led the House of Commons, and having been entrusted with the business of forming a ministry, was indeed a great descent. But a punctilious sense of personal dignity was no part of the character of Henry Fox.

We have not time to enumerate all the other men of weight who were, by some tie or other, attached to the government. We may mention Hardwicke, reputed the first lawyer of the age; Legge, reputed the first financier of the age; the acute and ready Oswald; the bold and humorous Nugent; Charles

Townshend, the most brilliant and versatile of mankind; Elliot, Barrington, North, Pratt. Indeed, as far as we recollect, there were in the whole House of Commons only two men of distinguished abilities who were not connected with the government; and those two men stood so low in public estimation, that the only service which they could have rendered to any government would have been to oppose it. We speak of Lord George Sackville and Bubb Dodington.

Though most of the official men, and all the members of the cabinet, were reputed Whigs, the Tories were by no means excluded from employment. Pitt had gratified many of them with commands in the militia, which increased both their income and their importance in their own counties; and they were therefore in better humour than at any time since the death of Anne. Some of the party still continued to grumble over their punch at the Cocoa Tree; but in the House of Commons not a single one of the malecontents durst lift his eyes above the buckle of Pitt's shoe.

Thus there was absolutely no opposition. Nay, there was no sign from which it could be guessed in what quarter opposition was likely to arise. Several years passed during which Parliament seemed to have abdicated its chief functions. The Journals of the House of Commons, during four sessions, contain no trace of a division on a party question. The supplies, though beyond precedent great, were voted without discussion. The most animated debates of that period were on road bills and inclosure bills.

The old King was content; and it mattered little whether he were content or not. It would have been impossible for him to emancipate himself from a ministry so powerful, even if he had been inclined to do so. But he had no such inclination. He had once, indeed, been strongly prejudiced against Pitt, and had repeatedly been ill used by Newcastle; but the vigour and success with which the war had been waged in Germany, and the smoothness with which all public business was carried on, had produced a favourable change in the royal mind.

Such was the posture of affairs when, on the twenty-fifth of October, 1760, George the Second suddenly died, and George the Third, then twenty-two years old, became King. The situation of George the Third differed widely from that of his grandfather and that of his greatgrandfather. Many years had elapsed since a sovereign of England had been an object of affection to any part of his people. The first two Kings of the House of Hanover had neither those hereditary rights which have often supplied the defect of merit, nor those personal qualities which have often supplied the defect of title. A prince may be popular with little virtue or capacity, if he reigns by birthright derived from a long line of illustrious predecessors. An usurper may be popular, if his genius has saved or aggrandised the nation which he governs. Perhaps no rulers have in our time had a stronger hold on the affection of subjects than the Emperor Francis, and his son-in-law the Emperor Napoleon. But imagine a ruler with no better title than Napoleon, and no better understanding than Francis. Richard Cromwell was such a ruler; and, as soon as an arm was lifted up against him, he fell without a struggle, amidst universal derision. George the First and George the Second were in a situation which bore some resemblance to that of Richard Cromwell. They were saved from the fate of Richard Cromwell by the strenuous and able exertions of the Whig party, and by the general conviction that the nation had no choice but between the House of Brunswick and Popery. But by no class were the Guelphs regarded with *that devoted* affection, of which Charles the First, Charles the Second, and James the Second, in spite of the greatest faults, and in the midst of the greatest misfortunes, received innumerable proofs. Those Whigs who stood by the new dynasty so manfully with purse and sword did so on principles independent of, and indeed almost incompatible with, the sentiment of devoted loyalty. The moderate Tories regarded the foreign dynasty as a great evil, which must be endured for fear of a greater evil. In the eyes of the high Tories, the Elector was the most hateful of robbers and tyrants. The crown of another was on his head; the blood of the brave and loyal was on his hands. Thus, during many years, the Kings of England were objects of strong personal aversion to many of their subjects, and of strong personal attachment to none. They found, indeed, firm and cordial support against the pretender to their throne; but this support was given, not at all for their sake, but for the sake of a religious and political system which would have been endangered by their fall. This support, too, they were compelled to purchase by perpetually sacrificing their private inclinations to the party which had set them on the throne, and which maintained them there.

At the close of the reign of George the Second, the feeling of aversion with which the House of Brunswick had long been regarded by half the nation had died away; but no feeling of affection to that house had yet sprung up. There was little, indeed, in the old King's character to inspire esteem or tenderness. He was not our countryman. He never set foot on our soil till he was more than thirty years old. His speech bewrayed his foreign origin and breeding. His love for his native land, though the most amiable part of his character, was not likely to endear him to his British subjects. He was never so happy as when he could exchange St. James's for Herrenhausen. Year after year, our fleets were employed to *convoy him to the Continent*, and the interests of his kingdom were as nothing to him when compared with the interests of his Electorate. As to the rest, he had neither the qualities which make dulness respectable, nor the qualities which make libertinism attractive. He had been a bad son and a worse father, an unfaithful husband and an ungraceful lover. Not one magnanimous or humane action is recorded of him; but many instances of meanness, and of a harshness which, but for the strong constitutional restraints under which he was placed, might have made the misery of his people.

He died; and at once a new world opened. The young King was a born Englishman. All his tastes and habits, good or bad, were English. No portion of his subjects had anything to reproach him with. Even the remaining adherents of the House of Stuart could scarcely impute to him the guilt of usurpation. He was not responsible for the Revolution, for the Act of Settlement, for the suppression of the risings of 1715 and of 1745. He was innocent of the blood of Derwentwater and Kilmarnock, of Balmerino and Cameron. Born fifty years after the old line had been expelled, fourth in descent and third in succession of the Hanoverian dynasty, he might plead some show of hereditary right. His age, his appearance, and all that was known of his character, conciliated public favour. He was in the bloom of youth; his person and address were pleasing. Scandal imputed to him no vice; and flattery might, without any glaring absurdity, ascribe to him many princely virtues.

It is not strange, therefore, that the sentiment of loyalty, a sentiment which had lately seemed to be as much out of date as the belief in witches or the practice of pilgrimage, should, from the day of his accession, have begun to revive. The Tories in particular, who had always been inclined to King-worship, and who had long felt with pain the want of an idol *before whom* they could bow themselves down, were as joyful as the priest of Apis, when, after a long interval, they had found a new calf to adore. It was soon clear that George the Third was regarded by a portion of the nation with a very different feeling from that which his two predecessors had inspired. They had been merely First Magistrates, Doges, Stadtholders; he was emphatically a King, the anointed of heaven, the breath of his people's nostrils. The years of the widowhood and mourning of the Tory party were over. Dido had kept faith long enough to the cold ashes of a former lord; she had at last found a comforter, and recognised the vestiges of the old flame. The golden days of Harley would return. The Somersets, the Lees, and the Wyndhams would again surround the throne. The latitudinarian Prelates, who had not been ashamed to correspond with Doddridge and to shake hands with Whiston, would be succeeded by divines of the temper of South and Atterbury. The devotion which had been so signally shown to the House of Stuart, which had been proof against defeats, confiscations, and proscriptions, which perfidy, oppression, ingratitude, could not weary out, was now transferred entire to the House of Brunswick. If George the Third would but accept the homage of the Cavaliers and High Churchmen, he should be to them all that Charles the First and Charles the Second had been.

The Prince, whose accession was thus hailed by a great party long estranged from his house, had received from nature a strong will, a firmness of temper to which a harsher name might perhaps be given, and an understanding not, indeed, acute or enlarged, but such as qualified him to be a good man of business. But his character had not yet fully developed itself. He had been brought up in strict seclusion. The detractors of the Princess Dowager of Wales affirmed that she had kept her children from commerce with society, *in order that she might* hold an undivided empire over their minds. She gave a very different explanation of her conduct. She would gladly, she said, see her sons and daughters mix in the world, if they could do so without risk to their morals. But the profligacy of the people of quality alarmed her. The young men were all rakes; the young women made love, instead of waiting till it was made to them. She could not bear to expose those whom she loved best to the contaminating influence of such society. The moral advantages of the system of education which formed the Duke of York, the Duke of Cumberland, and the Queen of Denmark, may perhaps be questioned. George the Third was indeed no libertine; but he brought to the throne a mind only half opened, and was for some time entirely under the influence of his mother and of his Groom of the Stole, John Stuart, Earl of Bute.

The Earl of Bute was scarcely known, even by name, to the country which he was soon to govern. He had indeed, a short time after he came of age, been chosen to fill a vacancy which, in the middle of a parliament, had taken place among the Scotch representative peers. He had disobliged the Whig ministers by giving some silent votes with the Tories, had consequently lost his seat at the next dissolution, and had never been reelected. Near twenty years had elapsed since he had borne any part in politics. He had passed some of those years at his seat in one of the Hebrides, and from that retirement he had emerged as one of the household of Prince Frederic. Lord Bute, excluded from public life, had found out many ways of amusing his leisure. He was a tolerable actor in private theatricals, and was particularly successful in the part of Lothario. A handsome leg, to which both painters and satirists took care to give prominence, was among his chief qualifications for the stage. He devised quaint dresses for masquerades. He dabbled in geometry, mechanics, and botany. He paid some attention to antiquities and works of art, and was considered in his own circle as a judge of painting, architecture, and poetry. It is said that his spelling was incorrect. But though, in our time, incorrect spelling is justly considered as a proof of sordid ignorance, it would be unjust to apply the same rule to people who lived a century ago. The novel of Sir Charles Grandison was published about the time at which Lord Bute made his appearance at Leicester House. Our readers may perhaps remember the account which Charlotte Grandison gives of her two lovers. One of them, a fashionable baronet who talks French and Italian fluently, cannot write a line in his own language without some sin against orthography; the other, who is represented as a most respectable specimen of the young aristocracy, and something of a virtuoso, is described as spelling pretty well for a lord. On the whole, the Earl of Bute might fairly be called a man of cultivated mind. He was also a man of undoubted honour. But his understanding was narrow, and his manners cold and haughty. His qualifications for the part of a statesman were best described by Frederic, who often indulged in the unprincely luxury of sneering at his dependents. "Bute," said his Royal Highness, "you are the very man to be envoy at some small proud German court where there is nothing to do."

Scandal represented the Groom of the Stole as the favoured lover of the Princess Dowager. He was undoubtedly her confidential friend. The influence which the two united exercised over the mind of the King was for a time unbounded. The Princess, a woman and a foreigner, was not likely to be a judicious adviser about affairs of state. The Earl could scarcely be said to have served even a noviciate in politics. His notions of government had been acquired in *the society* which had been in the habit of assembling round

Frederic at Kew and Leicester House. That society consisted principally of Tories, who had been reconciled to the House of Hanover by the civility with which the Prince had treated them, and by the hope of obtaining high preferment when he should come to the throne. Their political creed was a peculiar modification of Toryism. It was the creed neither of the Tories of the seventeenth nor of the Tories of the nineteenth century; it was the creed, not of Filmer and Sacheverell, not of Perceval and Eldon, but of the sect of which Bolingbroke may be considered as the chief doctor. This sect deserves commendation for having pointed out and justly reprobated some great abuses which sprang up during the long domination of the Whigs. But it is far easier to point out and reprobate abuses than to propose beneficial reforms: and the reforms which Bolingbroke proposed would either have been utterly inefficient, or would have produced much more mischief than they would have removed.

The Revolution had saved the nation from one class of evils, but had at the same time — such is the imperfection of all things human — engendered or aggravated another class of evils which required new remedies. Liberty and property were secure from the attacks of prerogative. Conscience was respected. No government ventured to infringe any of the rights solemnly recognised by the instrument which had called William and Mary to the throne. But it cannot be denied that, under the new system, the public interests and the public morals were seriously endangered by corruption and faction. During the long struggle against the Stuarts, the chief object of the most enlightened statesmen had been to strengthen the *House of* Commons. The struggle was over; the victory was *won; the* House of Commons was supreme in the state; and *all the vices* which had till then been latent in the representative system were rapidly developed by prosperity and power. Scarcely had the executive government become really responsible to the House of Commons, when it began to appear that the House of Commons was not really responsible to the nation. Many of the constituent bodies were under the absolute control of individuals; many were notoriously at the command of the highest bidder. The debates were not published. It was very seldom known out of doors how a gentleman had voted. Thus, while the ministry was accountable to the Parliament, the majority of the Parliament was accountable to nobody. Under such circumstances, nothing could be more natural than that the members should insist on being paid for their votes, should form themselves into combinations for the purpose of raising the price of their votes, and should at critical conjunctures extort large wages by threatening a strike. Thus the Whig ministers of George the First and George the Second were compelled to reduce corruption to a system, and to practise it on a gigantic scale.

If we are right as to the cause of these abuses, we can scarcely be wrong as to the remedy. The remedy was surely not to deprive the House of Commons of its weight in the state. Such a course would undoubtedly have put an end to parliamentary corruption and to parliamentary factions: for, when votes cease to be of importance, they will cease to be bought; and, when knaves can get nothing by combining, they will cease to combine. But to destroy corruption and faction by introducing despotism would have been to cure bad by worse. The proper remedy evidently was, to make the House of Commons responsible to the nation; and this was to be effected in two ways; first, by giving publicity to parliamentary proceedings, and thus placing every member on his trial before the tribunal of public opinion; and secondly, by so reforming the *constitution of the House* that no man should be able to sit in it who had not been returned by a respectable and independent body of constituents.

Bolingbroke and Bolingbroke's disciples recommended a very different mode of treating the diseases of the state. Their doctrine was, that a vigorous use of the prerogative by a patriot King would at once break all factious combinations, and supersede the pretended necessity of bribing members of Parliament. The King had only to resolve that he would be master, that he would not be held in thraldom by any set of men, that he would take for ministers any persons in whom he had confidence, without distinction of party, and that he would restrain his servants from influencing by immoral means, either the constituent bodies or the representative body. This childish scheme proved that those who proposed it knew nothing of the nature of the evil with which they pretended to deal. The real cause of the prevalence of corruption and faction was that a House of Commons, not accountable to the people, was more powerful than the King. Bolingbroke's remedy could be applied only by a King more powerful than the House of Commons. How was the patriot Prince to govern in defiance of the body without whose consent he could not equip a sloop, keep a battalion under arms, send an embassy, or defray even the charges of his own household? Was he to dissolve the Parliament? And what was he likely to gain by appealing to Sudbury and Old Sarum against the venality of their representatives? Was he to send out privy seals? Was he to levy ship-money? If so, this boasted reform must commence in all probability by civil war, and, if consummated, must be consummated by the establishment of absolute monarchy. Or was the patriot King to carry the House of Commons with him in his upright designs? By what means? Interdicting himself from the use *of corrupt* influence, what motive was he to address to the Dodingtons and Winningtons? Was cupidity, strengthened by habit, to be laid asleep by a few fine sentences about virtue and union?

Absurd as this theory was, it had many admirers, particularly among men of letters. It was now to be reduced to practice; and the result was, as any man of sagacity must have foreseen, the most piteous and ridiculous of failures.

On the very day of the young King's accession, appeared some signs which indicated the approach of a great change. The speech which he made to his council was not submitted to the cabinet. It was drawn up by Bute, and contained some expressions which might be construed into reflections on the conduct of affairs during the late reign. Pitt remonstrated, and begged that these expressions might be softened down in the printed copy; but it was not till after some hours of altercation that Bute yielded; and, even after Bute had yielded, the King affected to hold out till the following afternoon. On the same day on which this singular contest took place, Bute was not only sworn of the privy council, but introduced into the cabinet.

Soon after this, Lord Holdernesse, one of the Secretaries of State, in pursuance of a plan concerted with the court, resigned the seals. Bute was instantly appointed to the vacant place. A general election speedily followed, and the new Secretary entered parliament in the only way in which he then could enter it, as one of the sixteen representative peers of Scotland.*

Had the ministers been firmly united it can scarcely be doubted that they would have been able to withstand the court. The parliamentary influence of the Whig aristocracy, combined with the genius, the virtue, and the fame of Pitt, would have

* In the reign of Anne, the House of Lords had resolved that, under the 23d article of Union, no Scotch peer could be created a peer of Great Britain. This resolution was not annulled till the year 1782.

been irresistible. But there had been in the cabinet of George the Second latent jealousies and enmities, which now began to show themselves. Pitt had been estranged from his old ally Legge, the Chancellor of the Exchequer. Some of the ministers were envious of Pitt's popularity. Others were, not altogether without cause, disgusted by his imperious and haughty demeanour. Others, again, were honestly opposed to some parts of his policy. They admitted that he had found the country in the depths of humiliation, and had raised it to the height of glory; they admitted that he had conducted the war with energy, ability, and splendid success. But they began to hint that the drain on the resources of the state was unexampled, and that the public debt was increasing with a speed at which Montague or Godolphin would have stood aghast. Some of the acquisitions made by our fleets and armies were, it was acknowledged, profitable as well as honourable; but, now that George the Second was dead, a courtier might venture to ask why England was to become a party in a dispute between two German powers. What was it to her whether the House of Hapsburg or the House of Brandenburg ruled in Silesia? Why were the best English regiments fighting on the Main? Why were the Prussian battalions paid with English gold? The great minister seemed to think it beneath him to calculate the price of victory. As long as the Tower guns were fired, as the streets were illuminated, as French banners were carried in triumph through London, it was to him matter of indifference to what extent the public burdens were augmented. Nay, he seemed to glory in the magnitude of those sacrifices which the people, fascinated by his eloquence and success, had too readily made, and would long and bitterly regret. There was no check on *waste* or *embezzlement*. Our commissaries returned from the *camp of Prince Ferdinand* to buy boroughs, to rear palaces, to rival the magnificence of the old aristocracy of the realm. Already had we borrowed, in four years of war, more than the most skilful and economical government would pay in forty years of peace. But the prospect of peace was as remote as ever. It could not be doubted that France, smarting and prostrate, would consent to fair terms of accommodation; but this was not what Pitt wanted. War had made him powerful and popular; with war, all that was brightest in his life was associated: for war his talents were peculiarly fitted. He had at length begun to love war for its own sake, and was more disposed to quarrel with neutrals than to make peace with enemies.

Such were the views of the Duke of Bedford and of the Earl of Hardwicke; but no member of the government held these opinions so strongly as George Grenville, the treasurer of the navy. George Grenville was brother-in-law of Pitt, and had always been reckoned one of Pitt's personal and political friends. But it is difficult to conceive two men of talents and integrity more utterly unlike each other. Pitt, as his sister often said, knew nothing accurately except Spenser's Fairy Queen. He had never applied himself steadily to any branch of knowledge. He was a wretched financier. He never became familiar even with the rules of that House of which he was the brightest ornament. He had never studied public law as a system; and was, indeed, so ignorant of the whole subject, that George the Second, on one occasion, complained bitterly that a man who had never read Vattel should presume to undertake the direction of foreign affairs. But these defects were more than redeemed by high and rare gifts, by a strange power of inspiring great masses of men with confidence and affection, by an eloquence which not only delighted the ear, but stirred the blood, and brought tears into the eyes, by originality in devising plans, by vigour in executing them. Grenville, on the other hand, was by nature and habit a man of details. He had been bred a lawyer; and he had brought the industry and acuteness of the Temple into official and parliamentary life. He was supposed to be intimately acquainted with the whole fiscal system of the country. He had paid especial attention to the law of Parliament, and was so learned in all things relating to the privileges and orders of the House of Commons that those who loved him least pronounced him the only person competent to succeed Onslow in the Chair. His speeches were generally instructive, and sometimes, from the gravity and earnestness with which he spoke, even impressive, but never brilliant, and generally tedious. Indeed, even when he was at the head of affairs, he sometimes found it difficult to obtain the ear of the House. In disposition as well as in intellect, he differed widely from his brother-in-law. Pitt was utterly regardless of money. He would scarcely stretch out his hand to take it; and, when it came, he threw it away with childish profusion. Grenville, though strictly upright, was grasping and parsimonious. Pitt was a man of excitable nerves, sanguine in hope, easily elated by success and popularity, keenly sensible of injury, but prompt to forgive; Grenville's character was stern, melancholy, and pertinacious. Nothing was more remarkable in him than his inclination always to look on the dark side of things. He was the raven of the House of Commons, always croaking defeat in the midst of triumphs, and bankruptcy with an overflowing exchequer. Burke, with general applause, compared him, in a time of quiet and plenty, to the evil spirit whom Ovid described looking down on the stately temples and wealthy haven of Athens, and scarce able to refrain from *weeping* because she could find nothing at which to weep,

Such a man was not likely to be popular. But to unpopularity Grenville opposed a dogged determination, which sometimes forced even those who hated him to respect him.

It was natural that Pitt and Grenville, being such as they were, should take very different views of the situation of affairs. Pitt could see nothing but the trophies; Grenville could see nothing but the bill. Pitt boasted that England was victorious at once in America, in India, and in Germany, the umpire of the Continent, the mistress of the sea. Grenville cast up the subsidies, sighed over the army extraordinaries, and groaned in spirit to think that the nation had borrowed eight millions in one year.

With a ministry thus divided it was not difficult for Bute to deal. Legge was the first who fell. He had given offence to the young King in the late reign, by refusing to support a creature of Bute at a Hampshire election. He was now not only turned out, but in the closet, when he delivered up his seal of office, was treated with gross incivility.

Pitt, who did not love Legge, saw this event with indifference. But the danger was now fast approaching himself. Charles the Third of Spain had early conceived a deadly hatred of England. Twenty years before, when he was King of the Two Sicilies, he had been eager to join the coalition against Maria Theresa. But an English fleet had suddenly appeared in the Bay of Naples. An English captain had landed, had proceeded to the palace, had laid a watch on the table, and had told his majesty that, within an hour, a treaty of neutrality must be signed, or a bombardment would commence. The treaty was signed; the squadron sailed out of the bay twenty-four hours after it had sailed in; and from that day the ruling passion of the humbled Prince was aversion to the English name. He was at length in a situation in which he might *hope* to gratify that passion. He had recently become King of Spain and the Indies. He saw, with envy and apprehension, the triumphs of our navy, and the rapid extension of our colonial Empire. He was a Bourbon, and sympathised with the distress of the house from which he sprang. He was a Spaniard; and no Spaniard could bear to see Gibraltar and Minorca in the possession of a foreign power. Impelled by such feelings, Charles concluded a secret treaty with France. By this treaty, known as the Family Compact, the two powers bound themselves, not in express words, but by the clearest implication, to make war on England in common. Spain postponed the declaration of hostilities only till her fleet, laden with the treasures of America, should have arrived.

The existence of the treaty could not be kept a secret from Pitt. He acted as a man of his capacity and energy might be expected to act. He at once proposed to declare war against Spain, and to intercept the American fleet. He had determined, it is said, to attack without delay both Havanna and the Philippines.

His wise and resolute counsel was rejected. Bute was foremost in opposing it, and was supported by almost the whole cabinet. Some of the ministers doubted, or affected to doubt, the correctness of Pitt's intelligence; some shrank from the responsibility of advising a course so bold and decided as that which he proposed; some were weary of his ascendency, and were glad to be rid of him on any pretext. One only of his colleagues agreed with him, his brother-in-law, Earl Temple.

Pitt and Temple resigned their offices. To Pitt the young King behaved at parting in the most gracious manner. Pitt, who, proud and fiery every where else, was always meek and humble in the closet, was moved even to tears. The King and the favourite urged him to accept some substantial mark of royal gratitude. Would he like to be appointed governor of Canada? A salary of five thousand pounds a-year should be annexed to the office. Residence would not be required. It was true that the governor of Canada, as the law then stood, could not be a member of the House of Commons. But a bill should be brought in, authorising Pitt to hold his government together with a seat in Parliament, and in the preamble should be set forth his claims to the gratitude of his country. Pitt answered, with all delicacy, that his anxieties were rather for his wife and family than for himself, and that nothing would be so acceptable to him as a mark of royal goodness which might be beneficial to those who were dearest to him. The hint was taken. The same Gazette which announced the retirement of the Secretary of State announced also that, in consideration of his great public services, his wife had been created a peeress in her own right, and that a pension of three thousand pounds a-year, for three lives, had been bestowed on himself. It was doubtless thought that the rewards and honours conferred on the great minister would have a conciliatory effect on the public mind. Perhaps, too, it was thought that his popularity, which had partly arisen from the contempt which he had always shown for money, would be damaged by a pension; and, indeed, a crowd of libels instantly appeared, in which he was accused of having sold his country. Many of his true friends thought that he would have best consulted the dignity of his character by refusing to accept any pecuniary reward from the court. Nevertheless, the general opinion of his talents, virtues, and services, remained unaltered. Addresses were presented to him from several large towns. London showed its admiration and affection in a still more marked manner. Soon after his resignation came the Lord Mayor's day. The King and *the royal family* dined at Guildhall. Pitt was one of the guests. The young sovereign, seated by his bride in his state coach, received a remarkable lesson. He was scarcely noticed. All eyes were fixed on the fallen minister; all acclamations directed to him. The streets, the balconies, the chimney tops, burst into a roar of delight as his chariot passed by. The ladies waved their handkerchiefs from the windows. The common people clung to the wheels, shook hands with the footmen, and even kissed the horses. Cries of "No Bute!" "No Newcastle salmon!" were mingled with the shouts of "Pitt for ever!" When Pitt entered Guildhall, he was welcomed by loud huzzas and clapping of hands, in which the very magistrates of the city joined. Lord Bute, in the mean time, was hooted and pelted through Cheapside, and would, it was thought, have been in some danger, if he had not taken the precaution of surrounding his carriage with a strong body guard of boxers. Many persons blamed the conduct of Pitt on this occasion as disrespectful to the King. Indeed, Pitt himself afterwards owned that he had done wrong. He was led into this error, as he was afterwards led into more serious errors, by the influence of his turbulent and mischievous brother-in-law, Temple.

The events which immediately followed Pitt's retirement raised his fame higher than ever. War with Spain proved to be, as he had predicted, inevitable. News came from the West Indies that Martinique had been taken by an expedition which he had sent forth. Havanna fell; and it was known that he had planned an attack on Havanna. Manilla capitulated; and it was believed that he had meditated a blow against Manilla. The American fleet, which he had proposed to intercept, had unloaded an immense cargo of bullion in the haven of Cadiz, before Bute could be convinced that the court of Madrid really entertained hostile intentions.

The session of Parliament which followed Pitt's retirement

passed over without any violent storm. Lord Bute took on himself the most prominent part in the House of Lords. He had become Secretary of State, and indeed prime minister, without having once opened his lips in public except as an actor. There was, therefore, no small curiosity to know how he would acquit himself. Members of the House of Commons crowded the bar of the Lords, and covered the steps of the throne. It was generally expected that the orator would break down; but his most malicious hearers were forced to own that he had made a better figure than they expected. They, indeed, ridiculed his action as theatrical, and his style as tumid. They were especially amused by the long pauses which, not from hesitation, but from affectation, he made at all the emphatic words, and Charles Townshend cried out, "Minute guns!" The general opinion however was, that, if Bute had been early practised in debate, he might have become an impressive speaker.

In the Commons, George Grenville had been entrusted with the lead. The task was not, as yet, a very difficult one: for Pitt did not think fit to raise the standard of opposition. His speeches at this time were distinguished, not only by that eloquence in which he excelled all his rivals, but also by a temperance and a modesty which had too often been wanting to his character. When war was declared against Spain, he justly laid claim to the merit of having foreseen what had at length become manifest to all, but he carefully abstained from arrogant and acrimonious expressions; and this abstinence was the more honourable to him, because his temper, never very placid, was now severely tried, both by gout and by calumny. The courtiers had adopted a mode of warfare, which was soon turned with far more formidable effect against themselves. Half the inhabitants of the Grub Street garrets *paid their milk scores, and got their shirts out of pawn,* by abusing Pitt. His German war, his subsidies, his pension, his wife's peerage, were shin of beef and gin, blankets and baskets of small coal, to the starving poetasters of the Fleet. Even in the House of Commons, he was, on one occasion during this session, assailed with an insolence and malice which called forth the indignation of men of all parties; but he endured the outrage with majestic patience. In his younger days he had been but too prompt to retaliate on those who attacked him; but now, conscious of his great services, and of the space which he filled in the eyes of all mankind, he would not stoop to personal squabbles. "This is no season," he said, in the debate on the Spanish war, "for altercation and recrimination. A day has arrived when every Englishman should stand forth for his country. Arm the whole; be one people; forget every thing but the public. I set you the example. Harassed by slanderers, sinking under pain and disease, for the public I forget both my wrongs and my infirmities!" On a general review of his life, we are inclined to think that his genius and virtue never shone with so pure an effulgence as during the session of 1762.

The session drew towards the close; and Bute, emboldened by the acquiescence of the Houses, resolved to strike another great blow, and to become first minister in name as well as in reality. That coalition, which a few months before had seemed all powerful, had been dissolved. The retreat of Pitt had deprived the government of popularity. Newcastle had exulted in the fall of the illustrious colleague whom he envied and dreaded, and had not foreseen that his own doom was at hand. He still tried to flatter himself that he was at the head of the government; but insults heaped on *insults* at length undeceived him. Places which had always *been considered* as in his gift, were bestowed without any reference to him. His expostulations only called forth significant hints that it was time for him to retire. One day he pressed on Bute the claims of a Whig Prelate to the archbishopric of York. "If your grace thinks so highly of him," answered Bute, "I wonder that you did not promote him when you had the power." Still the old man clung with a desperate grasp to the wreck. Seldom, indeed, have Christian meekness and Christian humility equalled the meekness and humility of his patient and abject ambition. At length he was forced to understand that all was over. He quitted that court where he had held high office during forty-five years, and hid his shame and regret among the cedars of Claremont. Bute became first lord of the treasury.

The favourite had undoubtedly committed a great error. It is impossible to imagine a tool better suited to his purposes than that which he thus threw away, or rather put into the hands of his enemies. If Newcastle had been suffered to play at being first minister, Bute might securely and quietly have enjoyed the substance of power. The gradual introduction of Tories into all the departments of the government might have been effected without any violent clamour, if the chief of the great Whig connection had been ostensibly at the head of affairs. This was strongly represented to Bute by Lord Mansfield, a man who may justly be called the father of modern Toryism, of Toryism modified to suit an order of things under which the House of Commons is the most powerful body in the state. The theories which had dazzled Bute could not impose on the fine intellect of Mansfield. The temerity with which Bute provoked the hostility of powerful and deeply rooted interests, was displeasing to Mansfield's cold and timid nature. Expostulation, however, was vain. Bute was impatient of advice, drunk with success, eager to be, in show as well as in reality, the head of the government. He had engaged in *an undertaking* in which a screen was absolutely necessary to his success, and even to his safety. He found an excellent screen ready in the very place where it was most needed; and he rudely pushed it away.

And now the new system of government came into full operation. For the first time since the accession of the House of Hanover, the Tory party was in the ascendant. The prime minister himself was a Tory. Lord Egremont, who had succeeded Pitt as Secretary of State, was a Tory, and the son of a Tory. Sir Francis Dashwood, a man of slender parts, of small experience, and of notoriously immoral character, was made Chancellor of the Exchequer, for no reason that could be imagined, except that he was a Tory, and had been a Jacobite. The royal household was filled with men whose favourite toast, a few years before, had been the King over the water. The relative position of the two great national seats of learning was suddenly changed. The university of Oxford had long been the chief seat of disaffection. In troubled times, the High Street had been lined with bayonets; the colleges had been searched by the King's messengers. Grave doctors were in the habit of talking very Ciceronian treason in the theatre; and the undergraduates drank bumpers to Jacobite toasts, and chanted Jacobite airs. Of four successive Chancellors of the University, one had notoriously been in the Pretender's service; the other three were fully believed to be in secret correspondence with the exiled family. Cambridge had therefore been especially favoured by the Hanoverian Princes, and had shown herself grateful for their patronage. George the First had enriched her library; George the Second had contributed munificently to her Senate House. Bishoprics and deaneries were showered on her children. Her Chancellor was Newcastle, the chief of the Whig aristocracy; *her High* Steward was Hardwicke, the Whig head of the law. *Both her burgesses* had held office under the Whig ministry.

Times had now changed. The University of Cambridge was received at St. James's with comparative coldness. The answers to the addresses of Oxford were all graciousness and warmth.

The watchwords of the new government were prerogative and purity. The sovereign was no longer to be a puppet in the hands of any subject, or of any combination of subjects. George the Third would not be forced to take ministers whom he disliked, as his grandfather had been forced to take Pitt. George the Third would not be forced to part with any whom he delighted to honour, as his grandfather had been forced to part with Carteret. At the same time, the system of bribery which had grown up during the late reigns was to cease. It was ostentatiously proclaimed that, since the accession of the young King, neither constituents nor representatives had been bought with the secret service money. To free Britain from corruption and oligarchical cabals, to detach her from continental connections, to bring the bloody and expensive war with France and Spain to a close, such were the specious objects which Bute professed to procure.

Some of these objects he attained. England withdrew, at the cost of a deep stain on her faith, from her German connections. The war with France and Spain was terminated by a peace, honourable indeed and advantageous to our country, yet less honourable and less advantageous than might have been expected from a long and almost unbroken series of victories, by land and sea, in every part of the world. But the only effect of Bute's domestic administration was to make faction wilder, and corruption fouler than ever.

The mutual animosity of the Whig and Tory parties had begun to languish after the fall of Walpole, and had seemed to be almost extinct at the close of the reign of George the Second. It now revived in all its force. Many Whigs, it is true, were still in office. The Duke of Bedford had signed the treaty with France. The Duke of Devonshire, though much out of humour, still continued to be Lord Chamberlain. Grenville, who led the House of Commons, and Fox, who still enjoyed in silence the immense gains of the Pay Office, had always been regarded as strong Whigs. But the bulk of the party throughout the country regarded the new minister with abhorrence. There was, indeed, no want of popular themes for invective against his character. He was a favourite; and favourites have always been odious in this country: No mere favourite had been at the head of the government since the dagger of Felton had reached the heart of the Duke of Buckingham. After that event the most arbitrary and the most frivolous of the Stuarts had felt the necessity of confiding the chief direction of affairs to men who had given some proof of parliamentary or official talent. Strafford, Falkland, Clarendon, Clifford, Shaftesbury, Lauderdale, Danby, Temple, Halifax, Rochester, Sunderland, whatever their faults might be, were all men of acknowledged ability. They did not owe their eminence merely to the favour of the sovereign. On the contrary, they owed the favour of the sovereign to their eminence. Most of them, indeed, had first attracted the notice of the court by the capacity and vigour which they had shown in opposition. The Revolution seemed to have for ever secured the state against the domination of a Carr or a Villiers. Now, however, the personal regard of the King had at once raised a man who had seen nothing of public business, who had never opened his lips in Parliament, over the heads of a crowd of eminent orators, financiers, diplomatists. From a private gentleman, this fortunate minion had at once been turned into a Secretary of State. He *had made* his maiden speech when at the head of the administration. The vulgar resorted to a simple explanation of the phenomenon, and the coarsest ribaldry against the Princess Mother was scrawled on every wall and sung in every alley.

This was not all. The spirit of party, roused by impolitic provocation from its long sleep, roused in turn a still fiercer and more malignant Fury, the spirit of national animosity. The grudge of Whig against Tory was mingled with the grudge of Englishman against Scot. The two sections of the great British people had not yet been indissolubly blended together. The events of 1715 and of 1745 had left painful and enduring traces. The tradesmen of Cornhill had been in dread of seeing their tills and warehouses plundered by barelegged mountaineers from the Grampians. They still recollected that Black Friday, when the news came that the rebels were at Derby, when all the shops in the city were closed, and when the Bank of England began to pay in sixpences. The Scots, on the other hand, remembered with natural resentment, the severity with which the insurgents had been chastised, the military outrages, the humiliating laws, the heads fixed on Temple Bar, the fires and quartering blocks on Kennington Common. The favourite did not suffer the English to forget from what part of the island he came. The cry of all the south was that the public offices, the army, the navy, were filled with high-cheeked Drummonds and Erskines, Macdonalds and Macgillivrays, who could not talk a Christian tongue, and some of whom had but lately begun to wear Christian breeches. All the old jokes on hills without trees, girls without stockings, men eating the food of horses, pails emptied from the fourteenth story, were pointed against these lucky adventurers. To the honour of the Scots it must be said, that their prudence and their pride restrained them from retaliation. Like the princess in the Arabian tale, they stopped their ears *tight*, and, unmoved by the shrillest notes of abuse, walked on, without once looking round, straight towards the Golden Fountain.

Bute, who had always been considered as a man of taste and reading, affected, from the moment of his elevation, the character of a Mæcenas. If he expected to conciliate the public by encouraging literature and art, he was grievously mistaken. Indeed, none of the objects of his munificence, with the single exception of Johnson, can be said to have been well selected; and the public, not unnaturally, ascribed the selection of Johnson rather to the Doctor's political prejudices than to his literary merits: for a wretched scribbler named Shebbeare, who had nothing in common with Johnson except violent Jacobitism, and who had stood in the pillory for a libel on the Revolution, was honoured with a mark of royal approbation, similar to that which was bestowed on the author of the English Dictionary, and of the Vanity of Human Wishes. It was remarked that Adam, a Scotchman, was the court architect, and that Ramsay, a Scotchman, was the court painter, and was preferred to Reynolds. Mallet, a Scotchman, of no high literary fame, and of infamous character, partook largely of the liberality of the government. John Home, a Scotchman, was rewarded for the tragedy of Douglas, both with a pension and with a sinecure place. But, when the author of the Bard, and of the Elegy in a Country Churchyard, ventured to ask for a Professorship, the emoluments of which he much needed, and for the duties of which he was, in many respects, better qualified than any man living, he was refused; and the post was bestowed on the pedagogue under whose care the favourite's son-in-law, Sir James Lowther, had made such signal proficiency in the graces and in the humane virtues.

*Thus*, the first lord of the treasury was detested by many *as a Tory*, by many as a favourite, and by many as a Scot.

All the hatred which flowed from these various sources soon mingled, and was directed in one torrent of obloquy against the treaty of peace. The Duke of Bedford, who negotiated that treaty, was hooted through the streets. Bute was attacked in his chair, and was with difficulty rescued by a troop of guards. He could hardly walk the streets in safety without disguising himself. A gentleman who died not many years ago used to say that he once recognised the favourite Earl in the piazza of Covent Garden, muffled in a large coat, and with a hat and wig drawn down over his brows. His lordship's established type with the mob was a jack boot, a wretched pun on his Christian name and title. A jack boot, generally accompanied by a petticoat, was sometimes fastened on a gallows, and sometimes committed to the flames. Libels on the court, exceeding in audacity and rancour any that had been published for many years, now appeared daily both in prose and verse. Wilkes, with lively insolence, compared the mother of George the Third to the mother of Edward the Third, and the Scotch minister to the gentle Mortimer. Churchill, with all the energy of hatred, deplored the fate of his country, invaded by a new race of savages, more cruel and ravenous than the Picts or the Danes, the poor, proud children of Leprosy and Hunger. It is a slight circumstance, but deserves to be recorded, that in this year pamphleteers first ventured to print at length the names of the great men whom they lampooned. George the Second had always been the K—. His ministers had been Sir R— W—, Mr. P—, and the Duke of N—. But the libellers of George the Third, of the Princess Mother, and of Lord Bute did not give quarter to a single vowel.

It was supposed that Lord Temple secretly encouraged the most scurrilous assailants of the government. In truth, those *who knew his habits* tracked him as men track a mole. It was his nature to grub underground. Whenever a heap of dirt was flung up, it might well be suspected that he was at work in some foul crooked labyrinth below. Pitt turned away from the filthy work of opposition, with the same scorn with which he had turned away from the filthy work of government. He had the magnanimity to proclaim every where the disgust which he felt at the insults offered by his own adherents to the Scottish nation, and missed no opportunity of extolling the courage and fidelity which the Highland regiments had displayed through the whole war. But, though he disdained to use any but lawful and honourable weapons, it was well known that his fair blows were likely to be far more formidable than the privy thrusts of his brother-in-law's stiletto.

Bute's heart began to fail him. The Houses were about to meet. The treaty would instantly be the subject of discussion. It was probable that Pitt, the great Whig connection, and the multitude, would all be on the same side. The favourite had professed to hold in abhorrence those means by which preceding ministers had kept the House of Commons in good humour. He now began to think that he had been too scrupulous. His Utopian visions were at an end. It was necessary, not only to bribe, but to bribe more shamelessly and flagitiously than his predecessors, in order to make up for lost time. A majority must be secured, no matter by what means. Could Grenville do this? Would he do it? His firmness and ability had not yet been tried in any perilous crisis. He had been generally regarded as a humble follower of his brother Temple, and of his brother-in-law Pitt, and was supposed, though with little reason, to be still favourably inclined towards them. Other aid must be called in. And where was other aid to be found?

*There* was one man, whose sharp and manly logic had *often in* debate been found a match for the lofty and impassioned rhetoric of Pitt, whose talents for jobbing were not inferior to his talents for debate, whose dauntless spirit shrank from no difficulty or danger, and who was as little troubled with scruples as with fears. Henry Fox, or nobody, could weather the storm which was about to burst. Yet was he a person to whom the court, even in that extremity, was unwilling to have recourse. He had always been regarded as a Whig of the Whigs. He had been the friend and disciple of Walpole. He had long been connected by close ties with William Duke of Cumberland. By the Tories he was more hated than any man living. So strong was their aversion to him that when, in the late reign, he attempted to form a party against the Duke of Newcastle, they had thrown all their weight into Newcastle's scale. By the Scots, Fox was abhorred as the confidential friend of the conqueror of Culloden. He was, on personal grounds, most obnoxious to the Princess Mother. For he had, immediately after her husband's death, advised the late King to take the education of her son, the heir apparent, entirely out of her hands. He had recently given, if possible, still deeper offence; for he had indulged, not without some ground, the ambitious hope that his beautiful sister-in-law, the Lady Sarah Lennox, might be queen of England. It had been observed that the King at one time rode every morning by the grounds of Holland House, and that, on such occasions, Lady Sarah, dressed like a shepherdess at a masquerade, was making hay close to the road, which was then separated by no wall from the lawn. On account of the part which Fox had taken in this singular love affair, he was the only member of the Privy Council who was not summoned to the meeting at which his Majesty announced his intended marriage with the Princess of Mecklenburg. Of all the statesmen of the age, therefore, it seemed that Fox was *the last with* whom Bute, the Tory, the Scot, the favourite of the Princess Mother, could, under any circumstances, act. Yet to Fox Bute was now compelled to apply.

Fox had many noble and amiable qualities, which in private life shone forth in full lustre, and made him dear to his children, to his dependents, and to his friends; but as a public man he had no title to esteem. In him the vices which were common to the whole school of Walpole appeared, not perhaps in their worst, but certainly in their most prominent form; for his parliamentary and official talents made all his faults conspicuous. His courage, his vehement temper, his contempt for appearances, led him to display much that others, quite as unscrupulous as himself, covered with a decent veil. He was the most unpopular of the statesmen of his time, not because he sinned more than many of them, but because he canted less.

He felt his unpopularity; but he felt it after the fashion of strong minds. He became, not cautious, but reckless, and faced the rage of the whole nation with a scowl of inflexible defiance. He was born with a sweet and generous temper; but he had been goaded and baited into a savageness which was not natural to him, and which amazed and shocked those who knew him best. Such was the man to whom Bute, in extreme need, applied for succour.

That succour Fox was not unwilling to afford. Though by no means of an envious temper, he had undoubtedly contemplated the success and popularity of Pitt with bitter mortification. He thought himself Pitt's match as a debater, and Pitt's superior as a man of business. They had long been regarded as well-paired rivals. They had started fair in the career of ambition. They had long run side by side. At length Fox had taken the lead, and Pitt had fallen behind. Then had come a sudden turn of fortune, like that in Virgil's foot-race. Fox had stumbled in the mire, and had not only been defeated, but befouled. Pitt had reached the goal, and received the prize. The emoluments of the Pay Office might induce the defeated statesman to submit in silence to the ascendency of his competitor, but could not satisfy a mind conscious of great powers, and sore from great vexations. As soon, therefore, as a party arose adverse to the war and to the supremacy of the great war minister, the hopes of Fox began to revive. His feuds with the Princess Mother, with the Scots, with the Tories, he was ready to forget, if, by the help of his old enemies, he could now regain the importance which he had lost, and confront Pitt on equal terms.

The alliance was, therefore, soon concluded. Fox was assured that, if he would pilot the government out of its embarrassing situation, he should be rewarded with a peerage, of which he had long been desirous. He undertook on his side to obtain, by fair or foul means, a vote in favour of the peace. In consequence of this arrangement he became leader of the House of Commons; and Grenville, stifling his vexation as well as he could, sullenly acquiesced in the change.

Fox had expected that his influence would secure to the court the cordial support of some eminent Whigs who were his personal friends, particularly of the Duke of Cumberland and of the Duke of Devonshire. He was disappointed, and soon found that, in addition to all his other difficulties, he must reckon on the opposition of the ablest prince of the blood, and of the great house of Cavendish.

But he had pledged himself to win the battle; and he was not a man to go back. It was no time for squeamishness. Bute was made to comprehend that the ministry could be saved only by practising the tactics of Walpole to an extent at which Walpole himself would have stared. The Pay Office was turned into a mart for votes. Hundreds of members were closeted there with Fox, and, as there is too much reason to believe, departed carrying with them the wages of infamy. It was affirmed by persons who had the best opportunities of obtaining information, that twenty-five thousand pounds were thus paid away in a single morning. The lowest bribe given, it was said, was a bank-note for two hundred pounds.

Intimidation was joined with corruption. All ranks, from the highest to the lowest, were to be taught that the King would be obeyed. The Lords Lieutenants of several counties were dismissed. The Duke of Devonshire was especially singled out as the victim by whose fate the magnates of England were to take warning. His wealth, rank, and influence, his stainless private character, and the constant attachment of his family to the House of Hanover, did not secure him from gross personal indignity. It was known that he disapproved of the course which the government had taken; and it was accordingly determined to humble the Prince of the Whigs, as he had been nicknamed by the Princess Mother. He went to the palace to pay his duty. "Tell him," said the King to a page, "that I will not see him." The page hesitated. "Go to him," said the King, "and tell him those very words." The message was delivered. The Duke tore off his gold key, and went away boiling with anger. His relations who were in office instantly resigned. A few days later, the King called for the list of Privy Councillors, and with his own hand struck out the Duke's name.

In this step there was at least courage, though little wisdom or good nature. But, as nothing was too high for the revenge of the court, so also was nothing too low. A persecution, such as had never been known before and has never been known since, raged in every public department. Great numbers of humble and laborious clerks were deprived of *their bread*, not because they had neglected their duties, not *because* they had taken an active part against the ministry, but merely because they had owed their situations to the recommendation of some nobleman or gentleman who was against the peace. The proscription extended to tidewaiters, to gaugers, to door-keepers. One poor man to whom a pension had been given for his gallantry in a fight with smugglers, was deprived of it because he had been befriended by the Duke of Grafton. An aged widow, who, on account of her husband's services in the navy, had, many years before, been made housekeeper to a public office, was dismissed from her situation, because it was imagined that she was distantly connected by marriage with the Cavendish family. The public clamour, as may well be supposed, grew daily louder and louder. But the louder it grew, the more resolutely did Fox go on with the work which he had begun. His old friends could not conceive what had possessed him. "I could forgive," said the Duke of Cumberland, "Fox's political vagaries, but I am quite confounded by his inhumanity. Surely he used to be the best-natured of men."

At last Fox went so far as to take a legal opinion on the question, whether the patents granted by George the Second were binding on George the Third. It is said that, if his colleagues had not flinched, he would at once have turned out the Tellers of the Exchequer and Justices in Eyre.

Meanwhile the Parliament met. The ministers, more hated by the people than ever, were secure of a majority, and they had also reason to hope that they would have the advantage in the debates as well as in the divisions; for Pitt was confined to his chamber by a severe attack of gout. His friends moved to defer the consideration of the treaty till he should be able to attend: but the motion was rejected. The great day arrived. The discussion had lasted some time, when a loud huzza was heard in Palace Yard. The noise came nearer and nearer, up the stairs, through the lobby. The door opened, and from the midst of a shouting multitude came forth Pitt, borne in the arms of his attendants. His face was thin and ghastly, his limbs swathed in flannel, his crutch in his hand. The bearers set him down within the bar. His friends instantly surrounded him, and with their help he crawled to his seat near the table. In this condition he spoke three hours and a half against the peace. During that time he was repeatedly forced to sit down and to use cordials. It may well be supposed that his voice was faint, that his action was languid, and that his speech, though occasionally brilliant and impressive, was feeble when compared with his best oratorical performances. But those who remembered what he had done, and who saw what he suffered, listened to him with emotions stronger than any that mere eloquence can produce. He was unable to stay for the division, and was carried away from the House amidst shouts as loud as those which had announced his arrival.

A large majority approved the peace. The exultation of the court was boundless. "Now," exclaimed the Princess Mother, "my son is really King." The young sovereign spoke of himself as freed from the bondage in which his grandfather had been held. On one point, it was announced, his mind was unalterably made up. Under no circumstances whatever should those Whig grandees, who had enslaved his predecessors and endeavoured to enslave himself, be restored to power.

This vaunting was premature. The real strength of the favourite was by no means proportioned to the number of votes which he had, on one particular division, been able to command. He was soon again in difficulties. The most important part of his budget was a tax on cider. This measure was opposed, not only by those who were generally hostile to his administration, but also by many of his supporters. The name of excise had always been hateful to the Tories. One of the chief crimes of Walpole, in their eyes, had been his partiality for this mode of raising money. The Tory Johnson had in his Dictionary given so scurrilous a definition of the word Excise, that the Commissioners of Excise had seriously thought of prosecuting him. The counties which the new impost particularly affected had always been Tory counties. It was the boast of John Philips, the poet of the English vintage, that the Cider-land had ever been faithful to the throne, and that all the pruning-hooks of her thousand orchards had been beaten into swords for the service of the ill fated Stuarts. The effect of Bute's fiscal scheme was to produce an union between the gentry and yeomanry of the Ciderland and the Whigs of the capital. Herfordshire and Worcestershire were in a flame. The city of London, though not so directly interested, was, if possible, still more excited. The debates on this question irreparably damaged the government. Dashwood's financial statement had been confused and absurd beyond belief, and had been received by the House with roars of laughter. He had sense enough to be conscious of his unfitness for the high situation which he held, and exclaimed in a comical fit of despair, "What shall I do? The boys will point at me in the street, and cry, 'There goes the worst Chancellor of the Exchequer that ever was.'" George Grenville came to the rescue, and spoke strongly on his favourite theme, the profusion with which the late war had been carried on. That profusion, he said, had made taxes necessary. He called on the gentlemen opposite to him to say where they would have a tax laid, and dwelt on this topic with his usual prolixity. "Let them tell me where," he repeated in a monotonous and somewhat fretful tone. "I say, Sir, let them tell me where. I repeat it, Sir; I am entitled to say to them, *Tell me where.*" Unluckily for him, Pitt had come down to the House that night, and had been bitterly provoked by the reflections thrown on the war. He revenged himself by murmuring, in a whine resembling Grenville's, a line of a well known song, "Gentle Shepherd, tell me where." "If," cried Grenville, "gentlemen are to be treated in this way —" Pitt, as was his fashion, when he meant to mark extreme contempt, rose deliberately, made his bow, and walked out of the House, leaving his brother-in-law in convulsions of rage, and every body else in convulsions of laughter. It was long before Grenville lost the nickname of the Gentle Shepherd.

But the ministry had vexations still more serious to endure. The hatred which the Tories and Scots bore to Fox was implacable. In a moment of extreme peril, they had consented to put themselves under his guidance. But the aversion with which they regarded him broke forth as soon as the crisis seemed to be over. Some of them attacked him about the accounts of the Pay Office. Some of them rudely interrupted him when speaking, by laughter and ironical cheers. He was naturally desirous to escape from so disagreeable a situation, and demanded the peerage which had been promised as the reward of his services.

It was clear that there must be some change in the composition of the ministry. But scarcely any, even of those who, from their situation, might be supposed to be in all the secrets of the government, anticipated what really took place. To the amazement of the Parliament and the nation, it was suddenly announced that Bute had resigned.

Twenty different explanations of this strange step were suggested. Some attributed it to profound design, and some to sudden panic. Some said that the lampoons of the opposition had driven the Earl from the field; some that he had *taken* office only in order to bring the war to a close, and had *always* meant to retire when that object had been accomplished. He publicly assigned ill health as his reason for quitting business, and privately complained that he was not cordially seconded by his colleagues, and that Lord Mansfield, in particular, whom he had himself brought into the cabinet, gave him no support in the House of Peers. Mansfield was, indeed, far too sagacious not to perceive that Bute's situation was one of great peril, and far too timorous to thrust himself into peril for the sake of another. The probability, however, is that Bute's conduct on this occasion, like the conduct of most men on most occasions, was determined by mixed motives. We suspect that he was sick of office; for this is a feeling much more common among ministers than persons who see public life from a distance are disposed to believe; and nothing could be more natural than that this feeling should take possession of the mind of Bute. In general, a statesman climbs by slow degrees. Many laborious years elapse before he reaches the topmost pinnacle of preferment. In the earlier part of his career, therefore, he is constantly lured on by seeing something above him. During his ascent he gradually becomes inured to the annoyances which belong to a life of ambition. By the time that he has attained the highest point, he has become patient of labour and callous to abuse. He is kept constant to his vocation, in spite of all its discomforts, at first by hope, and at last by habit. It was not so with Bute. His whole public life lasted little more than two years. On the day on which he became a politician he became a cabinet minister. In a few months he was, both in name and in show, chief of the administration. Greater than he had been he could not be. If what he already possessed was vanity and vexation of spirit, no delusion remained to entice him onward. He had been cloyed with the pleasures of ambition before he had been seasoned to its pains. His habits had not been such as were likely *to fortify his mind against* obloquy and public hatred. He had reached his forty-eighth year in dignified ease, without knowing, by personal experience, what it was to be ridiculed and slandered. All at once, without any previous initiation, he had found himself exposed to such a storm of invective and satire as had never burst on the head of any statesman. The emoluments of office were now nothing to him; for he had just succeeded to a princely property by the death of his father-in-law. All the honours which could be bestowed on him he had already secured. He had obtained the Garter for himself, and a British peerage for his son. He seems also to have imagined that by quitting the treasury he should escape from danger and abuse without really resigning power, and should still be able to exercise in private supreme influence over the royal mind.

Whatever may have been his motives, he retired. Fox at the same time took refuge in the House of Lords; and George Grenville became First Lord of the Treasury and Chancellor of the Exchequer.

We believe that those who made this arrangement fully intended that Grenville should be a mere puppet in the hands of Bute; for Grenville was as yet very imperfectly known even to those who had observed him long. He passed for a mere official drudge; and he had all the industry, the minute accuracy, the formality, the tediousness, which belong to the character. But he had other qualities which had not yet shown themselves, devouring ambition, dauntless courage, self-confidence amounting to presumption, and a temper which could not endure opposition. He was not disposed to be any body's tool; and he had no attachment, political or personal, to Bute. The two men had, indeed, nothing in common, except a strong propensity towards harsh and unpopular courses. Their principles were fundamentally different. Bute was a Tory. Grenville would have been very angry with any person who should have denied his claim to be a Whig. He was more prone to tyrannical measures than Bute; but he loved tyranny only when disguised under the forms of constitutional liberty. He mixed up, after a fashion then not very unusual, the theories of the republicans of the seventeenth century with the technical maxims of English law, and thus succeeded in combining anarchical speculation with arbitrary practice. The voice of the people was the voice of God; but the only legitimate organ through which the voice of the people could be uttered was the Parliament. All power was from the people; but to the Parliament the whole power of the people had been delegated. No Oxonian divine had ever, even in the years which immediately followed the Restoration, demanded for the king so abject, so unreasoning a homage, as Grenville, on what he considered as the purest Whig principles, demanded for the Parliament. As he wished to see the Parliament despotic over the nation, so he wished to see it also despotic over the court. In his view the prime minister, possessed of the confidence of the House of Commons, ought to be Mayor of the Palace. The King was a mere Childeric or Chilperic, who might well think himself lucky in being permitted to enjoy such handsome apartments at Saint James's, and so fine a park at Windsor.

Thus the opinions of Bute and those of Grenville were diametrically opposed. Nor was there any private friendship between the two statesmen. Grenville's nature was not forgiving; and he well remembered how, a few months before, he had been compelled to yield the lead of the House of Commons to Fox.

We are inclined to think, on the whole, that the worst administration which has governed England since the Revolution was that of George Grenville. His public acts may be classed under two heads, outrages on the liberty of the people, and *outrages on the dignity* of the crown.

He began by making war on the press. John Wilkes, member of Parliament for Aylesbury, was singled out for persecution. Wilkes had, till very lately, been known chiefly as one of the most profane, licentious, and agreeable rakes about town. He was a man of taste, reading, and engaging manners. His sprightly conversation was the delight of green rooms and taverns, and pleased even grave hearers when he was sufficiently under restraint to abstain from detailing the particulars of his amours, and from breaking jests on the New Testament. His expensive debaucheries forced him to have recourse to the Jews. He was soon a ruined man, and determined to try his chance as a political adventurer. In Parliament he did not succeed. His speaking, though pert, was feeble, and by no means interested his hearers so much as to make them forget his face, which was so hideous that the caricaturists were forced, in their own despite, to flatter him. As a writer, he made a better figure. He set up a weekly paper, called the North Briton. This journal, written with some pleasantry, and great audacity and impudence, had a considerable number of readers. Forty-four numbers had been published when Bute resigned; and, though almost every number had contained matter grossly libellous, no prosecution had been instituted. The forty-fifth number was innocent when compared with the majority of those which had preceded it, and indeed contained nothing so strong as may in our time be found daily in the leading articles of the Times and Morning Chronicle. But Grenville was now at the head of affairs. A new spirit had been infused into the administration. Authority was to be upheld. The government was no longer to be braved with impunity. Wilkes was arrested under a general warrant, conveyed to the Tower, and confined there with circumstances of unusual severity. His papers *were seized*, and carried to the Secretary of State. These *harsh* and illegal measures produced a violent outbreak of popular rage, which was soon changed to delight and exultation. The arrest was pronounced unlawful by the Court of Common Pleas, in which Chief Justice Pratt presided, and the prisoner was discharged. This victory over the government was celebrated with enthusiasm both in London and in the cider counties.

While the ministers were daily becoming more odious to the nation, they were doing their best to make themselves also odious to the court. They gave the King plainly to understand that they were determined not to be Lord Bute's creatures, and exacted a promise that no secret adviser should have access to the royal ear. They soon found reason to suspect that this promise had not been observed. They remonstrated in terms less respectful than their master had been accustomed to hear, and gave him a fortnight to make his choice between his favourite and his cabinet.

George the Third was greatly disturbed. He had but a few weeks before exulted in his deliverance from the yoke of the great Whig connection. He had even declared that his honour would not permit him ever again to admit the members of that connection into his service. He now found that he had only exchanged one set of masters for another set still harsher and more imperious. In his distress he thought on Pitt. From Pitt it was possible that better terms might be obtained than either from Grenville, or from the party of which Newcastle was the head.

Grenville, on his return from an excursion into the country, repaired to Buckingham House. He was astonished to find at the entrance a chair, the shape of which was well known to him, and indeed to all London. It was distinguished by a large boot, made for the purpose of accommodating the great Commoner's gouty leg. Grenville guessed the whole. His brother-in-law was closeted with the King. Bute, provoked by what he considered as the unfriendly and ungrateful conduct of his successors, had himself proposed that Pitt should be summoned to the palace.

Pitt had two audiences on two successive days. What passed at the first interview led him to expect that the negotiation would be brought to a satisfactory close; but on the morrow he found the King less complying. The best account, indeed the only trustworthy account of the conference, is that which was taken from Pitt's own mouth by Lord Hardwicke. It appears that Pitt strongly represented the importance of conciliating those chiefs of the Whig party who had been so unhappy as to incur the royal displeasure. They had, he said, been the most constant friends of the House of Hanover. Their power was great; they had been long versed in public business. If they were to be under sentence of exclusion, a solid administration could not be formed. His Majesty could not bear to think of putting himself into the hands of those whom he had recently chased from his court with the strongest marks of anger. "I am sorry, Mr. Pitt," he said, "but I see this will not do. My honour is concerned. I must support my honour." How his Majesty succeeded in supporting his honour, we shall soon see.

Pitt retired, and the King was reduced to request the ministers, whom he had been on the point of discarding, to remain in office. During the two years which followed, Grenville, now closely leagued with the Bedfords, was the master of the court; and a hard master he proved. He knew that he was kept in place only because there was no choice except between himself and the Whigs. That, under any circumstances, the Whigs would be forgiven, he thought impossible. The late attempt to get rid of him had roused his resentment; *the failure of* that attempt had liberated him from all fear. *He had* never been very courtly. He now began to hold a language, to which, since the days of Cornet Joyce and President Bradshaw, no English King had been compelled to listen.

In one matter, indeed, Grenville, at the expense of justice and liberty, gratified the passions of the court while gratifying his own. The persecution of Wilkes was eagerly pressed. He had written a parody on Pope's Essay on Man, entitled the Essay on Woman, and had appended to it notes, in ridicule of Warburton's famous Commentary.

This composition was exceedingly profligate, but not more so, we think, than some of Pope's own works, the imitation of the second satire of the first book of Horace, for example; and, to do Wilkes justice, he had not, like Pope, given his ribaldry to the world. He had merely printed at a private press a very small number of copies, which he meant to present to some of his boon companions, whose morals were in no more danger of being corrupted by a loose book than a negro of being tanned by a warm sun. A tool of the government, by giving a bribe to the printer, procured a copy of this trash, and placed it in the hands of the ministers. The ministers resolved to visit Wilkes's offence against decorum with the utmost rigour of the law. What share piety and respect for morals had in dictating this resolution, our readers may judge from the fact that no person was more eager for bringing the libertine poet to punishment than Lord March, afterwards Duke of Queensberry. On the first day of the session of Parliament, the book, thus disgracefully obtained, was laid on the table of the Lords by the Earl of Sandwich, whom the Duke of Bedford's interest had made Secretary of State. The unfortunate author had not the slightest suspicion that his licentious poem had ever been seen, except by his printer and by a few of his dissipated companions, till it was *produced in full* Parliament. Though he was a man of easy temper, averse from danger, and not very susceptible of shame, the surprise, the disgrace, the prospect of utter ruin, put him beside himself. He picked a quarrel with one of Lord Bute's dependents, fought a duel, was seriously wounded, and, when half recovered, fled to France. His enemies had now their own way both in the Parliament and in the King's Bench. He was censured, expelled from the House of Commons, outlawed. His works were ordered to be burned by the common hangman. Yet was the multitude still true to him. In the minds even of many moral and religious men, his crime seemed light when compared with the crime of his accusers. The conduct of Sandwich, in particular, excited universal disgust. His own vices were notorious; and, only a fortnight before he laid the Essay on Woman before the House of Lords, he had been drinking and singing loose catches with Wilkes at one of the most dissolute clubs in London. Shortly after the meeting of Parliament, the Beggar's Opera was acted at Covent Garden theatre. When Macheath uttered the words — "That Jemmy Twitcher should peach me I own surprised me," — pit, boxes, and galleries, burst into a roar which seemed likely to bring the roof down. From that day Sandwich was universally known by the nickname of Jemmy Twitcher. The ceremony of burning the North Briton was interrupted by a riot. The constables were beaten; the paper was rescued; and, instead of it, a jackboot and a petticoat were committed to the flames. Wilkes had instituted an action for the seizure of his papers against the Undersecretary of State. The jury gave a thousand pounds damages. But neither these nor any other indications of public feeling had power to move Grenville. He had the Parliament with him: and, according to his political creed, the sense of the nation was to be collected from the Parliament alone.

Soon, however, he found reason to fear that even the Parliament might fail him. On the question of the legality of general warrants, the Opposition, having on its side all sound principles, all constitutional authorities, and the voice of the whole nation, mustered in great force, and was joined by many who did not ordinarily vote against the government. On one occasion the ministry, in a very full house, had a majority of only fourteen votes. The storm, however, blew over. The spirit of the Opposition, from whatever cause, began to flag at the moment when success seemed almost certain. The session ended without any change. Pitt, whose eloquence had shone with its usual lustre in all the principal debates, and whose popularity was greater than ever, was still a private man. Grenville, detested alike by the court and by the people, was still minister.

As soon as the Houses had risen, Grenville took a step which proved, even more signally than any of his past acts, how despotic, how acrimonious, and how fearless his nature was. Among the gentlemen not ordinarily opposed to the government, who, on the great constitutional question of general warrants, had voted with the minority, was Henry Conway, brother of the Earl of Hertford, a brave soldier, a tolerable speaker, and a well-meaning, though not a wise or vigorous politician. He was now deprived of his regiment, the merited reward of faithful and gallant service in two wars. It was confidently asserted that in this violent measure the King heartily concurred.

But whatever pleasure the persecution of Wilkes, or the dismissal of Conway, may have given to the royal mind, it is certain that his Majesty's aversion to his ministers increased day by day. Grenville was as frugal of the public money as of his own, and morosely refused to accede to the King's request, that a few thousand pounds might be expended in buying some open fields to the west of the gardens of Buckingham House. In consequence of this refusal, the fields were soon covered with buildings, and the King and Queen were overlooked in their most private walks by the upper windows of a hundred houses. Nor was this the worst. Grenville was as liberal of words as he was sparing of guineas. Instead of explaining himself in that clear, concise, and lively manner, which alone could win the attention of a young mind new to business, he spoke in the closet just as he spoke in the House of Commons. When he had harangued two hours, he looked at his watch, as he had been in the habit of looking at the clock opposite the Speaker's chair, apologised for the length of his discourse, and then went on for an hour more. The members of the House of Commons can cough an orator down, or can walk away to dinner; and they were by no means sparing in the use of these privileges when Grenville was on his legs. But the poor young King had to endure all this eloquence with mournful civility. To the end of his life he continued to talk with horror of Grenville's orations.

About this time took place one of the most singular events in Pitt's life. There was a certain Sir William Pynsent, a Somersetshire baronet of Whig politics, who had been a Member of the House of Commons in the days of Queen Anne, and had retired to rural privacy when the Tory party, towards the end of her reign, obtained the ascendency in her councils. His manners were eccentric. His morals lay under very odious imputations. But his fidelity to his political opinions was unalterable. During fifty years of seclusion he continued to brood over the circumstances which had driven him from public life, the dismissal of the Whigs, the peace of Utrecht, the desertion of our allies. He now thought that he perceived a close analogy between the well remembered events of his youth and the events which he had witnessed in extreme old age; between the disgrace of Marlborough and the disgrace of Pitt; between the elevation of Harley and the elevation of Bute; between the treaty negotiated by St. John and the treaty negotiated by Bedford; between the wrongs of the House of Austria in 1712 and the wrongs of the House of Brandenburg in 1762. This fancy took such possession of the old man's mind that he determined to leave his whole property to Pitt. In this way Pitt unexpectedly came into possession of near three thousand pounds a-year. Nor could all the malice of his enemies find any ground for reproach in the transaction. Nobody could call him a legacy hunter. Nobody could accuse him of seizing that to which others had a better claim. For he had never in his life seen Sir William; and Sir William had left no relation so near as to be entitled to form any expectations respecting the estate.

The fortunes of Pitt seemed to flourish; but his health was worse than ever. We cannot find that, during the session which began in January 1765, he once appeared in parliament. He remained some months in profound retirement at Hayes, his favourite villa, scarcely moving except from his arm-chair to his bed, and from his bed to his arm-chair, and often employing his wife as his amanuensis in his most confidential correspondence. Some of his detractors whispered that his invisibility was to be ascribed quite as much to affectation as to gout. In truth his character, high and splendid as it was, wanted simplicity. With genius which did not need the aid of stage tricks, and with a spirit which should have been far above them, he had yet been, through life, in the habit of practising them. It was, therefore, now surmised that, having acquired all the consideration which could be derived from eloquence and from great services to the state, he had determined not to make himself cheap by often appearing in public, but, under the pretext of ill health, to surround himself with mystery, to emerge only at long intervals and on momentous occasions, and at other times to deliver his oracles only to a few favoured votaries, who were suffered to make pilgrimages to his shrine. If such were his object, it was for a time fully attained. Never was the magic of his name so powerful, never was he regarded by his country with such superstitious veneration, as during this year of silence and seclusion.

While Pitt was thus absent from Parliament, Grenville proposed a measure destined to produce a great revolution, the effects of which will long be felt by the whole human race. We speak of the act for imposing stamp duties on the North American colonies. The plan was eminently characteristic of its author. Every feature of the parent was found in the child. A timid statesman would have shrunk from a step, of which Walpole, at a time when the colonies were far less powerful, had said — "He who shall propose it, will be a much bolder man than I." But the nature of Grenville was insensible to fear. A statesman of large views would have felt that to lay taxes at Westminster on New England and New York, was a course opposed, not indeed to the letter of the Statute Book, or to any decision contained in the Term Reports, but to the principles of good government, and to the spirit of the constitution. A statesman of large views would also have felt that ten times the estimated produce of the American stamps would have been dearly purchased by even a transient quarrel between the mother country and the colonies. But Grenville knew of no spirit of the constitution distinct from the letter of the law, and of no national interests except those which are expressed by pounds, shillings, and pence. That his policy might give birth to deep discontents in all the provinces, from the shore of the Great Lakes to the

Mexican sea; that France and Spain might seize the opportunity of revenge; that the Empire might be dismembered; that the debt, that debt with the amount of which he perpetually reproached Pitt, might, in consequence of his own policy, be doubled; these were possibilities which never occurred to that small, sharp mind.

The Stamp Act will be remembered as long as the globe lasts. But, at the time, it attracted much less notice in this country than another Act which is now almost utterly forgotten. The King fell ill, and was thought to be in a dangerous state. His complaint, we believe, was the same which, at a later period, repeatedly incapacitated him for the performance of his regal functions. The heir apparent was only two years old. It was clearly proper to make provision for the administration of the government, in case of a minority. The discussions on this point brought the quarrel between the court and the ministry to a crisis. The King wished to be entrusted with the power of naming a regent by will. The ministers feared, or affected to fear, that, if this power were conceded to him, he would name the Princess Mother, nay, possibly the Earl of Bute. They, therefore, insisted on introducing into the bill words confining the King's choice to the royal family. Having thus excluded Bute, they urged the King to let them, in the most marked manner, exclude the Princess Dowager also. They assured him that the House of Commons would undoubtedly strike her name out, and by this threat they wrung from him a reluctant assent. In a few days, it appeared that the representations by which they had induced the King to put this gross and public affront on his mother were unfounded. The friends of the Princess in the House of Commons moved that her name should be inserted. The ministers could not decently attack the parent of their master. They hoped that the Opposition would come to their help, and put on them a force to which they would gladly have yielded. But the majority of the Opposition, though hating the Princess, hated Grenville more, beheld his embarrassment with delight, and would do nothing to extricate him from it. The Princess's name was accordingly placed in the list of persons qualified to hold the regency.

The King's resentment was now at the height. The present evil seemed to him more intolerable than any other. Even the junta of Whig grandees could not treat him worse than he had been treated by his present ministers. In his distress he poured out his whole heart to his uncle, the Duke of Cumberland. The Duke was not a man to be loved; but he was eminently a man to be trusted. He had an intrepid temper, a strong understanding, and a high sense of honour and duty. As a general, he belonged to a remarkable class of captains; captains, we mean, whose fate it has been to lose almost all the battles which they have fought, and yet to be reputed stout and skilful soldiers. Such captains were Coligni and William the Third. We might, perhaps, add Marshal Soult to the list. The bravery of the Duke of Cumberland was such as distinguished him even among the princes of his brave house. The indifference with which he rode about amidst musket balls and cannon balls was not the highest proof of his fortitude. Hopeless maladies, horrible surgical operations, far from unmanning him, did not even discompose him. With courage, he had the virtues which are akin to courage. He spoke the truth, was open in enmity and friendship, and upright in all his dealings. But his nature was hard; and what seemed to him justice was rarely tempered with mercy. He was, therefore, during many years one of the most unpopular men in England. The severity with which he had treated the *rebels* after the battle of Culloden, had gained for him the *name* of the Butcher. His attempts to introduce into the army of England, then in a most disorderly state, the rigorous discipline of Potsdam, had excited still stronger disgust. Nothing was too bad to be believed of him. Many honest people were so absurd as to fancy that, if he were left Regent during the minority of his nephews, there would be another smothering in the Tower. These feelings, however, had passed away. The Duke had been living, during some years, in retirement. The English, full of animosity against the Scots, now blamed his Royal Highness only for having left so many Camerons and Macphersons to be made gaugers and customhouse officers. He was, therefore, at present, a favourite with his countrymen, and especially with the inhabitants of London.

He had little reason to love the King, and had shown clearly, though not obtrusively, his dislike of the system which had lately been pursued. But he had high and almost romantic notions of the duty which, as a prince of the blood, he owed to the head of his house. He determined to extricate his nephew from bondage, and to effect a reconciliation between the Whig party and the throne, on terms honourable to both.

In this mind he set off for Hayes, and was admitted to Pitt's sick room; for Pitt would not leave his chamber, and would not communicate with any messenger of inferior dignity. And now began a long series of errors on the part of the illustrious statesman, errors which involved his country in difficulties and distresses more serious even than those from which his genius had formerly rescued her. His language was haughty, unreasonable, almost unintelligible. The only thing which could be discerned through a cloud of vague and not very gracious phrases, was that he would not at that moment take office. The truth, we believe, was this. Lord Temple, who was Pitt's evil genius, had just formed a new *scheme of politics*. Hatred of Bute and of the Princess had,

it should seem, taken entire possession of Temple's soul. [He]
had quarrelled with his brother George, because George h[ad]
been connected with Bute and the Princess. Now that Geor[ge]
appeared to be the enemy of Bute and of the Princess, Temp[le]
was eager to bring about a general family reconciliation. T[he]
three brothers, as Temple, Grenville, and Pitt, were p[o-]
pularly called, might make a ministry, without leaning f[or]
aid either on Bute or on the Whig connection. With su[ch]
views, Temple used all his influence to dissuade Pitt from a[c-]
ceding to the propositions of the Duke of Cumberland. Pi[tt]
was not convinced. But Temple had an influence over hi[m]
such as no other person had ever possessed. They were ve[ry]
old friends, very near relations. If Pitt's talents and fam[e]
had been useful to Temple, Temple's purse had formerly, [in]
times of great need, been useful to Pitt. They had nev[er]
been parted in politics. Twice they had come into the cabin[et]
together; twice they had left it together. Pitt could not be[ar]
to think of taking office without his chief ally. Yet he felt th[at]
he was doing wrong, that he was throwing away a great o[p-]
portunity of serving his country. The obscure and unco[n-]
ciliatory style of the answers which he returned to the ove[r-]
tures of the Duke of Cumberland, may be ascribed to t[he]
embarrassment and vexation of a mind not at peace with itsel[f.]
It is said that he mournfully explained to Temple,

> "Extinxi te meque, soror, populumque, patresque
> Sidonios, urbemque tuam."

The prediction was but too just.

Finding Pitt impracticable, the Duke of Cumberland a[d-]
vised the King to submit to necessity, and to keep Grenvil[le]
and the Bedfords. It was, indeed, not a time at which o[f-]
fices could safely be left vacant. The unsettled state [of]
the government had produced a general relaxation throu[gh]
*all the departments* of the public service. Meetings, whi[ch]

at another time would have been harmless, now turned to riots, and rapidly rose almost to the dignity of rebellions. The Houses of Parliament were blockaded by the Spitalfields weavers. Bedford House was assailed on all sides by a furious rabble, and was strongly garrisoned with horse and foot. Some people attributed these disturbances to the friends of Bute, and some to the friends of Wilkes. But, whatever might be the cause, the effect was general insecurity. Under such circumstances the King had no choice. With bitter feelings of mortification, he informed the ministers that he meant to retain them.

They answered by demanding from him a promise on his royal word never more to consult Lord Bute. The promise was given. They then demanded something more. Lord Bute's brother, Mr. Mackenzie, held a lucrative office in Scotland. Mr. Mackenzie must be dismissed. The King replied that the office had been given under very peculiar circumstances, and that he had promised never to take it away while he lived. Grenville was obstinate; and the King, with a very bad grace, yielded.

The session of Parliament was over. The triumph of the ministers was complete. The King was almost as much a prisoner as Charles the First had been, when in the Isle of Wight. Such were the fruits of the policy which, only a few months before, was represented as having for ever secured the throne against the dictation of insolent subjects.

His Majesty's natural resentment showed itself in every look and word. In his extremity he looked wistfully towards that Whig connection, once the object of his dread and hatred. The Duke of Devonshire, who had been treated with such unjustifiable harshness, had lately died, and had been succeeded by his son, who was still a boy. The King condescended to express his regret for what had passed, and to invite the young Duke to court. The noble youth came, attended by his uncles, and was received with marked graciousness.

This and many other symptoms of the same kind irritated the ministers. They had still in store for their sovereign an insult which would have provoked his grandfather to kick them out of the room. Grenville and Bedford demanded an audience of him, and read him a remonstrance of many pages, which they had drawn up with great care. His Majesty was accused of breaking his word, and of treating his advisers with gross unfairness. The Princess was mentioned in language by no means eulogistic. Hints were thrown out that Bute's head was in danger. The King was plainly told that he must not continue to show, as he had done, that he disliked the situation in which he was placed, that he must frown upon the Opposition, that he must carry it fair towards his ministers in public. He several times interrupted the reading, by declaring that he had ceased to hold any communication with Bute. But the ministers, disregarding his denial, went on; and the King listened in silence, almost choked by rage. When they ceased to read, he merely made a gesture expressive of his wish to be left alone. He afterwards owned that he thought he should have gone into a fit.

Driven to despair, he again had recourse to the Duke of Cumberland; and the Duke of Cumberland again had recourse to Pitt. Pitt was really desirous to undertake the direction of affairs, and owned, with many dutiful expressions, that the terms offered by the King were all that any subject could desire. But Temple was impracticable; and Pitt, with great regret, declared that he could not, without the concurrence of his brother-in-law, undertake the administration.

The Duke now saw only one way of delivering his nephew.

An administration must be formed of the Whigs in opposition, without Pitt's help. The difficulties seemed almost insuperable. Death and desertion had grievously thinned the ranks of the party lately supreme in the state. Those among whom the Duke's choice lay might be divided into two classes, men too old for important offices, and men who had never been in any important office before. The cabinet must be composed of broken invalids or of raw recruits.

This was an evil, yet not an unmixed evil. If the new Whig statesmen had little experience in business and debate, they were, on the other hand, pure from the taint of that political immorality which had deeply infected their predecessors. Long prosperity had corrupted that great party which had expelled the Stuarts, limited the prerogatives of the Crown, and curbed the intolerance of the Hierarchy. Adversity had already produced a salutary effect. On the day of the accession of George the Third, the ascendency of the Whig party terminated; and on that day the purification of the Whig party began. The rising chiefs of that party were men of a very different sort from Sandys and Winnington, from Sir William Yonge and Henry Fox. They were men worthy to have charged by the side of Hampden at Chalgrove, or to have exchanged the last embrace with Russell on the scaffold in Lincoln's Inn Fields. They carried into politics the same high principles of virtue which regulated their private dealings, nor would they stoop to promote even the noblest and most salutary ends by means which honour and probity condemn. Such men were Lord John Cavendish, Sir George Savile, and others whom we hold in honour as the second founders of the Whig party, as the restorers of its pristine health and energy after half a century of degeneracy.

The chief of this respectable band was the Marquess of

Rockingham, a man of splendid fortune, excellent sense, and stainless character. He was indeed nervous to such a degree that, to the very close of his life, he never rose without great reluctance and embarrassment to address the House of Lords. But, though not a great orator, he had in a high degree some of the qualities of a statesman. He chose his friends well; and he had, in an extraordinary degree, the art of attaching them to him by ties of the most honourable kind. The cheerful fidelity with which they adhered to him through many years of almost hopeless opposition was less admirable than the disinterestedness and delicacy which they showed when he rose to power.

We are inclined to think that the use and the abuse of party cannot be better illustrated than by a parallel between two of the connections of that time, the Rockingham party and the Bedfords. The Rockingham party was, in our opinion, such as a party should be. It consisted of men united together by common opinions, by common public objects, by common esteem. That they desired to obtain, by strictly constitutional means, the direction of affairs they did not deny. But, though often invited to accept the emoluments of office, they steadily refused to accept them on conditions inconsistent with their principles. The Bedfords, as a party, had, as far as we can discover, no principle whatever. Rigby and Sandwich wanted places; and thought that they should fetch a higher price by sticking together than singly. They therefore acted in concert, and prevailed on a much more important and a much better man than themselves to act with them.

It was now intimated to Rockingham that the Duke of Cumberland now wished to see him. The Marquess consented to take the treasury. Newcastle, so long the recognised chief of the Whigs, could not be excluded from the ministry. He was appointed keeper of the privy seal. A very honest clear-headed country gentleman, of the name of Dowdeswell, became Chancellor of the Exchequer. General Conway, who had served under the Duke of Cumberland, and was strongly attached to his royal highness, was made Secretary of State, with the lead in the House of Commons. A great Whig nobleman, in the prime of manhood, from whom much was at that time expected, Augustus Duke of Grafton, was the other Secretary.

The oldest man living could remember no government so weak in oratorical talents and in official experience. The general opinion was, that the ministers might hold office during the recess, but that the first day of debate in Parliament would be the last day of their power. Charles Townshend was asked what he thought of the new administration. "It is," said he, "mere lute-string; pretty summer wear. It will never do for the winter."

At this conjuncture Lord Rockingham had the wisdom to discern the value, and secure the aid, of an ally, who, to eloquence surpassing the eloquence of Pitt, and to industry which shamed the industry of Grenville, united an amplitude of comprehension to which neither Pitt nor Grenville could lay claim. A young Irishman had, some time before, come over to push his fortune in London. He had written much for the booksellers; but he was best known by a little treatise, in which the style and reasoning of Bolingbroke were mimicked with exquisite skill, and by a theory, of more ingenuity than soundness, touching the pleasures which we receive from the objects of taste. He had also attained a high reputation as a talker, and was regarded by the men of letters who supped together at the Turk's Head as the only match in conversation for Dr. Johnson. He now became private secretary to Lord Rockingham, and was brought into Parliament by his patron's influence. These arrangements, indeed, were not made without some difficulty. The Duke of Newcastle, who was always meddling and chattering, adjured the first lord of the treasury to be on his guard against this adventurer, whose real name was O'Bourke, and whom his grace knew to be a wild Irishman, a Jacobite, a Papist, a concealed Jesuit. Lord Rockingham treated the calumny as it deserved; and the Whig party was strengthened and adorned by the accession of Edmund Burke.

The party, indeed, stood in need of accessions; for it sustained about this time an almost irreparable loss. The Duke of Cumberland had formed the government, and was its main support. His exalted rank and great name in some degree balanced the fame of Pitt. As mediator between the Whigs and the Court, he held a place which no other person could fill. The strength of his character supplied that which was the chief defect of the new ministry. Conway, in particular, who, with excellent intentions and respectable talents, was the most dependent and irresolute of human beings, drew from the counsels of that masculine mind a determination not his own. Before the meeting of Parliament the Duke suddenly died. His death was generally regarded as the signal of great troubles, and on this account, as well as from respect for his personal qualities, was greatly lamented. It was remarked that the mourning in London was the most general ever known, and was both deeper and longer than the Gazette had prescribed.

In the mean time, every mail from America brought alarming tidings. The crop which Grenville had sown his successors had now to reap. The colonies were in a state bordering on rebellion. The stamps were burned. The revenue officers were tarred and feathered. All traffic between *the discontented* provinces and the mother country was interrupted of London was in dismay. Half the firms of Bristol and Liverpool were threatened with bankruptcy. In Leeds, Manchester, Nottingham, it was said that three artisans out of every ten had been turned adrift. Civil war seemed to be at hand; and it could not be doubted that, if once the British nation were divided against itself, France and Spain would soon take part in the quarrel.

Three courses were open to the ministers. The first was to enforce the Stamp Act by the sword. This was the course on which the King, and Grenville, whom the King hated beyond all living men, were alike bent. The natures of both were arbitrary and stubborn. They resembled each other so much that they could never be friends; but they resembled each other also so much that they saw almost all important practical questions in the same point of view. Neither of them would bear to be governed by the other; but they were perfectly agreed as to the best way of governing the people.

Another course was that which Pitt recommended. He held that the British Parliament was not constitutionally competent to pass a law for taxing the colonies. He therefore considered the Stamp Act as a nullity, as a document of no more validity than Charles's writ of shipmoney, or James's proclamation dispensing with the penal laws. This doctrine seems to us, we must own, to be altogether untenable.

Between these extreme courses lay a third way. The opinion of the most judicious and temperate statesmen of those times was that the British constitution had set no limit whatever to the legislative power of the British King, Lords, and Commons, over the whole British Empire. Parliament, they held, was legally competent to tax America, as Parliament was legally competent to commit any other act of folly or wickedness, to confiscate the property of all the merchants in Lombard Street, or to attaint any man in the kingdom of high treason, without examining witnesses against him, or hearing him in his own defence. The most atrocious act of confiscation or of attainder is just as valid an act as the Toleration Act or the Habeas Corpus Act. But from acts of confiscation and acts of attainder lawgivers are bound, by every obligation of morality, systematically to refrain. In the same manner ought the British legislature to refrain from taxing the American colonies. The Stamp Act was indefensible, not because it was beyond the constitutional competence of Parliament, but because it was unjust and impolitic, sterile of revenue, and fertile of discontents. These sound doctrines were adopted by Lord Rockingham and his colleagues, and were, during a long course of years, inculcated by Burke, in orations, some of which will last as long as the English language.

The winter came; the Parliament met; and the state of the colonies instantly became the subject of fierce contention. Pitt, whose health had been somewhat restored by the waters of Bath, reappeared in the House of Commons, and, with ardent and pathetic eloquence, not only condemned the Stamp Act, but applauded the resistance of Massachusetts and Virginia, and vehemently maintained, in defiance, we must say, of all reason and of all authority, that, according to the British constitution, the supreme legislative power does not include the power to tax. The language of Grenville, on the other hand, was such as Strafford might have used at the council table of Charles the First, when news came of the resistance to the liturgy at Edinburgh. The colonists were traitors; those who excused them were little better. Frigates, mortars, bayonets, sabres, were the proper remedies for such distempers.

The ministers occupied an intermediate position; they proposed to declare that the legislative authority of the British *Parliament* over the whole Empire was in all cases supreme;

and they proposed, at the same time, to repeal the Stamp Act. To the former measure Pitt objected; but it was carried with scarcely a dissentient voice. The repeal of the Stamp Act Pitt strongly supported; but against the Government was arrayed a formidable assemblage of opponents. Grenville and the Bedfords were furious. Temple, who had now allied himself closely with his brother, and separated himself from Pitt, was no despicable enemy. This, however, was not the worst. The ministry was without its natural strength. It had to struggle, not only against its avowed enemies, but against the insidious hostility of the King, and of a set of persons who, about this time, began to be designated as the King's friends.

The character of this faction has been drawn by Burke with even more than his usual force and vivacity. Those who know how strongly, through his whole life, his judgment was biassed by his passions, may not unnaturally suspect that he has left us rather a caricature than a likeness; and yet there is scarcely, in the whole portrait, a single touch of which the fidelity is not proved by facts of unquestionable authenticity.

The public generally regarded the King's friends as a body of which Bute was the directing soul. It was to no purpose that the Earl professed to have done with politics, that he absented himself year after year from the levee and the drawing-room, that he went to the north, that he went to Rome. The notion that, in some inexplicable manner, he dictated all the measures of the court, was fixed in the minds, not only of the multitude, but of some who had good opportunities of obtaining information, and who ought to have been superior to vulgar prejudices. Our own belief is that these suspicions were unfounded, and that he ceased to have any communication with the King on political matters some time *before the dismissal of* George Grenville. The supposition of Bute's influence is, indeed, by no means necessary to *explain* the phenomena. The King, in 1765, was no longer the ignorant and inexperienced boy who had, in 1760, been managed by his mother and his Groom of the Stole. He had, during several years, observed the struggles of parties, and conferred daily on high questions of state with able and experienced politicians. His way of life had developed his understanding and character. He was now no longer a puppet, but had very decided opinions both of men and things. Nothing could be more natural than that he should have high notions of his own prerogatives, should be impatient of opposition, and should wish all public men to be detached from each other and dependent on himself alone; nor could anything be more natural than that, in the state in which the political world then was, he should find instruments fit for his purposes.

Thus sprang into existence and into note a reptile species of politicians never before and never since known in our country. These men disclaimed all political ties, except those which bound them to the throne. They were willing to coalesce with any party, to abandon any party, to undermine any party, to assault any party, at a moment's notice. To them, all administrations, and all oppositions were the same. They regarded Bute, Grenville, Rockingham, Pitt, without one sentiment either of predilection or of aversion. They were the King's friends. It is to be observed that this friendship implied no personal intimacy. These people had never lived with their master, as Dodington at one time lived with his father, or as Sheridan afterwards lived with his son. They never hunted with him in the morning, or played cards with him in the evening, never shared his mutton or walked with him among his turnips. Only one or two of them ever saw his *face, except* on public days. The whole band, however, *always had* early and accurate information as to his personal inclinations. None of these people were high in the administration. They were generally to be found in places of much emolument, little labour, and no responsibility; and these places they continued to occupy securely while the cabinet was six or seven times reconstructed. Their peculiar business was not to support the ministry against the opposition, but to support the King against the ministry. Whenever his Majesty was induced to give a reluctant assent to the introduction of some bill which his constitutional advisers regarded as necessary, his friends in the House of Commons were sure to speak against it, to vote against it, to throw in its way every obstruction compatible with the forms of Parliament. If his Majesty found it necessary to admit into his closet a Secretary of State or a First Lord of the Treasury whom he disliked, his friends were sure to miss no opportunity of thwarting and humbling the obnoxious minister. In return for these services, the King covered them with his protection. It was to no purpose that his responsible servants complained to him that they were daily betrayed and impeded by men who were eating the bread of the government. He sometimes justified the offenders, sometimes excused them, sometimes owned that they were to blame, but said that he must take time to consider whether he could part with them. He never would turn them out; and, while every thing else in the state was constantly changing, these sycophants seemed to have a life estate in their offices.

It was well known to the King's friends that, though his Majesty had consented to the repeal of the Stamp Act, he had consented with a very bad grace, and that though he had eagerly welcomed the Whigs, when, in his extreme need and at his earnest entreaty, they had undertaken to free him from an insupportable yoke, he had by no means got over his early *prejudices against his* deliverers. The ministers soon found that, while they were encountered in front by the whole force of a strong opposition, their rear was assailed by a large body of those whom they had regarded as auxiliaries.

Nevertheless, Lord Rockingham and his adherents went on resolutely with the bill for repealing the Stamp Act. They had on their side all the manufacturing and commercial interests of the realm. In the debates the government was powerfully supported. Two great orators and statesmen, belonging to two different generations, repeatedly put forth all their powers in defence of the bill. The House of Commons heard Pitt for the last time, and Burke for the first time, and was in doubt to which of them the palm of eloquence should be assigned. It was indeed a splendid sunset and a splendid dawn.

For a time the event seemed doubtful. In several divisions the ministers were hard pressed. On one occasion, not less than twelve of the King's friends, all men in office, voted against the government. It was to no purpose that Lord Rockingham remonstrated with the King. His Majesty confessed that there was ground for complaint, but hoped that gentle means would bring the mutineers to a better mind. If they persisted in their misconduct, he would dismiss them.

At length the decisive day arrived. The gallery, the lobby, the Court of Requests, the staircases, were crowded with merchants from all the great ports of the island. The debate lasted till long after midnight. On the division, the ministers had a great majority. The dread of civil war, and the outcry of all the trading towns of the kingdom, had been too strong for the combined strength of the court and the opposition.

It was in the first dim twilight of a February morning that *the doors* were thrown open, and that the chiefs of the hostile *parties* showed themselves to the multitude. Conway was received with loud applause. But, when Pitt appeared, all eyes were fixed on him alone. All hats were in the air. Loud and long huzzas accompanied him to his chair, and a train of admirers escorted him all the way to his home. Then came forth Grenville. As soon as he was recognised, a storm of hisses and curses broke forth. He turned fiercely on the crowd, and caught one man by the throat. The bystanders were in great alarm. If a scuffle began, none could say how it might end. Fortunately the person who had been collared only said, "If I may not hiss, Sir, I hope I may laugh," and laughed in Grenville's face.

The majority had been so decisive, that all the opponents of the ministry, save one, were disposed to let the bill pass without any further contention. But solicitation and expostulation were thrown away on Grenville. His indomitable spirit rose up stronger and stronger under the load of public hatred. He fought out the battle obstinately to the end. On the last reading he had a sharp altercation with his brother-in-law, the last of their many sharp altercations. Pitt thundered in his loftiest tones against the man who had wished to dip the ermine of a British King in the blood of the British people. Grenville replied with his wonted intrepidity and asperity. "If the tax," he said, "were still to be laid on, I would lay it on. For the evils which it may produce my accuser is answerable. His profusion made it necessary. His declarations against the constitutional powers of King, Lords, and Commons, have made it doubly necessary. I do not envy him the huzza. I glory in the hiss. If it were to be done again, I would do it."

The repeal of the Stamp Act was the chief measure of Lord Rockingham's government. But that government is entitled to the praise of having put a stop to two oppressive practices, which, in Wilkes's case, had attracted the notice and excited the just indignation of the public. The House of Commons was induced by the ministers to pass a resolution condemning the use of general warrants, and another resolution, condemning the seizure of papers in cases of libel.

It must be added, to the lasting honour of Lord Rockingham, that his administration was the first which, during a long course of years, had the courage and the virtue to refrain from bribing members of Parliament. His enemies accused him and his friends of weakness, of haughtiness, of party spirit; but calumny itself never dared to couple his name with corruption.

Unhappily his government, though one of the best that has ever existed in our country, was also one of the weakest. The King's friends assailed and obstructed the ministers at every turn. To appeal to the King was only to draw forth new promises and new evasions. His Majesty was sure that there must be some misunderstanding. Lord Rockingham had better speak to the gentlemen. They should be dismissed on the next fault. The next fault was soon committed, and his Majesty still continued to shuffle. It was too bad. It was quite abominable; but it mattered less as the prorogation was at hand. He would give the delinquents one more chance. If they did not alter their conduct next session, he should not have one word to say for them. He had already resolved that, long before the commencement of the next session, Lord Rockingham should cease to be minister.

We have now come to a part of our story which, admiring as we do the genius and the many noble qualities of Pitt, we cannot relate without much pain. We believe that, at this conjuncture, he had it in his power to give the victory either to the Whigs or to the King's friends. If he had allied himself *closely* with Lord Rockingham, what could the court have *done?* There would have been only one alternative, the

Whigs or Grenville; and there could be no doubt what the King's choice would be. He still remembered, as well he might, with the utmost bitterness, the thraldom from which his uncle had freed him, and said about this time, with great vehemence, that he would sooner see the Devil come into his closet than Grenville.

And what was there to prevent Pitt from allying himself with Lord Rockingham? On all the most important questions their views were the same. They had agreed in condemning the peace, the Stamp Act, the general warrants, the seizure of papers. The points on which they differed were few and unimportant. In integrity, in disinterestedness, in hatred of corruption, they resembled each other. Their personal interests could not clash. They sat in different Houses, and Pitt had always declared that nothing should induce him to be first lord of the treasury.

If the opportunity of forming a coalition beneficial to the state, and honourable to all concerned, was suffered to escape, the fault was not with the Whig ministers. They behaved towards Pitt with an obsequiousness which, had it not been the effect of sincere admiration and of anxiety for the public interests, might have been justly called servile. They repeatedly gave him to understand that, if he chose to join their ranks, they were ready to receive him, not as an associate, but as a leader. They had proved their respect for him by bestowing a peerage on the person who, at that time, enjoyed the largest share of his confidence, Chief Justice Pratt. What then was there to divide Pitt from the Whigs? What, on the other hand, was there in common between him and the King's friends, that he should lend himself to their purposes, he who had never owed any thing to flattery or intrigue, he whose eloquence and independent spirit had overawed two generations *of slaves* and jobbers, he who had twice been forced by the enthusiasm of an admiring nation on a reluctant Prince?

Unhappily the court had gained Pitt, not, it is true, by those ignoble means which were employed when such men as Rigby and Wedderburn were to be won, but by allurements suited to a nature noble even in its aberrations. The King set himself to seduce the one man who could turn the Whigs out without letting Grenville in. Praise, caresses, promises, were lavished on the idol of the nation. He, and he alone, could put an end to faction, could bid defiance to all the powerful connections in the land united, Whigs and Tories, Rockinghams, Bedfords, and Grenvilles. These blandishments produced a great effect. For though Pitt's spirit was high and manly, though his eloquence was often exerted with formidable effect against the court, and though his theory of government had been learned in the school of Locke and Sidney, he had always regarded the person of the sovereign with profound veneration. As soon as he was brought face to face with royalty, his imagination and sensibility were too strong for his principles. His Whiggism thawed and disappeared; and he became, for the time, a Tory of the old Ormond pattern. Nor was he by any means unwilling to assist in the work of dissolving all political connections. His own weight in the state was wholly independent of such connections. He was therefore inclined to look on them with dislike, and made far too little distinction between gangs of knaves associated for the mere purpose of robbing the public, and confederacies of honourable men for the promotion of great public objects. Nor had he the sagacity to perceive that the strenuous efforts which he made to annihilate all parties tended only to establish the ascendency of one party, and *that the basest* and most hateful of all.

It he doubted whether he would have been thus

misled, if his mind had been in full health and vigour. But the truth is that he had for some time been in an unnatural state of excitement. No suspicion of this sort had yet got abroad. His eloquence had never shone with more splendour than during the recent debates. But people afterwards called to mind many things which ought to have roused their apprehensions. His habits were gradually becoming more and more eccentric. A horror of all loud sounds, such as is said to have been one of the many oddities of Wallenstein, grew upon him. Though the most affectionate of fathers, he could not at this time bear to hear the voices of his own children, and laid out great sums at Hayes in buying up houses contiguous to his own, merely that he might have no neighbours to disturb him with their noise. He then sold Hayes, and took possession of a villa at Hampstead, where he again began to purchase houses to right and left. In expense, indeed, he vied, during this part of his life, with the wealthiest of the conquerors of Bengal and Tanjore. At Burton Pynsent, he ordered a great extent of ground to be planted with cedars. Cedars enough for the purpose were not to be found in Somersetshire. They were therefore collected in London, and sent down by land carriage. Relays of labourers were hired; and the work went on all night by torchlight. No man could be more abstemious than Pitt; yet the profusion of his kitchen was a wonder even to epicures. Several dinners were always dressing; for his appetite was capricious and fanciful; and at whatever moment he felt inclined to eat, he expected a meal to be instantly on the table. Other circumstances might be mentioned, such as separately are of little moment, but such as, when taken together, and when viewed in connection with the strange events which followed, justify us in believing that his mind was already in a morbid state.

Soon after the close of the session of Parliament, Lord

Rockingham received his dismissal. He retired, accompanied by a firm body of friends, whose consistency and uprightness enmity itself was forced to admit. None of them had asked or obtained any pension or any sinecure, either in possession or in reversion. Such disinterestedness was then rare among politicians. Their chief, though not a man of brilliant talents, had won for himself an honourable fame, which he kept pure to the last. He had, in spite of difficulties which seemed almost insurmountable, removed great abuses and averted a civil war. Sixteen years later, in a dark and terrible day, he was again called upon to save the state, brought to the very brink of ruin by the same perfidy and obstinacy which had embarrassed, and at length overthrown, his first administration.

Pitt was planting in Somersetshire when he was summoned to court by a letter written by the royal hand. He instantly hastened to London. The irritability of his mind and body were increased by the rapidity with which he travelled; and when he reached his journey's end he was suffering from fever. Ill as he was, he saw the King at Richmond, and undertook to form an administration.

Pitt was scarcely in the state in which a man should be who has to conduct delicate and arduous negotiations. In his letters to his wife, he complained that the conferences in which it was necessary for him to bear a part heated his blood and accelerated his pulse. From other sources of information we learn, that his language, even to those whose cooperation he wished to engage, was strangely peremptory and despotic. Some of his notes written at this time have been preserved, and are in a style which Lewis the Fourteenth would have been too well bred to employ in addressing any French gentleman.

*In the attempt to dissolve all parties, Pitt met with some* difficulties. Some Whigs, whom the court would gladly have detached from Lord Rockingham, rejected all offers. The Bedfords were perfectly willing to break with Grenville; but Pitt would not come up to their terms. Temple, whom Pitt at first meant to place at the head of the treasury, proved intractable. A coldness indeed had, during some months, been fast growing between the brothers-in-law, so long and so closely allied in politics. Pitt was angry with Temple for opposing the repeal of the Stamp Act. Temple was angry with Pitt for refusing to accede to that family league which was now the favourite plan at Stowe. At length the Earl proposed an equal partition of power and patronage, and offered, on this condition, to give up his brother George. Pitt thought the demand exorbitant, and positively refused compliance. A bitter quarrel followed. Each of the kinsmen was true to his character. Temple's soul festered with spite, and Pitt's swelled into contempt. Temple represented Pitt as the most odious of hypocrites and traitors. Pitt held a different and perhaps a more provoking tone. Temple was a good sort of man enough, whose single title to distinction was, that he had a large garden, with a large piece of water, and a great many pavilions and summer-houses. To his fortunate connection with a great orator and statesman he was indebted for an importance in the state which his own talents could never have gained for him. That importance had turned his head. He had begun to fancy that he could form administrations, and govern empires. It was piteous to see a well meaning man under such a delusion.

In spite of all these difficulties, a ministry was made such as the King wished to see, a ministry in which all his Majesty's friends were comfortably accommodated, and which, with the exception of his Majesty's friends, contained no four *persons who had* ever in their lives been in the habit of acting together. Men who had never concurred in a single vote found themselves seated at the same board. The office of paymaster was divided between two persons who had never exchanged a word. Most of the chief posts were filled either by personal adherents of Pitt, or by members of the late ministry, who had been induced to remain in place after the dismissal of Lord Rockingham. To the former class belonged Pratt, now Lord Camden, who accepted the great seal, and Lord Shelburne, who was made one of the Secretaries of State. To the latter class belonged the Duke of Grafton, who became First Lord of the Treasury, and Conway, who kept his old position both in the government and in the House of Commons. Charles Townshend, who had belonged to every party, and cared for none, was Chancellor of the Exchequer. Pitt himself was declared prime minister, but refused to take any laborious office. He was created Earl of Chatham, and the privy seal was delivered to him.

It is scarcely necessary to say, that the failure, the complete and disgraceful failure, of this arrangement, is not to be ascribed to any want of capacity in the persons whom we have named. None of them were deficient in abilities; and four of them, Pitt himself, Shelburne, Camden, and Townshend, were men of high intellectual eminence. The fault was not in the materials, but in the principle on which the materials were put together. Pitt had mixed up these conflicting elements, in the full confidence that he should be able to keep them all in perfect subordination to himself, and in perfect harmony with each other. We shall soon see how the experiment succeeded.

On the very day on which the new prime minister kissed hands, three fourths of that popularity which he had long enjoyed with ____ ____ and ____ which he owed the greater ____ A violent outcry was raised, not against that part of his conduct which really deserved severe condemnation, but against a step in which we can see nothing to censure. His acceptance of a peerage produced a general burst of indignation. Yet surely no peerage had ever been better earned; nor was there ever a statesman who more needed the repose of the Upper House. Pitt was now growing old. He was much older in constitution than in years. It was with imminent risk to his life that he had, on some important occasions, attended his duty in Parliament. During the session of 1764, he had not been able to take part in a single debate. It was impossible that he should go through the nightly labour of conducting the business of the government in the House of Commons. His wish to be transferred, under such circumstances, to a less busy and a less turbulent assembly, was natural and reasonable. The nation, however, overlooked all these considerations. Those who had most loved and honoured the great Commoner were loudest in invective against the new made Lord. London had hitherto been true to him through every vicissitude. When the citizens learned that he had been sent for from Somersetshire, that he had been closeted with the King at Richmond, and that he was to be first minister, they had been in transports of joy. Preparations were made for a grand entertainment and for a general illumination. The lamps had actually been placed round the Monument, when the Gazette announced that the object of all this enthusiasm was an Earl. Instantly the feast was countermanded. The lamps were taken down. The newspapers raised the roar of obloquy. Pamphlets, made up of calumny and scurrility, filled the shops of all the booksellers; and of those pamphlets, the most galling were written under the direction of the malignant Temple. It was now the fashion to compare the two Williams, William Pulteney and William Pitt. Both, it was said, had, by eloquence and simulated patriotism, acquired a great ascendency in the House of Commons and in the country. Both had been entrusted with the office of reforming the government. Both had, when at the height of power and popularity, been seduced by the splendour of the coronet. Both had been made earls, and both had at once become objects of aversion and scorn to the nation which a few hours before had regarded them with affection and veneration.

The clamour against Pitt appears to have had a serious effect on the foreign relations of the country. His name had till now acted like a spell at Versailles and Saint Ildefonso. English travellers on the Continent had remarked that nothing more was necessary to silence a whole room full of boasting Frenchmen than to drop a hint of the probability that Mr. Pitt would return to power. In an instant there was deep silence: all shoulders rose, and all faces were lengthened. Now, unhappily, every foreign court, in learning that he was recalled to office, learned also that he no longer possessed the hearts of his countrymen. Ceasing to be loved at home, he ceased to be feared abroad. The name of Pitt had been a charmed name. Our envoys tried in vain to conjure with the name of Chatham.

The difficulties which beset Chatham were daily increased by the despotic manner in which he treated all around him. Lord Rockingham had, at the time of the change of ministry, acted with great moderation, had expressed a hope that the new government would act on the principles of the late government, and had even interfered to prevent many of his friends from quitting office. Thus Saunders and Keppel, two naval commanders of great eminence, had been induced to remain at the Admiralty, where their services were much *needed.* The Duke of Portland was still Lord Chamberlain, and Lord Besborough Postmaster. But within a quarter of a year, Lord Chatham had so deeply affronted these men, that they all retired in disgust. In truth, his tone, submissive in the closet, was at this time insupportably tyrannical in the cabinet. His colleagues were merely his clerks for naval, financial, and diplomatic business. Conway, meek as he was, was on one occasion provoked into declaring that such language as Lord Chatham's had never been heard west of Constantinople, and was with difficulty prevented by Horace Walpole from resigning, and rejoining the standard of Lord Rockingham.

The breach which had been made in the government by the defection of so many of the Rockinghams, Chatham hoped to supply by the help of the Bedfords. But with the Bedfords he could not deal as he had dealt with other parties. It was to no purpose that he bade high for one or two members of the faction, in the hope of detaching them from the rest. They were to be had; but they were to be had only in the lot. There was indeed for a moment some wavering and some disputing among them. But at length the counsels of the shrewd and resolute Rigby prevailed. They determined to stand firmly together, and plainly intimated to Chatham that he must take them all, or that he should get none of them. The event proved that they were wiser in their generation than any other connection in the state. In a few months they were able to dictate their own terms.

The most important public measure of Lord Chatham's administration was his celebrated interference with the corn trade. The harvest had been bad; the price of food was high; and he thought it necessary to take on himself the responsibility of laying an embargo on the exportation of grain. When Parliament met, this proceeding was attacked by the opposition as unconstitutional, and defended by the ministers as indispensably necessary. At last an act was passed to indemnify all who had been concerned in the embargo.

The first words uttered by Chatham, in the House of Lords, were in defence of his conduct on this occasion. He spoke with a calmness, sobriety, and dignity, well suited to the audience which he was addressing. A subsequent speech which he made on the same subject was less successful. He bade defiance to aristocratical connections, with a superciliousness to which the Peers were not accustomed, and with tones and gestures better suited to a large and stormy assembly than to the body of which he was now a member. A short altercation followed, and he was told very plainly that he should not be suffered to browbeat the old nobility of England.

It gradually became clearer and clearer that he was in a distempered state of mind. His attention had been drawn to the territorial acquisitions of the East India Company, and he determined to bring the whole of that great subject before Parliament. He would not, however, confer on the subject with any of his colleagues. It was in vain that Conway, who was charged with the conduct of business in the House of Commons, and Charles Townshend, who was responsible for the direction of the finances, begged for some glimpse of light as to what was in contemplation. Chatham's answers were sullen and mysterious. He must decline any discussion with them; he did not want their assistance; he had fixed on a person to take charge of his measure in the House of Commons. This person was a member who was not connected with the government, and who neither had, nor deserved to have, the ear of the House, a noisy, purseproud, illiterate demagogue, whose Cockney English and scraps of mispronounced Latin were the *jest of the* newspapers, Alderman Beckford. It may well be *supposed* that these strange proceedings produced a ferment through the whole political world. The city was in commotion. The East India Company invoked the faith of charters. Burke thundered against the ministers. The ministers looked at each other and knew not what to say. In the midst of the confusion, Lord Chatham proclaimed himself gouty, and retired to Bath. It was announced, after some time, that he was better, that he would shortly return, that he would soon put every thing in order. A day was fixed for his arrival in London. But when he reached the Castle inn at Marlborough, he stopped, shut himself up in his room, and remained there some weeks. Every body who travelled that road was amazed by the number of his attendants. Footmen and grooms, dressed in his family livery, filled the whole inn, though one of the largest in England, and swarmed in the streets of the little town. The truth was that the invalid had insisted that, during his stay, all the waiters and stable-boys of the Castle should wear his livery.

His colleagues were in despair. The Duke of Grafton proposed to go down to Marlborough in order to consult the oracle. But he was informed that Lord Chatham must decline all conversation on business. In the mean time, all the parties which were out of office, Bedfords, Grenvilles, and Rockinghams, joined to oppose the distracted government on the vote for the land tax. They were reinforced by almost all the county members, and had a considerable majority. This was the first time that a ministry had been beaten on an important division in the House of Commons since the fall of Sir Robert Walpole. The administration, thus furiously assailed from without, was torn by internal dissensions. It had been formed on no principle whatever. From the very first, nothing but Chatham's authority had prevented the hostile contingents which made up his ranks from going to blows with each other. That authority was now withdrawn, and every thing was in commotion.

Conway, a brave soldier, but in civil affairs the most timid and irresolute of men, afraid of disobliging the King, afraid of being abused in the newspapers, afraid of being thought factious if he went out, afraid of being thought interested if he stayed in, afraid of every thing, and afraid of being known to be afraid of any thing, was beaten backwards and forwards like a shuttlecock between Horace Walpole who wished to make him prime minister, and Lord John Cavendish who wished to draw him into opposition. Charles Townshend, a man of splendid talents, of lax principles, and of boundless vanity and presumption, would submit to no control. The full extent of his parts, of his ambition, and of his arrogance, had not yet been made manifest; for he had always quailed before the genius and the lofty character of Pitt. But now that Pitt had quitted the House of Commons, and seemed to have abdicated the part of chief minister, Townshend broke loose from all restraint.

While things were in this state, Chatham at length returned to London. He might as well have remained at Marlborough. He would see nobody. He would give no opinion on any public matter. The Duke of Grafton begged piteously for an interview, for an hour, for half an hour, for five minutes. The answer was, that it was impossible. The King himself repeatedly condescended to expostulate and implore. "Your duty," he wrote, "your own honour, require you to make an effort." The answers to these appeals were commonly written in Lady Chatham's hand, from her lord's dictation, for he had not energy even to use a pen. He flings himself at the King's feet. He is penetrated by the royal goodness, so signally shown to the most unhappy of men. He implores a little more indulgence. He cannot as yet transact business. He cannot see *his colleagues*. Least of all can he bear the excitement of an *interview* with majesty.

Some were half inclined to suspect that he was, to use a military phrase, malingering. He had made, they said, a great blunder, and had found it out. His immense popularity, his high reputation for statesmanship, were gone for ever. Intoxicated by pride, he had undertaken a task beyond his abilities. He now saw nothing before him but distresses and humiliations; and he had therefore simulated illness, in order to escape from vexations which he had not fortitude to meet. This suspicion, though it derived some colour from that weakness which was the most striking blemish of his character, was certainly unfounded. His mind, before he became first minister, had been, as we have said, in an unsound state; and physical and moral causes now concurred to make the derangement of his faculties complete. The gout, which had been the torment of his whole life, had been suppressed by strong remedies. For the first time since he was a boy at Oxford, he passed several months without a twinge. But his hand and foot had been relieved at the expense of his nerves. He became melancholy, fanciful, irritable. The embarrassing state of public affairs, the grave responsibility which lay on him, the consciousness of his errors, the disputes of his colleagues, the savage clamours raised by his detractors, bewildered his enfeebled mind. One thing alone, he said, could save him. He must repurchase Hayes. The unwilling consent of the new occupant was extorted by Lady Chatham's entreaties and tears; and her lord was somewhat easier. But if business were mentioned to him, he, once the proudest and boldest of mankind, behaved like a hysterical girl, trembled from head to foot, and burst into a flood of tears.

His colleagues for a time continued to entertain the expectation that his health would soon be restored, and that he would emerge from his retirement. But month followed month, and still he remained hidden in mysterious seclusion, and sunk, as far as they could learn, in the deepest dejection of spirits. They at length ceased to hope or to fear any thing from him; and, though he was still nominally Prime Minister, took without scruple steps which they knew to be diametrically opposed to all his opinions and feelings, allied themselves with those whom he had proscribed, disgraced those whom he most esteemed, and laid taxes on the colonies, in the face of the strong declarations which he had recently made.

When he had passed about a year and three quarters in gloomy privacy, the King received a few lines in Lady Chatham's hand. They contained a request, dictated by her lord, that he might be permitted to resign the Privy Seal. After some civil show of reluctance, the resignation was accepted. Indeed Chatham was, by this time, almost as much forgotten as if he had already been lying in Westminster Abbey.

At length the clouds which had gathered over his mind broke and passed away. His gout returned, and freed him from a more cruel malady. His nerves were newly braced. His spirits became buoyant. He woke as from a sickly dream. It was a strange recovery. Men had been in the habit of talking of him as of one dead, and, when he first showed himself at the King's levee, started as if they had seen a ghost. It was more than two years and a half since he had appeared in public.

He, too, had cause for wonder. The world which he now entered was not the world which he had quitted. The administration which he had formed had never been, at any one moment, entirely changed. But there had been so many losses and so many accessions, that he could scarcely recognise his own work. Charles Townshend was dead. Lord Shelburne had been dismissed. Conway had sunk into utter insignificance. The Duke of Grafton had fallen into the hands of the Bedfords. The Bedfords had deserted Grenville, had made their peace with the King and the King's friends, and had been admitted to office. Lord North was Chancellor of the Exchequer, and was rising fast in importance. Corsica had been given up to France without a struggle. The disputes with the American colonies had been revived. A general election had taken place. Wilkes had returned from exile, and outlaw as he was, had been chosen knight of the shire for Middlesex. The multitude was on his side. The court was obstinately bent on ruining him, and was prepared to shake the very foundations of the constitution for the sake of a paltry revenge. The House of Commons, assuming to itself an authority which of right belongs only to the whole legislature, had declared Wilkes incapable of sitting in Parliament. Nor had it been thought sufficient to keep him out. Another must be brought in. Since the freeholders of Middlesex had obstinately refused to choose a member acceptable to the Court, the House had chosen a member for them. This was not the only instance, perhaps not the most disgraceful instance, of the inveterate malignity of the Court. Exasperated by the steady opposition of the Rockingham party, the King's friends had tried to rob a distinguished Whig nobleman of his private estate, and had persisted in their mean wickedness till their own servile majority had revolted from mere disgust and shame. Discontent had spread throughout the nation, and was kept up by stimulants such as had rarely been applied to the public mind. Junius had taken the field, had trampled Sir William Draper in the dust, had well-nigh broken the heart of Blackstone, and had so mangled the reputation of the Duke of Grafton, that his grace had become sick of office, and was beginning to look wistfully towards the shades of Euston. Every principle of foreign, domestic, and colonial policy which was dear to the heart of Chatham had, during the eclipse of his genius, been violated by the government which he had formed.

The remaining years of his life were spent in vainly struggling against that fatal policy which, at the moment when he might have given it a death blow, he had been induced to take under his protection. His exertions redeemed his own fame, but they effected little for his country.

He found two parties arrayed against the government, the party of his own brothers-in-law, the Grenvilles, and the party of Lord Rockingham. On the question of the Middlesex election these parties were agreed. But on many other important questions they differed widely; and they were, in truth, not less hostile to each other than to the Court. The Grenvilles had, during several years, annoyed the Rockinghams with a succession of acrimonious pamphlets. It was long before the Rockinghams could be induced to retaliate. But an ill natured tract, written under Grenville's direction, and, entitled a State of the Nation, was too much for their patience. Burke undertook to defend and avenge his friends, and executed the task with admirable skill and vigour. On every point he was victorious, and nowhere more completely victorious than when he joined issue on those dry and minute questions of statistical and financial detail in which the main strength of Grenville lay. The official drudge, even on his own chosen ground, was utterly unable to maintain the fight against the great orator and philosopher. When Chatham reappeared, Grenville was still writhing with the recent shame and smart of this well merited chastisement. Cordial cooperation between the two sections of the Opposition was impossible. Nor could Chatham easily connect himself with either. His feelings, in spite of many affronts given and received, drew him towards the Grenvilles. For he had strong domestic affections; and his nature, which, though haughty, was by no means obdurate, had been softened by *affliction.* But from his kinsmen he was separated by a wide difference of opinion on the question of colonial taxation. A reconciliation, however, took place. He visited Stowe: he shook hands with George Grenville; and the Whig freeholders of Buckinghamshire, at their public dinners, drank many bumpers to the union of the three brothers.

In opinions, Chatham was much nearer to the Rockinghams than to his own relatives. But between him and the Rockinghams there was a gulf not easily to be passed. He had deeply injured them, and in injuring them, had deeply injured his country. When the balance was trembling between them and the Court, he had thrown the whole weight of his genius, of his renown, of his popularity, into the scale of misgovernment. It must be added, that many eminent members of the party still retained a bitter recollection of the asperity and disdain with which they had been treated by him at the time when he assumed the direction of affairs. It is clear from Burke's pamphlets and speeches, and still more clear from his private letters, and from the language which he held in conversation, that he regarded Chatham with a feeling not far removed from dislike. Chatham was undoubtedly conscious of his error, and desirous to atone for it. But his overtures of friendship, though made with earnestness, and even with unwonted humility, were at first received by Lord Rockingham with cold and austere reserve. Gradually the intercourse of the two statesmen became courteous and even amicable. But the past was never wholly forgotten.

Chatham did not, however, stand alone. Round him gathered a party, small in number, but strong in great and various talents. Lord Camden, Lord Shelburne, Colonel Barré, and Dunning, afterwards Lord Ashburton, were the principal

ion.

. to believe that, from this time till atham's death, his intellect suffered any decay. His eloquence was almost to the last heard with delight. But it was not exactly the eloquence of the House of Lords. That lofty and passionate, but somewhat desultory declamation, in which he excelled all men, and which was set off by looks, tones, and gestures, worthy of Garrick or Talma, was out of place in a small apartment where the audience often consisted of three or four drowsy prelates, three or four old judges, accustomed during many years to disregard rhetoric, and to look only at facts and arguments, and three or four listless and supercilious men of fashion, whom any thing like enthusiasm moved to a sneer. In the House of Commons, a flash of his eye, a wave of his arm, had sometimes cowed Murray. But, in the House of Peers, his utmost vehemence and pathos produced less effect than the moderation, the reasonableness, the luminous order, and the serene dignity, which characterized the speeches of Lord Mansfield.

On the question of the Middlesex election, all the three divisions of the Opposition acted in concert. No orator in either House defended what is now universally admitted to have been the constitutional cause with more ardour or eloquence than Chatham. Before this subject had ceased to occupy the public mind, George Grenville died. His party rapidly melted away; and in a short time most of his adherents appeared on the ministerial benches.

Had George Grenville lived many months longer, the friendly ties which, after years of estrangement and hostility, had been renewed between him and his brother-in-law, would, in all probability, have been a second time violently dissolved. For now the quarrel between England and the North American colonies took a gloomy and terrible aspect. Oppression provoked resistance; resistance was made the pretext for fresh oppression. The warnings of all the greatest statesmen of the age were lost on an imperious court and a deluded nation.

Soon a colonial senate ...
Then the colonial militia ...
regiments. At length the ...
Two millions of Englishmen ...
been as loyal to their princes ...
the people of Kent or ...
solemn act from the danger ...
insurgents would struggle ...
financial and military ...
disasters, following ...
dispelled the illusion ...
British force ...
by a hostile power ...
These governments ...
signally ...

...ed,
...who
...h was
...vet coat.
...rge, and
...uld be dis-
...eyes, which

..., Chatham rose.
...t length his tones
Here and there his
...sion which reminded
...hat he was not himself,
...hesitated, repeated the
...o confused that, in speak-
...ould not recall the name of
...e listened in solemn silence,

who had hoped to profit by our domestic dissensions. Lord Rockingham, therefore, and those who acted with him, conceived that the wisest course now open to England was to acknowledge the independence of the United States, and to turn her whole force against her European enemies.

Chatham, it should seem, ought to have taken the same side. Before France had taken any part in our quarrel with the colonies, he had repeatedly, and with great energy of language, declared that it was impossible to conquer America; and he could not without absurdity maintain that it was easier to conquer France and America together than America alone. But his passions overpowered his judgment, and made him blind to his own inconsistency. The very circumstances which made the separation of the colonies inevitable made it to him altogether insupportable. The dismemberment of the Empire seemed to him less ruinous and humiliating, when produced by domestic dissensions, than when produced by foreign interference. His blood boiled at the degradation of his country. Whatever lowered her among the nations of the earth, he felt as a personal outrage to himself. And the feeling was natural. He had made her so great. He had been so proud of her; and she had been so proud of him. He remembered how, more than twenty years before, in a day of gloom and dismay, when her possessions were torn from her, when her flag was dishonoured, she had called on him to save her. He remembered the sudden and glorious change which his energy had wrought, the long series of triumphs, the days of thanksgiving, the nights of illumination. Fired by such recollections, he determined to separate himself from those who advised that the independence of the colonies should be acknowledged. That he was in error will *scarcely*, we think, be disputed by his warmest admirers. *Indeed*, the treaty, by which, a few years later, the republic of the United States was recognised, was the work of his most attached adherents and of his favourite son.

The Duke of Richmond had given notice of an address to the throne, against the further prosecution of hostilities with America. Chatham had, during some time, absented himself from Parliament, in consequence of his growing infirmities. He determined to appear in his place on this occasion, and to declare that his opinions were decidedly at variance with those of the Rockingham party. He was in a state of great excitement. His medical attendants were uneasy, and strongly advised him to calm himself, and to remain at home. But he was not to be controlled. His son William, and his son-in-law Lord Mahon, accompanied him to Westminster. He rested himself in the Chancellor's room till the debate commenced, and then, leaning on his two young relations, limped to his seat. The slightest particulars of that day were remembered, and have been carefully recorded. He bowed, it was remarked, with great courtliness to those peers who rose to make way for him and his supporters. His crutch was in his hand. He wore, as was his fashion, a rich velvet coat. His legs were swathed in flannel. His wig was so large, and his face so emaciated, that none of his features could be discerned, except the high curve of his nose, and his eyes, which still retained a gleam of the old fire.

When the Duke of Richmond had spoken, Chatham rose. For some time his voice was inaudible. At length his tones became distinct and his action animated. Here and there his hearers caught a thought or an expression which reminded them of William Pitt. But it was clear that he was not himself. He lost the thread of his discourse, hesitated, repeated the same words several times, and was so confused that, in speaking of the Act of Settlement, he could not recall the name of the Electress Sophia. The House listened in solemn silence, and with the aspect of profound respect and compassion. The stillness was so deep that the dropping of a handkerchief would have been heard. The Duke of Richmond replied with great tenderness and courtesy; but while he spoke, the old man was observed to be restless and irritable. The Duke sat down. Chatham stood up again, pressed his hand on his breast, and sank down in an apoplectic fit. Three or four lords who sat near him caught him in his fall. The House broke up in confusion. The dying man was carried to the residence of one of the officers of Parliament, and was so far restored as to be able to bear a journey to Hayes. At Hayes, after lingering a few weeks, he expired in his seventieth year. His bed was watched to the last, with anxious tenderness, by his wife and children; and he well deserved their care. Too often haughty and wayward to others, to them he had been almost effeminately kind. He had through life been dreaded by his political opponents, and regarded with more awe than love even by his political associates. But no fear seems to have mingled with the affection which his fondness, constantly overflowing in a thousand endearing forms, had inspired in the little circle at Hayes.

Chatham, at the time of his decease, had not, in both Houses of Parliament, ten personal adherents. Half the public men of the age had been estranged from him by his errors, and the other half by the exertions which he had made to repair his errors. His last speech had been an attack at once on the policy pursued by the government, and on the policy recommended by the opposition. But death restored him to his old place in the affection of his country. Who could hear unmoved of the fall of that which had been so great, and which had stood so long? The circumstances, too, seemed rather to belong to the tragic stage than to real life. A great statesman, full of years and honours, led forth to the Senate

House by a son of rare hopes, and stricken down in full council while straining his feeble voice to rouse the drooping spirit of his country, could not but be remembered with peculiar veneration and tenderness. Detraction was overawed. The voice even of just and temperate censure was mute. Nothing was remembered but the lofty genius, the unsullied probity, the undisputed services, of him who was no more. For once, all parties were agreed. A public funeral, a public monument, were eagerly voted. The debts of the deceased were paid. A provision was made for his family. The City of London requested that the remains of the great man whom she had so long loved and honoured might rest under the dome of her magnificent cathedral. But the petition came too late. Every thing was already prepared for the interment in Westminster Abbey.

Though men of all parties had concurred in decreeing posthumous honours to Chatham, his corpse was attended to the grave almost exclusively by opponents of the government. The banner of the lordship of Chatham was borne by Colonel Barré, attended by the Duke of Richmond and Lord Rockingham. Burke, Savile, and Dunning upheld the pall. Lord Camden was conspicuous in the procession. The chief mourner was young William Pitt. After the lapse of more than twenty-seven years, in a season as dark and perilous, his own shattered frame and broken heart were laid, with the same pomp, in the same consecrated mould.

Chatham sleeps near the northern door of the Church, in a spot which has ever since been appropriated to statesmen, as the other end of the same transept has long been to poets. Mansfield rests there, and the second William Pitt, and Fox, and Grattan, and Canning, and Wilberforce. In no other cemetery do so many great citizens lie within so narrow a space. *High over those venerable graves towers the stately* monument of Chatham, and from above, his effigy, graven by a cunning hand, seems still, with eagle face and outstretched arm, to bid England be of good cheer, and to hurl defiance at her foes. The generation which reared that memorial of him has disappeared. The time has come when the rash and indiscriminate judgments which his contemporaries passed on his character may be calmly revised by history. And history, while, for the warning of vehement, high, and daring natures, she notes his many errors, will yet deliberately pronounce, that, among the eminent men whose bones lie near his, scarcely one has left a more stainless, and none a more splendid name.

# INDEX.

## A.

Abbé and abbot, difference between, II. 115.

Academy, character of its doctrines, III. 97.

Adam, Robert, court architect to George III., V. 198.

Addison, Joseph, review of Miss Aikin's life of, V. 68—161; his character, V. 70; sketch of his father's life, V. 71; his birth and early life, V. 72; appointed to a scholarship in Magdalene College, Oxford, V. 73; his classical attainments, V. 74; his Essay on the Evidences of Christianity, V. 76. 154; contributes a preface to Dryden's Georgics, V. 80; his intention to take orders frustrated, V. 81; sent by the government to the Continent, V. 84; his introduction to Boileau, V. 85; leaves Paris and proceeds to Venice, V. 89; his residence in Italy, V. 90—95; composes his Epistle to Montague (then Lord Halifax), V. 94; his prospects clouded by the death of William III, V. 95; becomes tutor to a young English traveller, V. 95; writes his Treatise on Medals, V. 95; repairs to Holland, V. 96; returns to England, V. 96; his cordial reception and introduction into the Kit Cat Club, V. 96; his pecuniary difficulties, V. 96; engaged by Godolphin to write a poem in honour of Marlborough's exploits, V. 99; is appointed to a Commissionership, V. 99; merits of his "Campaign," V. 100; criticism of his Travels in Italy, V. 75. 103; his opera of Rosamond, V. 104; is made Undersecretary of State, and accompanies the Earl of Halifax to Hanover, V. 105; his election to the House of Commons, V. 106; his failure as a speaker, V. 106; his popularity and talents for conversation, V. 109; his timidity and constraint among strangers, V. 110; his favourite associates V. 111—114; becomes Chief Secretary for Ireland under Wharton, V. 114; origination of the Tatler, V. 116; his characteristics as a writer, V. 118—122; compared with Swift and Voltaire as a master of the art of ridicule, V. 119; his pecuniary losses, V. 125; loss of his Secretaryship, V. 125; resignation of his Fellowship, V. 125; encouragement and disappointment of his advances towards a great lady, V. 152; returned to Parliament without a contest, V. 125; his Whig Examiner, V. 126; intercedes with the Tories on behalf of Ambrose Phillipps and Steele, V. 126; his discontinuance of the Tatler and commencement of the Spectator, V. 127; his part in the Spectator, V. 128; his commencement and discontinuance of the Guardian, V. 131; his Cato, III. 348. V. 91. 131; his intercourse with Pope, V. 135; his concern for Steele, V. 137; begins a new series of the Spectator, V. 138; appointed secretary to the Lords Justices of the Council on the death of Queen Anne, V. 138; again appointed Chief Secretary for Ireland, V. 139; his relations with Swift and Tickell, V. 141; removed to the Board of Trade, V. 142; production of his Drummer, V. 142; his Freeholder, V. 142; his estrangement from Pope, V. 143; his long courtship of the Countess Dowager of Warwick and union with her, V. 152; takes up his abode at Holland House, V. 152; appointed Secretary of State by Sunderland, V. 153; failure of his health, V. 153; resigns his post, V. 153; receives a pension, V. 153; his estrangement from Steele and other friends, V. 154; advocates the bill for limiting the number of Peers, V. 155; refutation of a calumny upon him, V. 156; entrusts his works to Tickell, and dedicates them to Craggs, V. 158; sends for Gay on his death-bed to ask his forgiveness, V. 159; his death and funeral, V. 160; Tickell's elegy on his death, V. 160; superb edition of his works, V. 160; his monument in Poet's Corner, Westminster Abbey, V. 161.

Addison, Dr. Lancelot, sketch of his life, V. 71.

*Adiaphorists*, a sect of German Protestants, II. 87, 108.

Adultery, how represented by the dramatists of the Restoration, IV. 150.

Advancement of Learning, by Bacon, its publication, III. 49.

Æschylus and the Greek drama, I. 14—26.

Afghanistan, the monarchy of, analogous to that of England in the 16th century, II. 98; bravery of its inhabitants, IV. 240—244; the English the only army in India which could compete with them, IV. 241; their devastations in India, IV. 13.

Agricultural and manufacturing labourers, comparison of their condition, I. 224. 225.

Agujari, the singer, V. 8.

Aikin, Miss, review of her Life of Addison, V. 68—161.

Aix, its capture, II. 266.

Akenside, his Epistle to Curio, II. 211.

Albigenses, IV. 107—109.

Alexander the Great, compared with Clive, IV. 95, 96.

Alfieri and Cowper, comparison between them, I. 324—326.

Allahabad, IV. 238, 239.

Allegories of Johnson and Addison, II. 3.

Allegory, difficulty of making it interesting, II. 3.

Allegro and Penseroso, I. 13.

Alphabetical writing, the greatest of human inventions, III. 108; comparative views of its value by Plato and Bacon, III. 108, 109.

America, acquisitions of the Catholic Church in, IV. 98; its capabilities, IV. 98.

American colonies, British, war with them, IV. 266; act for imposing stamp duties upon them, V. 220; their disaffection, V. 230; revival of the dispute with them, V. 251;

ess of their resistance, V.

tist, their origin, II. 90.
rsis, reputed contriver of the r's wheel, III. 94.
dy Khan, governor of the tic, IV. 16, 17.
his fortress of Gheriah re-l by Clive, IV. 32.
ueen, her political and reli- inclinations, II.164; changes r government in 1710, II.
relative estimation by the s and the Tories of her reign, 5—170. 174; state of parties r accession, V. 95; dismisses higs, V. 123; change in the ct of public affairs conse- on her death, V. 138.
, Grecian eloquence at, IV.

III. 78.
ical succession, Mr. Glad- claims it for the Church of nd, III. 298—322.
, Thomas, III. 131.
ble of the Great Pyramid, .
not's Satirical Works, V. 120.
edes, his slight estimate of ventions, III. 105.
s, rebuked by Plato, III.

Nabob of, his relations with nd, IV. 17—24. 94; his s recognised by the English, .
gitica, Milton's, allusion to,

Duke of, secedes from Wal- administration, II. 230.
, compared with Tasso, IV.

emus, IV. 100.
hanes, IV. 145.
e, his authority impaired by sformation, III. 101.

Arithmetic, comparative estimate of, by Plato and by Bacon, III. 103, 104.
Arlington, Lord, his character, III. 173; his coldness for the Triple Alliance, III. 180; his impeach- ment, III. 197.
Armies in the middle ages, how constituted, I. 72. 150; a power- ful restraint on the regal power, I. 150; subsequent change in this respect, I. 152.
Arms, British, successes of, against the French in 1758, II. 266—269.
Army (the), control of, by Charles I. or by the Parliament, I. 159; its triumph over both, I. 167; danger of a standing army becoming an instrument of despotism, II. 71.
Arne, Dr., set to music Addison's opera of Rosamond, V. 105.
Arragon and Castile, their old in- stitutions favourable to public liberty, II. 124.
Art of War, Machiavelli's, I. 96.
Arundel, Earl of, III. 90.
Asia, Central, its people, IV. 239.
Asiatic Society, commencement of its career under Warren Hastings, IV. 303.
Assemblies, deliberative, II. 263.
Association. See Catholic Associa- tion.
Astronomy, comparative estimate of, by Socrates and by Bacon, III. 107.
Athenian comedies, their impurity, IV. 145; reprinted at the two Uni- versities, IV. 145.
Athenians (the), Johnson's opinion of them, I. 387.
Attainder, an act of, warrantable, II. 56.
Atterbury, Bishop, his reply to Bentley to prove the genuineness of the Letters of Phalaris, III. 246; reads the funeral service

over the lady of Addison, V.
260.
Attila, IV. 94.
Attributes of God, subtle speculations touching them imply no high degree of intellectual culture, IV. 100—103.
Aubrey, his charge of corruption against Bacon, III. 72; Bacon's decision against him after his present, III. 87.
Augsburg, Confession of, its adoption in Sweden, IV. 125.
Augustin, St., IV. 98.
Aurungzebe, his policy, IV. 11.
Austen, Jane, notice of, V. 56.
Austin, Sarah, her character as a translator, IV. 97. 142.
Austria, success of her armies in the Catholic cause, IV. 131.
Authors, their present position, I. 263—264.
Avignon, the Papal Court transferred from Rome to, IV. 109.

### B.

Baber, founder of the Mogul empire, IV. 10.
Bacon, Lady, mother of Lord Bacon, III. 13.
Bacon, Lord, review of Basil Montagu's new edition of the works of, III. 1—146; his mother distinguished as a linguist, III. 13; his early years, III. 16—19; his services refused by government, III. 20—21; his admission at Gray's Inn, III. 20; his legal attainments, III. 21; sat in Parliament in 1593, III. 22; part he took in politics, III. 23; his friendship with the Earl of Essex, III. 20—25; examination of his conduct to Essex, III. 26—47; influence of King James on his fortunes, III. 44; his servility to Lord Southampton, III. 45; influence his talents had with the public, III. 45; his distinction in Parliament and in the courts of law, III. 46; his literary and philosophical works, III. 46; his "Novum Organum," and the admiration it excited, III. 46; his work of reducing and recompiling the laws of England, III. 46; his tampering with the judges on the trial of Peacham, III. 50—55; attaches himself to Buckingham, III. 56; his appointment as Lord Keeper, III. 59; his share in the vices of the administration, III. 60; his animosity towards Sir Edward Coke, III. 65—67; his town and country residences, III. 67, 68; his titles of Baron Verulam and Viscount St. Albans, III. 68; report against him of the Committee on the Courts of Justice, III. 71; nature of the charges, III. 71, 72; overwhelming evidence to them, III. 73; his admission of his guilt, III. 75; his sentence, III. 75; examination of Mr. Montagu's arguments in his defence, III. 75—88; mode in which he spent the last years of his life, III. 89—91; chief peculiarity of his philosophy, III. 92—103; his views compared with those of Plato, III. 104—115; to what his wide and durable fame is chiefly owing, III. 117; his frequent treatment of moral subjects, III. 121; his views as a theologian, III. 122; vulgar notion of him as inventor of the inductive method, III. 124; estimate of his analysis of that method, III. 124—134; union of audacity and sobriety in his temper, III. 134; his amplitude of comprehension, III. 134, 135; his freedom from the spirit of controversy, III. 135; his eloquence,

wit, and similitudes, III. 136; his disciplined imagination, III. 139; his boldness and originality, III. 139; unusual development in the order of his faculties, III. 141; his resemblance to the mind of Burke, III. 141; specimens of his two styles, III. 142, 143; value of his Essays, III. 143; his greatest performance the first book of the Novum Organum, III. 144; contemplation of his life, III. 145, 146.

Bacon, Sir Nicholas, his character, III. 7—13.

Baconian philosophy, its chief peculiarity, III. 91; its essential spirit, III. 95; its method and object differed from the ancient, III. 103; comparative views of Bacon and Plato, III. 103—114; its beneficent spirit, III. 110, 111. 118; its value compared with ancient philosophy, III. 113—124.

Baillie, Gen., destruction of his detachment by Hyder Ali, IV. 280.

Balance of power, interest of the Popes in preserving it, IV. 132.

Banim, Mr., his defence of James II. as a supporter of toleration, II.321.

Banking operations of Italy in the 14th century, I. 68.

Bar (the), its degraded condition in the time of James II., I. 188.

Barbary, work on, by Rev. Dr. Addison, V. 71.

Barcelona, capture of, by Peterborough, II. 150.

Baretti, his admiration for Miss Burney, V. 22.

Barillon, M., his pithy words on the new council proposed by Temple, III. 208. 216.

Barlow, Bishop, IV. 162.

Barrington, Lord, V. 173.

Barwell, Mr., IV. 245; his support of Hastings, IV. 249. 263, 265. 270.

Bastile, Burke's declamations on its capture, IV. 318.

Battle of the Cranes and Pygmies, Addison's, V. 77.

Bavaria, its contest between Protestantism and Catholicism, IV. 121.

Baxter's testimony to Hampden's excellence, II. 20.

Bayle, Peter, IV. 104.

Beaumarchais, his suit before the parliament of Paris, III. 87.

Beckford, Alderman, V. 248.

Bedford, Duke of, V. 171; his views of the policy of Chatham, V. 184. 199; presents remonstrance to George III., V. 226.

Bedford, Earl of, invited by Charles I. to form an administration, II. 58.

Bedfords (the), V. 171; their opposition to the Rockingham ministry on the Stamp Act, V. 233; their willingness to break with Grenville on Chatham's accession to office, V. 243; deserted Grenville and admitted to office, V. 252; parallel between them and the Rockinghams, V. 228.

Bedford House assailed by a rabble, V. 225.

Begums of Oude, their domains and treasures, IV. 293; disturbances in Oude imputed to them, IV. 294; their protestations, IV. 295; their spoliation charged against Hastings, IV. 325.

Belgium, its contest between Protestantism and Catholicism, IV. 121. 131.

Belial, IV. 148.

Bell, Peter, Byron's spleen against, I. 327.

Bellasys, the English general, II. 143.

Bellingham, his malevolence, V. 57.

Belphegor (the), of Machiavelli, I. 89.

Benares, its grandeur, IV. 281; its

annexation to the British dominions, IV. 291.
"Benefits of the Death of Christ," IV. 121.
Benevolences, Oliver St. John's opposition to, and Bacon's support of, III. 49.
Bengal, its resources, III. 33; *et seq.*
Bentham, his language on the French revolution, II. 285.
Bentham and Dumont, II. 184.
Bentinck, Lord William, his memory cherished by the Hindoos, IV. 96.
Bentivoglio, Cardinal, on the state of religion in England in the 16th century, II. 103.
Bentley, Richard, his quarrel with Boyle, and remarks on Temple's Essay on the Letters of Phalaris, III. 245; his edition of Milton, III. 248; his notes on Horace, III. 248; his reconciliation with Boyle and Atterbury, III. 249.
Berar, occupied by the Bonslas, IV. 267.
Berwick, Duke of, held the Allies in check, II. 145; his retreat before Galway, II. 154.
Bickerstaff, Isaac, astrologer, V. 117.
Biographia Britannica, refutation of a calumny on Addison in, V. 156.
Biography, tenure by which a writer of is bound to his subject, III. 241.
Bishops, claims of those of the Church of England to apostolical succession, III. 298—306.
Black Hole of Calcutta described, IV. 36, 37; retribution of the English for its horrors, IV. 38, 39. 44—47.
Blackmore, Sir Richard, his attainments in the ancient languages, V. 77.
*Blackstone*, II. 348.
*Blasphemous* publications, policy *of Government* in respect to, I. 245.

Blenheim, battle of, V. 97; Addison employed to write a poem in its honour, V. 99.
Blois, Addison's retirement to, V. 85.
"Bloomsbury gang," the denomination of the Bedfords, V. 171.
Bodley, Sir Thomas, founder of the Bodleian library, III. 49. 90.
Bohemia, influence of the doctrines of Wickliffe in, IV. 109, 110.
Boileau, Addison's intercourse with, V. 85; his opinion of modern Latin, V. 87; his literary qualities, V. 88.
Bolingbroke, Lord, the liberal patron of literature, I. 370; proposed to strengthen the royal prerogative, II. 200; his pretence of philosophy in his exile, III. 121; his jest on occasion of the first representation of Cato, V. 133; Pope's perfidy towards him, V. 149; his remedy for the diseases of the state, V. 180.
Bombay, its affairs thrown into confusion by the new council at Calcutta, IV. 250.
Book of the Church, Southey's, I. 214.
Books, puffing of, I. 265—270.
Booth, played the hero in Addison's Cato on its first representation, V. 132.
Borgia, Cæsar, I. 91.
Boroughs, rotten, the abolition of, a necessary reform in the time of George I., II. 209.
Boswell, James, his character, I. 362—367.
Boswell's Life of Johnson, by Croker, review of, I. 341—394; character of the work, I. 362.
Boswellism, I. 59.
Bourbon, the House of, their vicissitudes in Spain, II. 142—163.
Bourne, Vincent, V. 87; his Latin verses in celebration of Addison's restoration to health, V. 153.

Boyle, Charles, his nominal editorship of the Letters of Phalaris, III. 245; his book on Greek history and philology, V. 77.
Boyle, Rt. Hon. Henry, V. 99.
"Boys" (the), in opposition to Sir R. Walpole, II. 205.
Bracegirdle, Mrs., her celebrity as an actress, IV, 196; her intimacy with Congreve, IV. 196, 197.
Brahmins, IV. 103.
Breda, treaty of, III. 177, 178.
Bribery, foreign, in the time of Charles I., I. 193.
Bribuega, siege of, II. 162.
"Broad Bottom Administration" (the), II. 243.
Brothers, his prophecies as a test of faith, IV. 103.
Brown, Launcelot, IV. 83.
Brown's Estimate, II. 257.
Bruce, his appearance at Dr. Burney's concerts, V. 8.
Brunswick, the House of, V. 174.
Brussels, its importance as the seat of a vice-regal Court, III. 176.
Brydges, Sir Egerton, 676.
Buchanan, character of his writings, III. 102.
Buckhurst, IV. 147.
Buckingham, Duke of, the "Steenie" of James I., II. 30—32; Bacon's early discernment of his influence, III. 56—58; his return for Bacon's patronage, III. 59; his corruption, III. 61; his character and position, III. 63—67; his marriage, III. 70; his visit to Bacon, and report of his condition, III. 72.
Buckingham, Duke of, one of the Cabal ministry, IV. 166; his fondness for Wycherley, IV. 166; anecdote of his versatility, IV. 166.
Budgell, Eustace, one of Addison's friends, V. 111. 114.
Bunyan, John, his history and character, II. 10—14; his style, II. 16.

Bunyan's Pilgrim's Progress, review of Southey's edition, II. 1; peculiarity of the work, II. 4. 9. 14—16; not a perfect allegory, II. 8, 9.
Buonaparte, I. 174. II. 260. V. 101. See also Napoleon.
Burgoyne, Gen., chairman of the committee of inquiry on Lord Clive, IV. 90.
Burke, Edmund, his characteristics, I. 211; his opinion of the war with Spain on the question of maritime right, II. 241; resembles Bacon, III. 141; effect of his speeches on the House of Commons, III. 253; not the author of the Letters of Junius, IV. 247; his charges against Hastings, IV. 310—341; his kindness to Miss Burney, V. 38; her incivility to him at Hastings' trial, V. 38; his early political career, V. 229—233; his first speech in the House of Commons, V. 236; his opposition to Chatham's measures relating to India, V. 249; his defence of his party against Grenville's attacks, V. 254; his feeling towards Chatham, V. 255.
Burleigh and his Times, review of Rev. Dr. Nares's, II. 81; his early life and character, II. 83—88; his death, II. 89; importance of the times in which he lived, II. 89; the great stain on his character, II. 108; character of the class of statesmen he belonged to, III. 8; his conduct towards Bacon, III. 20, 21. 28; his apology for having resorted to torture, III. 53; Bacon's letter to him upon the department of knowledge he had chosen, III. 135.
Burnet, Bishop, III. 250.
Burney, Dr., his social position, V. 4—9; his conduct relative to his daughter's first publication, V.

19; his daughter's engagement at Court, V. 32.
Burney, Frances. *See* D'Arblay, Madame.
Bussy, his eminent merit and conduct in India, IV. 27.
Bute, Earl of, his character and education, V. 178; appointed Secretary of State, V. 183; opposes the proposal of war with Spain on account of the family compact, V. 188; his unpopularity on Chatham's resignation, V. 190; becomes Prime Minister, V. 192; his first speech in the House of Lords, V. 192; induces the retirement of the Duke of Newcastle, V. 193; becomes First Lord of the Treasury, V. 193; his foreign and domestic policy, V. 195—207; his resignation, V. 208; continues to advise the king privately, V. 213. 224. 233.
Butler, Addison not inferior to him in wit, V. 118.
Byng, Admiral, his failure at Minorca, II. 257; his trial, II. 259; opinion of his conduct, II. 259; Chatham's defence of him, II. 260.
Byron, Lord, his epistolary style, I. 302; his character I. 303; his early life, I. 304; his quarrel with and separation from his wife, I. 305—308; his expatriation, I. 309; decline of his intellectual powers, I. 310; his attachment to Italy and Greece, I. 310; his sickness and death, I. 311; general grief for his fate, I. 312; remarks on his poetry, I. 313; his admiration of the Pope school of poetry, I. 326; his opinion of Wordsworth and Coleridge, I. 327; of Peter Bell, I. 327; his estimate *of the poetry of the 18th and 19th centuries*, I. 327; his sensitive*ness to criticism*, I. 328; the interpreter between Wordsworth and the multitude, I. 330; the founder of an exoteric Lake school, I. 330; remarks on his dramatic works, I. 330—337; his egotism, I. 334; cause of his influence, I. 338—340.

C.

Cabal (the), their proceedings and designs, III. 189, 190. 198.
Cabinets, in modern times, III. 206.
Cadiz, exploit of Essex at the siege of, II. 143. III. 30; its pillage by the English expedition in 1702, II. 143.
Calcutta, its position on the Hoogley, IV. 34; scene of the Black Hole of, IV. 36, 37; resentment of the English at its fall IV. 38; again threatened by Surajah Dowlah, IV. 42; revival of its prosperity, IV. 53; its sufferings during the famine, IV. 84; its capture, IV. 229; its suburbs infested by robbers, IV. 250; its festivities on Hastings' marriage, IV. 265.
Calvinism, moderation of Bunyan's, II. 13; held by the Church of England at the end of the 16th century, III. 305; many of its doctrines contained in the Paulician theology, IV. 106.
Cambridge, University of, favoured by George I. and George II., V. 194; its superiority to Oxford in intellectual activity, III. 8; disturbances produced in, by the Civil War, III. 159.
Cambyses, story of his punishment of the corrupt judge, III. 81.
Camilla, Madame D'Arblay's, V. 59.
Campaign, The, by Addison, V. 99.
Canada, subjugation of, by the British in 1760, II. 268.

Canning, Mr., V. 53.
Cape Breton, reduction of, II. 266.
Caraffa, Gian Pietro, afterwards Pope Paul IV., his zeal and devotion, IV. 114. 120.
Carlisle, Lady, II. 64.
Carnatic (the), its resources, IV. 16—31; its invasion by Hyder Ali, IV. 279.
Carteret, Lord, his ascendency after the fall of Walpole, II. 212; Sir Horace Walpole's stories about him, II. 215; his defection from Sir Robert Walpole, II. 229; succeeds Walpole, II. 243; his character as a statesman, II. 244; created Earl Granville, II. 243.
Carthagena, surrender of the arsenal and ships of, to the Allies, II. 154.
Casina (the), of Plautus, I. 88.
Castile, Admiral of, II. 144.
Castile and Arragon, their old institutions favourable to public liberty, II. 124.
Castilians, their character in the 16th century, II. 119; their conduct in the War of the Succession, II. 156; their attachment to the faith of their ancestors, IV. 113.
Castracani, Castruccio, Life of, by Machiavelli, I. 105.
Catholic Association, attempt of the Tories to put it down, IV. 201.
Catholic Church. *See* Church of Rome.
Catholicism, causes of its success, IV. 99—126.
Catholics and Jews, the same reasoning employed against both, I. 289.
Catholics and Protestants, their relative numbers in the 16th century, II. 102.
Catholic Queen (a), precautions against, I. 158.
"Cato," Addison's play of, its merits,
and the contest it occasioned, II. 348; its first representation, V. 132; its performance at Oxford, V. 134.
Cavaliers, their successors in the reign of George I. turned demagogues, V. 165.
Cavendish, Lord, his conduct in the new council of Temple, III. 233; his merits, V. 227.
Cecil. *See* Burleigh.
Cecil, Robert, his rivalry with Francis Bacon, III. 19, 20. 28; his fear and envy of Essex, III. 24. 41; increase of his dislike for Bacon, III. 27; his conversation with Essex, III. 28; his interference to obtain knighthood for Bacon, III. 44.
Cecilia, Madame D'Arblay's, V. 57; specimen of its style, V. 62.
Censorship, existed in some form from Henry VIII. to the Revolution, II. 344.
Cervantes, II. 120.
Chalmers, Dr., Mr. Gladstone's opinion of his defence of the Church, III. 257.
Champion, Colonel, commander of the Bengal army, IV. 242.
Chandernagore, French settlement on the Hoogley, IV. 34; captured by the English, IV. 42.
Charlemagne, imbecility of his successors, IV. 11.
Charles, Archduke, his claim to the Spanish crown, II. 127; takes the field in support of it, II. 145; accompanies Peterborough in his expedition, II. 148; his success in the north-east of Spain, II. 151; is proclaimed king at Madrid, II. 156; his reverses and retreat, II. 158; his re-entry into Madrid, II. 160; his unpopularity, II. 161; concludes a peace, II. 165; forms an alliance with Philip of Spain, II. 171.

Charles I., lawfulness of the resistance to, I. 31. 37; Milton's defence of his execution, I. 41; his treatment of the Parliament of 1640, I. 131; his treatment of Strafford, I. 140; estimate of his character, I. 142. 169. 170. II. 31; his fall, I. 167; his condemnation and its consequences, I. 168—173; Hampden's opposition to him, and its consequences, II. 31—47; resistance of the Scots to him, II. 47. 48; his increasing difficulties, II. 49; his conduct towards the House of Commons, II. 63—67; his flight, II. 68; review of his conduct and treatment, II. 70—74; reaction in his favour during the Long Parliament, II. 318; cause of his political blunders, III. 69; effect of the victory over him on the national character, III. 153.

Charles I. and Cromwell, choice between, I. 166.

Charles II., character of his reign, I. 46; his foreign subsidies, I. 199; his situation in 1660 contrasted with that of Louis XVIII., II. 302—305; his character, II. 309. III. 174. 186. 188. 190. 219; his position towards the king of France, II. 314; consequences of his levity and apathy, II. 319; his court compared with that of his father, III. 172; his extravagance, III. 177; his subserviency to France, III. 180—202; his renunciation of the dispensing power, III. 197; his relations with Temple, III. 200. 203. 233; his system of bribery of the Commons, III. 211; his dislike of Halifax, III. 228; his dismissal of Temple, III. 235; his social disposition, IV. 166.

*Charles II. of Spain*, his unhappy *condition*, II. 125. 131—135; his difficulties in respect to the succession, II. 125—135.

Charles III. of Spain, his hatred of England, V. 187.

Charles V., IV. 112.

Charles VIII., III. 136.

Charles XII., compared with Clive, IV. 95.

Charlotte, Queen, obtains the attendance of Miss Burney, V. 31; her partizanship for Hastings, V. 40; her treatment of Miss Burney, V. 43—48.

Chatham, Earl of, character of his public life, II. 223; his early life, II. 225; his travels, II. 226; enters the army, II. 226; obtains a seat in Parliament, II. 226; attaches himself to the Whigs in opposition, II. 233; his qualities as an orator, II. 238—241; dismissed from the army, II. 240; is made Groom of the Bedchamber to the Prince of Wales, II. 241; declaims against the ministers, II. 242; his opposition to Carteret, II. 243; legacy left him by the Duchess of Marlborough, II. 243; supports the Pelham ministry, II. 245; appointed Vice-Treasurer of Ireland, II. 246; overtures made to him by Newcastle, II. 254; made Secretary of State, II. 254; defends Admiral Byng, II. 260; coalesces with the Duke of Newcastle, II. 254; success of his administration, II. 255—272; his appreciation of Clive, IV. 61. 86; breach between him and the great Whig connection, V. 87; review of his Correspondence, V. 162; in the zenith of prosperity and glory, V. 162; his coalition with Newcastle, V. 167; his strength in Parliament, V. 173; jealousies in his cabinet, V. 184; his defects V. 185; proposes to declare war against Spain on account of the family compact, V. 188; rejection of his counsel, V. 188; his resignation, V. 188; the king's gracious behaviour to him, V. 188; public enthusiasm towards him, V. 190; his conduct in opposition, V. 192—205; his speech against peace with France and Spain, V. 206; his unsuccessful audiences with George III. to form an administration, V. 214; Sir William Pynsent bequeaths his whole property to him, V. 219; bad state of his health, V. 219; is twice visited by the Duke of Cumberland with propositions from the king, V. 223; his condemnation of the American Stamp Act, V. 231; is induced by the king to assist in ousting Rockingham, V. 239; morbid state of his mind, V. 241. 248; undertakes to form an administration, V. 242; is created Earl of Chatham, V. 244; failure of his ministerial arrangements, V. 244—253; loss of his popularity, and of his foreign influence, V. 244—252; his despotic manners, V. 241. 246; lays an embargo on the exportation of corn, V. 247; his first speech in the House of Lords, V. 248; his supercilious conduct towards the Peers, V. 248; his retirement from office, V. 249; his policy violated, V. 251; resigns the privy seal, V. 252; state of parties and of public affairs on his recovery, V. 252; his political relations, V. 255; his eloquence not suited to the House of Lords, V. 256; opposed the recognition of the independence of the United States, V. 258; his last appearance in the House of Lords, V. 259; his death, V. 260; reflections on his fall, V. 260; his funeral in Westminster Abbey, V. 261.

Cherbourg, guns taken from, II. 266.

Chesterfield, Lord, his dismissal by Walpole, II. 230.

Cheyte Sing, a vassal of the government of Bengal, IV. 282; his large revenue and suspected treasure, IV. 286; Hastings' policy in desiring to punish him, IV. 286—292; his treatment made the successful charge against Hastings, IV. 322.

Chillingworth, his opinion on apostolical succession, III. 303; became a Catholic from conviction, IV. 104.

Chinsurah, Dutch settlement on the Hoogley, IV. 34; its siege by the English and capitulation, IV. 61.

Chivalry, its form in Languedoc in the 12th century, IV. 105.

Cholmondely, Mr., V. 22.

Christchurch College, Oxford, its repute after the Revolution, III. 245; issues a new edition of the Letters of Phalaris, III. 245.

Christianity, its alliance with the ancient philosophy, III. 99; light in which it was regarded by the Italians at the Reformation, IV. 112.

Church (the), in the time of James II., I. 188.

Church (the), Southey's Book of, I. 214.

Church, the English, persecutions in her name, I. 119; High and Low Church parties, V. 105.

Church of England, its origin, and connection with the state, I. 127. III. 321; its condition in the time of Charles I., I. 241. 245; endeavour of the leading Whigs at the Revolution to alter its Liturgy and Articles, II. 337. III. 310; its contest with the Scotch nation, II. 338; Mr. Gladstone's work in de-

*Macaulay, Essays. V.*

fence of it, III. 255; his arguments for its being the pure Catholic Church of Christ, III. 294. 298; its claims to apostolical succession discussed, III. 299—312; views respecting its alliance with the state, III. 313—323; contrast of its operations during the two generations succeeding the Reformation, with those of the Church of Rome, IV. 126—128.

Church of Rome, its alliance with ancient philosophy, III. 99; causes of its success and vitality, IV. 99; sketch of its history, IV. 102—142.

Churchill, Charles, I. 187. V. 199.

Cicero, partiality of Dr. Middleton towards, III. 4; the most eloquent and skilful of advocates, III. 6; his epistles in his banishment, III. 24; his opinion of the study of rhetoric, III. 126.

Cider, proposal of a tax on, by the Bute administration, V. 206.

Civilisation, England's progress in, due to the people, I. 260.

Civil privileges and political power identical, I. 288.

Civil war, its evils the price of our liberty, I. 38; conduct of the Long Parliament in reference to it, I. 143. 165.

Clarendon, Lord, his character, I. 187; his testimony in favour of Hampden, II. 36. 54. 58. 74. 77; his literary merit, III. 3; his position at the head of affairs, III. 171—181; his faulty style, III. 192; his opposition to the growing power of the Commons, III. 213; his temper, III. 214.

Clarke, Dr. Samuel, IV. 101.

Clarkson, Thomas, V. 57.

Classical learning, love of, in Italy in the 14th century, I. 70.

Clavering, General, IV. 245; his opposition to Hastings, IV. 250—256; his appointment as Governor-General, IV. 263; his defeat, IV. 265; his death, IV. 265.

Cleveland, Duchess of, her favour to Wycherley and Churchill, IV. 164.

Clifford, Lord, his character, III. 188; his retirement, III. 197; his talent for debate, III. 212.

Clive, Lord, review of Sir John Malcolm's Life of, IV. 1—96; his family and boyhood, IV. 3—5; his shipment to India, IV. 5; his arrival at Madras, and position there, IV. 7; obtains an ensign's commission in the Company's service, IV. 9; his attack, capture, and defence of Arcot, IV. 20—24; his subsequent proceedings, IV. 25, 26; his marriage and return to England, IV. 28, 29; his reception, IV. 29; enters Parliament, IV. 31; returns to India, IV. 32; his subsequent proceedings, IV. 32—50; his conduct towards Omichund, IV. 50; his pecuniary acquisitions, IV. 53; his transactions with Meer Jaffier, IV. 54—57; appointed Governor of the Company's possessions in Bengal, IV. 57; his dispersion of Shah Alum's army, IV. 59; responsibility of his position, IV. 60; his return to England, IV. 61; his reception, IV. 61, 62; his proceedings at the India House, IV. 64. 70; nominated Governor of the British possessions in Bengal, IV. 70; his arrival at Calcutta, IV. 70; suppresses a conspiracy, IV. 71—75; success of his foreign policy, IV. 76; his return to England, IV. 79; his unpopularity, and its causes, IV. 80—90; invested with the Grand Cross of the Bath, IV. 90; his speech in his defence, and its consequence, IV. 91; his life in retirement, IV. 92; reflections on his career, IV. 95; failing of his mind, and death by his own hand, IV. 94.

Clizia, Machiavelli's, I. 88.

Clodius, extensive bribery at the trial of, III. 78.

Club-room, Johnson's, I. 393.

Coalition of Chatham and Newcastle, II. 263.

Cobham, Lord, his malignity towards Essex, III. 41.

Cæsar Borgia, I. 91.

Cæsar, Claudius, resemblance of James I. to, II. 28.

Cæsar compared with Cromwell, I. 174.

Cæsars (the), parallel between them and the Tudors, not applicable, II. 99.

Coke, Sir E., his conduct towards Bacon, III. 21. 65; his opposition to Bacon in Peacham's case, III. 50; his experience in conducting state prosecutions, III. 54; his removal from the Bench, III. 65; his reconciliation with Buckingham, and agreement to marry his daughter to Buckingham's brother, III. 65; his reconciliation with Bacon, III. 67; his behaviour to Bacon at his trial, III. 84.

Coleridge, relative "correctness" of his poetry, I. 314; Byron's opinion of him, I. 327.

Coligni, Gaspar de, reference to, V. 222.

Collier, Jeremy, sketch of his life, IV. 183—190; his publication on the profaneness of the English stage, IV. 186. 193; his controversy with Congreve, IV. 192, *et seq.*

Colloquies on Society, Southey's, I. 210; plan of the work, I. 219.

Colonies, II. 121; question of the competency of Parliament to tax them, V. 232.

Colonna, Fabrizio, I. 96.

Comedy (the) of England, effect of the writings of Congreve and Sheridan upon, I. 85.

Comic Dramatists of the Restoration, IV. 144—199; have exercised a great influence on the human mind, IV. 145.

Comines, his testimony to the good government of England, II. 23.

Commerce and manufactures, condition of, during the war at the latter part of the reign of George II., II. 270; their extent in Italy in the 14th century, I. 68.

Commons, House of, increase of its power, I. 199; increase of its power by and since the Revolution, II. 339.

Commonwealth, IV. 158.

Comus, Milton's, I. 13. 15.

Condé, Marshal, compared with Clive, IV. 95.

Conflans, Admiral, his defeat by Hawke, II. 267.

Congreve, sketch of his career at the Temple, IV. 178; success of his "Love for Love," IV. 182; his "Mourning Bride," IV. 182; his controversy with Collier, IV. 190. 192; his "Way of the World," IV. 193; his position among men of letters, IV. 195; his attachment to Mrs. Bracegirdle, IV. 196; his friendship with the Duchess of Marlborough, IV. 198; his death and capricious will, IV. 197; his funeral in Westminster Abbey, IV. 198; cenotaph to his memory at Stowe, IV. 198; analogy between him and Wycherley, IV. 199.

Congreve and Sheridan, effect of their works upon the comedy of England, I. 85; contrasted with Shakspeare, I. 86.

Conquests of the British arms in 1758—60, II. 266—269.

Constance, council of, put an end to the Wickliffe schism, IV. 110.

Constitution (the) of England, in the 15th and 18th centuries, compared with those of other European states; I. 148; the argument that it would be destroyed by admitting the Jews to power, I. 285; its theory in respect to the three branches of the legislature, V. 156.

Constitutional government, decline of, on the Continent early in the 17th century, I. 156.

Constitutional History of England, review of Hallam's, I. 169—209.

Constitutional Royalists in the reign of Charles I., II. 60. 67.

Conway, Henry, V. 217; Secretary of State under Lord Rockingham, V. 229; returns to his position under Chatham, V. 244; sank into insignificance, V. 252.

Conway, Marshal, his character, IV. 62.

Cooke, Sir Anthony, his learning, III. 13.

Co-operation, advantages of, III. 268.

Coote, Sir Eyre, IV. 269; his character and conduct in council, IV. 270; his great victory of Porto Novo, IV. 281.

Corah, ceded to the Mogul, IV. 238.

"Correctness" in the fine arts and in the sciences, I. 315—319; in painting, I. 319; what is meant by it in poetry, I. 315—319.

Corruption, parliamentary, not necessary to the Tudors, II. 198; its extent in the reigns of George I. and II., V. 181.

Corsica given up to France, V. 253.

Cossimbazar, its situation and importance, IV. 220.

Council of York, its abolition, II. 55.

Country Wife of Wycherley, its character and merits, IV. 167; whence borrowed, IV. 176.

Courtenay, Rt. Hon. T. P., review of his Memoirs of Sir William Temple, III. 147—251; his concessions to Dr. Lingard in regard to the Triple Alliance, III. 184; his opinion of Temple's proposed new council, III. 205—208; his error as to Temple's residence, III. 237.

Cousinhood, nickname of the official members of the Temple family, III. 158.

Covenant, the Scotch, II. 47.

Covenanters (the), their conclusion of a treaty with Charles I., II. 48.

Coventry, Lady, V. 14.

Cowley, dictum of Denham concerning him, I. 2; deficient in imagination, I. 10; his wit, II. 192. V. 118; his admiration of Bacon, III. 144.

Cowper, Earl, Keeper of the Great Seal, V. 105.

Cowper, William, I. 324; his praise of Pope, I. 326; his friendship with Warren Hastings, IV. 217.

Cox, Archdeacon, his eulogium on Sir Robert Walpole, II. 202.

Coyer, Abbé, his imitation of Voltaire, V. 120.

Craggs, Secretary, II. 250; succeeds Addison, V. 153; Addison dedicates his works to him, V. 158.

Cranmer, Archbishop, estimate of his character, I. 122.

Crebillon the younger, II. 186.

Crisis, Steele's, V. 143.

Crisp, Samuel, his early career, V. 11; his tragedy of Virgina, V. 13; his retirement and seclusion, V. 15; his friendship with the Burneys, V. 17; his gratification at the success of Miss Burney's first work, V. 20; his advice to her

upon her comedy, V. 24; his applause of her "Cecilia," V. 25.
Criticism, remarks on Johnson's code of, I. 385.
Critics, professional, their influence over the reading public, I. 268.
Croker, Mr., his edition of Boswell's Life of Dr. Johnson, reviewed, I. 341—394.
Cromwell, Oliver, his elevation to power, I. 172; his character as a legislator, I. 175; as a general, I. 175; his administration and its results, I. 177; embarked with Hampden for America, but not suffered to proceed, II. 47; his qualities, II. 79; his administration, II. 305. 310; treatment of his remains, II. 308; his abilities displayed in Ireland, III. 168; anecdote of his sitting for his portrait, IV. 214.
Cromwell and Charles, choice between, I. 166.
Cromwell and Napoleon, remarks on Mr. Hallam's parallel between, I. 174—179.
Cromwell, Henry, description of, III. 161.
Cromwell, Richard, V. 174.
Crown (the), veto by, on Acts of Parliament, I. 158; its control over the army, I. 159; its power in the 16th century, II. 94; curtailment of its prerogatives, II. 199; its power predominant at the beginning of the 17th century, III. 208; decline of its power during the Pensionary Parliament, III. 211, 212; its long contest with the Parliament put an end to by the Revolution, III. 214. *See also* Prerogative.
Crusades (the), their beneficial effect upon Italy, I. 67.
Culpeper, Mr., II. 60.
Cumberland, *the dramatist*, his manner of acknowledging literary merit, V. 21.
Cumberland, Duke of, IV. 62; the confidential friend of Henry Fox, V. 201; confided in by George III., V. 222; his character, V. 222; mediated between the king and the Whigs, V. 225.

D.

Dacier, Madame, V. 84.
D'Alembert, Horace Walpole's opinion of him, II. 186.
Dallas, Chief Justice, one of the counsel for Hastings on his trial, IV. 331.
Danby, Earl, II. 198; his connection with Temple, abilities, and character, III. 198, 199; impeached and sent to the Tower, III. 204.
Danger, public, a certain amount of, will warrant a retrospective law, II. 56.
Dante, his Divine Comedy, I. 17. 69; comparison of him with Milton, I. 17, *et seq.;* "correctness" of his poetry, I. 313; story from, illustrative of the two great parties in England after the accession of the House of Hannover, V. 163.
D'Arblay, Madame, review of her Diary and Letters, V. 1—67; wide celebrity of her name, V. 1; her Diary, V. 3; her family, V. 3; her birth, and education, V. 4, 5; her father's social position, V. 9; her first literary efforts, V. 10; her friendship with Mr. Crisp, V. 11. 17; publication of her "Evelina," V. 18; her comedy, "The Witlings," V. 24; her second novel, "Cecilia," V. 25; death of her friends Crisp and Johnson, V. 26; her regard for Mrs. Delany, V. 27; her interview with the king

and queen, V. 28; accepts the situation of keeper of the robes, V. 29; sketch of her life in this position, V. 33—37; attends at Warren Hastings' trial, V. 37; her espousal of the cause of Hastings, V. 38; her incivility to Windham and Burke, V. 38; her sufferings during her keepership, V. 40. 45—48; her marriage, and close of the Diary, V. 50; publication of "Camilla," V. 50; subsequent events in her life, V. 50; her death, V. 52; character of her writings, V. 52—63; change in her style, V. 61; specimens of her three styles, 62—64; failure of her later works, V. 65; service she rendered to the English novel, V. 67.

Dashwood, Sir Francis, Chancellor of the Exchequer under Bute, V. 194; his inefficiency, V. 207.

Davies, Tom, I. 356.

Davila, one of Hampden's favourite authors, II. 38.

Daylesford, site of the estate of the Hastings' family, IV. 215; its purchase and adornment by Hastings, IV. 342, 343.

De Augmentis Scientiarum, by Bacon, III. 48. 90.

Debates in Parliament, effects of their publication, I. 204.

Debt, the national, effect of its abrogation, I. 230; England's capabilities in respect to it, I. 259.

Declaration of Right, II. 333.

"Declaration of the Practices and Treasons attempted and committed by Robert Earl of Essex," by Lord Bacon, III. 35.

Dedications, literary, more honest than formerly, I. 262.

De Guignes, V. 8.

Delany, Dr., his connection with Swift, V. 27; his widow, and her favour with the royal family, V. 27.

Delhi, its splendour during the Mogul empire, IV. 10.

Delium, battle of, III. 165.

Democracy, violence in its advocates induces reaction, II. 90.

Democritus, reputed the inventor of the arch, III. 94; Bacon's estimate of him, III. 95.

Demosthenes, III. 85.

Denham, dictum of, concerning Cowley, I. 2.

Denmark, contrast of its progress to the retrogression of Portugal, IV. 134.

Dennis, John, Pope's Narrative of his Frenzy, V. 136; his attack upon Addison's "Cato," V. 134.

Devonshire, Duchess of, IV. 330.

Devonshire, Duke of, forms an administration after the resignation of Newcastle, II. 258; Lord Chamberlain under Bute, V. 196; dismissed from his lord-lieutenancy, V. 204; invited to court by the king, V. 225.

Diary and Letters of Madame D'Arblay, reviewed, V. 1—67.

Dionysius, his inconsistency of character, IV. 346.

Discussion, free, its tendency, I. 242.

Dissent, cause of, in England, IV. 128; avoidance of in the Church of Rome, IV. 129; its extent in the time of Charles I., I. 241. See also Church of England.

Dissenters (the), examination of the reasoning of Mr. Gladstone for their exclusion from civil offices, III. 280—286.

Disturbances, public, during Grenville's administration, V. 224.

Divine Right, I. 82.

Division of labour, its necessity, III. 258; illustrations of the effects of disregarding it, III. 259.

Dodington, Bubb, V. 152.

Donne, John, comparison of his wit with Horace Walpole's, II. 192.

Dorset, the Earl of, the patron of literature in the reign of Charles II., I. 370. IV. 168.

Double Dealer, by Congreve, its reception, IV. 180; his defence of its profaneness, IV. 191.

Dover, Lord, review of his edition of Horace Walpole's Letters to Sir Horace Mann, II. 175—220. See Walpole, Sir Horace.

Dowdeswell, Mr., Chancellor of the Exchequer under Lord Rockingham, V. 229.

Drama (the), its origin in Greece, I. 13; causes of its dissolute character soon after the Restoration, IV. 159.

Dramas, Greek, compared with the English plays of the age of Elizabeth, I. 316.

Dramatic art, the unities violated in all the great masterpieces of, I. 316.

Dramatic literature shows the state of contemporary religious opinion, II. 106.

Dramatic Works (the) of Wycherley, Congreve, Vanbrugh, and Farquhar, review of Leigh Hunt's edition of, IV. 144—199.

Dramatists of the Elizabethan age, manner in which they treat religious subjects, II. 106.

Drogheda, Countess of, her character, acquaintance with Wycherley, and marriage, IV. 168; its consequences, IV. 169.

Drummond, Mr., V. 197.

Dryden, the original of his Father Dominic, I. 86; his merits not adequately appreciated in his day, I. 264; alleged improvement in English poetry since his time, I. 322; the connecting link of the literary schools of James I. and Anne, I. 329; his poetical genius, IV. 144; his excuse for the indecency and immorality of his writings, IV. 168; his generous admiration for the talents of others, IV. 180; censure on him by Collier for his language regarding heathen divinities, IV. 188, 189; complimentary verses to him by Addison, V. 78; obtained from Addison a critical preface to the Georgics, V. 80.

Dublin, Archbishop of, his work on Logic, III. 129.

Dumont, M., his opinion that Burke's work on the Revolution had saved Europe, II. 285; the interpreter of Bentham, II. 184.

Dundas, Mr., his character, and hostility to Hastings, IV. 313. 325.

Dupleix, governor of Pondicherry, his gigantic schemes for establishing French influence in India, IV. 9. 15. 18. 25—32.

E.

East India Company, its absolute authority in India, II. 268; its condition when Clive first went to India, IV. 5, 6; its war with the French East India Company, IV. 8; increase of its power, II. 28; its factories in Bengal, IV. 34; fortunes made by its servants in Bengal, IV. 65; its servants transformed into diplomatists and generals, IV. 219; nature of its government and power, IV. 229, 230; rights of the Nabob of Oude over Benares ceded to it, IV. 242; its financial embarrassments, IV. 287.

Ecclesiastical commission (the), II. 94.

Ecclesiastics, fondness of the old dramatists for the character of, II. 106.

Eden, pictures of, in old Bibles, I. 318; painting of, by a gifted master, I. 319.

Edinburgh, comparison of, with Florence, IV. 134.

Education in England in the 16th century, III. 18; duty of the government in promoting it, III. 315.

Education in Italy in the 14th century, I. 69.

Egerton, his charge of corruption against Bacon, III. 72; Bacon's decision against him after receiving his present, III. 87.

Egotism, why so unpopular in conversation, and so popular in writing, I. 338.

Elephants, use of, in war in India, IV. 23.

Eliot, Sir John, II. 36; his Treatise on Government, II. 37; died a martyr to liberty, II. 39.

Elizabeth (Queen), fallacy entertained respecting the persecutions under her, I. 115; her penal laws I. 115; arguments in favour of, on the head of persecution, apply with more force to Mary, I. 126; condition of the working classes in her reign, I. 249. II. 26; her rapid advance of Cecil, II. 88; character of her government, II. 94. 101. 112; a persecutor though herself indifferent, II. 108; her early notice of Lord Bacon, III. 16; her favour towards Essex, III. 25; factions at the close of her reign, III. 28, 29. 43; her pride and temper, III. 32. 57; and death, III. 43; progress in knowledge since her days, IV. 99; her Protestantism, IV. 123.

Ellenborough, Lord, one of the counsel for Hastings on his trial, IV. 331.

*Elphinstone*, Lord, IV. 96.

*Elwes*, V. 57.

Elwood, Milton's Quaker friend, allusion to, I. 58.

Emigration of Puritans to America, II. 46.

Emigration from England to Ireland under Cromwell, III. 170.

Empires, extensive, often more flourishing after a little pruning, II. 121.

England, her progress in civilisation due to the people, I. 260; her physical and moral condition in the 15th century, II. 23; never so rich and powerful as since the loss of her American colonies, II. 121; conduct of, in reference to the Spanish succession, II. 139; successive steps of her progress, II. 298, 299; influence of her revolution on the human race, II. 300. 337; her situation at the Restoration compared with France at the restoration of Louis XVIII., II. 303, 304; her situation in 1678, II. 308. 313. 317; character of her public men at the latter part of the 17th century, III. 154; difference in her situation under Charles II. and under the Protectorate, III. 175.

English (the), in the 16th century a free people, II. 97; their character, II. 310. 317.

English language, IV. 165.

English plays of the age of Elizabeth, I. 316.

"Englishman," Steele's, V. 143.

Enlightenment, its increase in the world not necessarily unfavourable to Catholicism, IV. 99.

Enthusiasts, dealings of the Church of Rome and the Church of England with them, IV. 127—130.

Epicureans, their peculiar doctrines, III. 98.

Epicurus, the lines on his pedestal, III. 99.

Epitaphs, Latin, I. 386.
Ercilla, Alonzode, a soldier as well as a poet, II. 120.
Essay on Government, Sir William Temple's, III. 192.
Essays, Lord Bacon's, value of them, III. 29. 49. 90. 134. 143.
Essex, Earl of, II. 112; his character, popularity, and favour with Elizabeth, III. 25—28. 57; his political conduct, III. 28; his friendship for Bacon, III. 27, 28. 36. 58; his conversation with Robert Cecil, III. 28; pleads for Bacon's marriage with Lady Hatton, III. 30. 65; his expedition to Spain, III. 30; his faults, III. 30. 58; decline of his fortunes, III. 31; his administration in Ireland, III. 31; Bacon's faithlessness to him, III. 32; his trial and execution, III. 34. 40; ingratitude of Bacon towards him, III. 32—43. 57; feeling of King James towards him, III. 45; his resemblance to Buckingham, III. 56.
Essex, Earl of, (*temp.* Ch. I.); II. 75, 76.
Etherege, Sir George, IV. 147.
Euripides, Milton's admiration of him, I. 15; emendation of a passage of, I. 353. *note.*
Europe, state of, at the peace of Utrecht, II. 170; want of union in, to arrest the designs of Louis XIV., III. 178; the distractions of, suspended for a short time by the treaty of Nimeguen, III. 201; its progress during the last seven centuries, IV. 105.
Evelina, Madame D'Arblay's, specimens of her style from, V. 62—65.
Evelyn, III. 174. 190.
Evils, natural and national, I. 234.
Exchequer, fraud of the Cabal ministry *in closing it,* III. 195.

F.

Fable (a) of Pilpay, I. 261.
Fairfax, reserved for him and Cromwell to terminate the civil war, II. 75.
Falkland, Lord, his conduct in respect to the bill of attainder against Strafford, I. 140; his character as a politician, I. 155; at the head of the Constitutional Royalists, II. 60.
Family Compact (the) between France and Spain, II. 171. V. 188.
Favourites, royal, always odious, V. 196.
Female Quixote (the), V. 66.
Fénélon, standard of morality in his Telemachus, IV. 152.
Ferdinand II., his devotion to Catholicism, IV. 124.
Ferdinand VII., resemblance between him and Charles I. of England, II. 73.
Fictions, literary, I. 59.
Fidelity, touching instance of, in the sepoys towards Clive, IV. 24.
Fielding, his contempt for Richardson, V. 13; case from his "Amelia," analogous to Addison's treatment of Steele, V. 113.
Filicaja, Vincenzio, V. 104.
Finance, Southey's theory of, I. 229—233.
Finch, Chief Justice to Charles I., II. 43; fled to Holland, II. 55.
Fine arts (the), encouragement of in Italy in the 14th century, I. 70; causes of their decline in England after the civil war, II. 188; government should promote them, III. 314.
Fletcher, the dramatist, IV. 150. 160.
Florence, state of, in the 14th century, I. 68; its History, by Machia-

velli, I. 104; compared with Edinburgh, IV. 134.

Foote, Charles, his stage character of an Anglo-Indian grandee, IV. 81; his mimicry, V. 54; his inferiority to Garrick, V. 54.

Forde, Colonel, IV. 57. 60.

Forms of government, I. 381—383.

Fox, the House of. *See* Holland, Lord.

Fox, Charles James, comparison of his History of James II. with Mackintosh's History of the Revolution, II. 274; his style, II. 276; characteristic of his oratory, II. 278; his bodily and mental constitution, IV. 203; his championship of arbitrary measures, and defiance of public opinion, IV. 207; his change after the death of his father, IV. 207; clamour raised against his India Bill, and his defence of it, IV. 312; his alliance with Burke, and call for peace with the American republic, IV. 315; his powerful party, IV. 319; his conflicts with Pitt, IV. 320; his motion on the charge against Hastings respecting his treatment of Cheyte Sing, IV. 321; his appearance on the trial of Hastings, IV. 331; his rupture with Burke, IV. 339.

Fox, Henry, sketch of his political character, II. 239. 251; accepts office, II. 253; directed to form an administration in concert with Chatham, II. 258; applied to by Bute to manage the House of Commons, V. 201; his private and public qualities, V. 202; became leader of the House of Commons, V. 203; obtains his promised peerage, V. 210.

*France*, illustration from the history of, since the Revolution, I. 183; her condition in 1783 and in 1832, II. 167; her state at the restoration of Louis XVIII., II. 302; enters into a compact with Spain against England, V. 188; her recognition of the independence of the United States, V. 257.

Francis, Sir Philip, councillor under the Regulating Act for India, IV. 245; his character and talents, IV. 246; probability of his being the author of the Letters of Junius, IV. 246—249; his opposition to Hastings, IV. 250—264; his patriotic feeling, and reconciliation with Hastings, IV. 271; his opposition to the arrangement with Sir Elijah Impey, IV. 276; renewal of his quarrel with Hastings, IV. 277; duel with Hastings, IV. 277; his return to England, IV. 281; his entrance into the House of Commons and character there, IV. 314. 321; his speech on Mr. Fox's motion relating to Cheyte Sing, IV. 321; his exclusion from the committee selected to conduct the impeachment of Hastings, IV. 327.

Francis, the Emperor, V. 174.

Franklin, Benjamin, IV. 101; his admiration for Miss Burney, V. 123.

Franks, rapid fall of their dominion after the death of Charlemagne, IV. 11.

Frederic the Great, inconsistencies in his character, IV. 346; his knowledge of the French language, V. 87.

Frederic II., IV. 168.

Free inquiry, right of, in religious matters, III. 295.

Free people (a) not easily reduced to servitude, I. 172.

Freeholder, Addison's, V. 92.

French Revolution (the), and the

Reformation, analogy between, II. 89.
Frenchmen, Johnson's opinion of, I. 388.
Froissart, his character of the English, II. 23.
Fulda, Hastings' Right to, IV. 220.
Funds, national. *See* National Debt.

## G.

Gabrielli, the singer, V. 8.
Galileo, IV. 102.
Galleons, Spanish, capture of at Vigo in 1702, II. 144.
Galway, Lord, commander of the allied army in Spain in 1704, II. 145. 154; defeated by the Bourbon army at Almanza, II. 157.
Ganges, the chief highway of Eastern commerce, IV. 33.
Garden of Eden, pictures of, in old Bibles, I. 318; painting of, by a gifted master, I. 319.
Garrick, David, his acquaintance with Johnson, I. 369; his power of amusing children, V. 7; his friendship for Crisp, V. 13; his advice as to Crisp's tragedy of Virginia, V. 13; his power of imitation, V. 54.
Garth, his epilogue to Cato, V. 133.
Gay, sent for by Addison on his deathbed to ask his forgiveness, V. 158.
Geneva, Addison's visit to, V. 95.
Genoa, Addison's admiration of, V. 90; its decay owing to Catholicism, IV. 134.
"Gentleman Dancing-Master," its production on the stage, IV. 167; its best scenes suggested by Calderon, IV. 176.
Geometry, comparative estimate of, by Plato and by Bacon, III. 104.
George I., his accession, II. 169.
George II., political state of the nation in his time, I. 201; his resentment against Chatham for his opposition to the payment of Hanoverian troops, II. 243; compelled to admit him to office, II. 246; his efforts for the protection of Hanover, II. 253; his relations towards his ministers, II. 264; reconciled to Chatham's possession of power, V. 173; his death, V. 174; his character, V. 176.
George III., his accession the commencement of a new historic era, I. 199. V. 162. 174; cause of the discontents in the early part of his reign, I. 201; his partiality to Clive, IV. 90; bright prospects at his accession, IV. 266. V. 162. 176; his interview with Miss Burney, V. 28; his opinions of Voltaire, Rousseau, and Shakspeare, V. 28; his partizanship for Hastings, V. 40; his illness and the view taken of it in the palace, V. 40; the history of the first ten years of his reign but imperfectly known, V. 162; his characteristics, V. 177; his favour to Lord Bute, V. 178; his notions of government, V. 179; slighted for Chatham at the Lord Mayor's dinner, V. 190; receives the resignation of Bute, and appoints George Grenville his successor, V. 210; his treatment by Grenville, V. 214; increase of his aversion to his ministers, V. 217; his illness, V. 221; disputes between him and his ministry on the regency question, V. 221; inclined to enforce the American Stamp Act by the sword, V. 231; the faction of the "King's friends," V. 233; his unwilling consent to the repeal of the Stamp Act, V. 235; dismisses Rockingham, and appoints Chatham his successor, V. 242.
George IV., V. 329.

Georgics (the), Addison's translation of a portion of, V. 78.
Germany, the literature of, little known in England sixty or seventy years ago, V. 86.
Germany and Switzerland, Addison's ramble in, V. 94.
Ghizni, peculiarity of the campaign in which it was taken, IV. 239.
Ghosts, Johnson's belief in, I. 379.
Gibbon, his alleged conversion to Mahommedanism, I. 347; his success as a historian, II. 274; his presence at Westminster Hall at the trial of Hastings, IV. 329; unlearned his native English during his exile, V. 62.
Gibraltar, capture of, by Sir George Rooke, II. 145.
Giffard, Lady, sister of Sir William Temple, III. 179. 181. 238; her death, III. 249.
Gifford, Byron's admiration of, I. 327.
Gladstone, W. E., review of "The State in its Relations with the Church," III. 252—324; quality of his mind, III. 255; grounds on which he rests his case for the defence of the Church, III. 258; his doctrine that the duties of government are paternal, III. 260; specimen of his arguments, III. 262; his argument that the profession of a national religion is imperative, III. 266; inconsequence of his reasoning, III. 277—286.
Gleig, Rev. G. R., review of his Life of Warren Hastings, IV. 213—349.
Godfrey, Sir E., II. 315.
Godolphin, Lord, his conversion to Whiggism, II. 163; engages Addison to write a poem in honour of the battle of Blenheim, V. 99.
Godolphin and Marlborough, their policy soon after the accession of Queen Anne, V. 97.
Goëzman, his bribery as a member of the parliament of Paris by Beaumarchais, III. 87.
Goldsmith, I. 364; unjust to estimate him by his History of Greece, V. 213.
Goordas, son of Nuncomar, his appointment as treasurer of the household, IV. 235.
Goree, conquest of, II. 267.
Gorhambury, the country residence of Lord Bacon, III. 67.
Government, various forms of, I. 381; changes in its form sometimes not felt till long after, II. 124; the science of, experimental and progressive, II. 165. 292; examination of Mr. Gladstone's treatise on the Philosophy of, III. 252. 308; doctrines of Southey on the duties and ends of, stated and examined, I. 233—244; its conduct in relation to infidel publications, I. 244; its proper functions, IV. 155. 159.
Grafton, Duke of, Secretary of State under Lord Rockingham, V. 229; First Lord of the Treasury under Chatham, V. 244; joined the Bedfords, V. 252.
Granby, Marquis of, his character, IV. 62.
Grand Alliance (the) against the Bourbons, II. 139.
Grand Remonstrance, debate on and passing of it, II. 61.
Granville, Lord. See Carteret, Lord.
Gray, his want of appreciation of Johnson, V. 13; his Latin verses, V. 87; his unsuccessful application for a professorship, V. 198.
"Great Commoner," the designation of Lord Chatham, II. 272. V. 170.
Greece, its history compared with

that of Italy, I. 73; its degradation and rise in modern times, I. 310; instances of the corruption of judges in the ancient commonwealths of, III. 78; its literature, IV. 106.
Greek drama, its origin, I. 13; compared with the English plays of the age of Elizabeth, I. 316.
Greeks, their social condition compared with that of the Italians of the middle ages, I. 100; their position and character in the 12th century, IV. 106; difference between them and the Romans, I. 79.
Gregory XIII., his austerity and zeal, V. 120.
Grenville, George, his character, V. 186; entrusted with the lead in the Commons under the Bute administration, V. 191; his support of the proposed tax on cider, V. 207; his nickname of "Gentle Shepherd," V. 208; appointed prime minister, V. 210; his opinions, V. 211; character of his public acts, V. 212; his treatment of the king, V. 214; his deprivation of Henry Conway of his regiment, V. 217; proposed the imposition of stamp duties on the North American colonies, V. 220; his embarrassment on the question of a regency, V. 221; his triumph over the king, V. 225; superseded by Lord Rockingham and his friends, V. 228; popular demonstration against him on the repeal of the Stamp Act, V. 237; deserted by the Bedfords, V. 244; his pamphlet against the Rockinghams, V. 255; his reconciliation with Catham, V. 255; his death, V. 256.
Grenvilles (the), V. 171; Richard Lord Temple at their head, V. 171.

Greville, Fulk, patron of Dr. Burney, his character, V. 4.
Grey, Earl, IV. 322. 339.
Grey, Lady Jane, her high classical acquirements, III. 13.
"Grievances," popular, on occasion of Walpole's fall, II. 208.
Grub Street, I. 375.
Guadaloupe, fall of, II. 267.
Guardian (the), its birth, V. 131; its discontinuance, V. 137.
Guelfs (the), their success greatly promoted by the ecclesiastical power, I. 65.
Guicciardini, II. 82.
Guicowar, its interpretation, IV. 267.
Guise, Henry, Duke of, his conduct on the day of the barricades at Paris, III. 34; his resemblances to Essex, III. 34.
Gunpowder, its inventor and the date of its discovery unknown, III. 100.
Gustavus Adolphus, IV. 133.

H.

Habeas Corpus Act, III. 222. 230.
Hale, Sir Matthew, his integrity, II. 79. III. 51.
Halifax, Lord, a trimmer both by intellect and by constitution, III. 225; compared with Shaftesbury, III. 225; his political tracts, III. 227; his oratorical powers, III. 228; the king's dislike to him, III. 228; his recommendation of Addison to Godolphin, V. 98; sworn of the Privy Council of Queen Anne, V. 105.
Hallam, Mr., review of his Constitutional History of England, I. 109—269; his qualifications as a historian, I. 111; his style, I. 111; character of his Constitutional History, I. 112; his impartiality, I. 112. 182; his description of the

proceedings of the third parliament of Charles I., and the measures which followed its dissolution, I. 130; his remarks on the impeachment of Strafford, I. 137; on the proceedings of the Long Parliament, and on the question of the justice of the civil war, I. 142—165; his opinion on the nineteen propositions of the Long Parliament, I. 157; on the veto of the crown on acts of parliament, I. 158; on the control over the army, V. 159; on the treatment of Laud, and on his correspondence with Strafford, I. 163; on the execution of Charles I., I. 167; his parallel between Cromwell and Napoleon, I. 175—181; his character of Clarendon, I. 190.

Hamilton, Gerard, his celebrated single speech, II. 255; his effective speaking in the Irish Parliament, V. 115.

Hammond, Henry, uncle of Sir William Temple, his designation by the new Oxonian sectaries, III. 159.

Hampden, John, his conduct in the ship-money affair approved by the Royalists, I. 132; effect of his loss on the Parliamentary cause, I. 166. II. 79; review of Lord Nugent's Memorial of him, II. 17; his public and private character, II. 18; Baxter's testimony to his excellence, II. 19; his origin and early history, II. 20; took his seat in the House of Commons in 1621, II. 22; joined the opposition to the Court, II. 22; his first appearance as a public man, II. 30; his first stand for the fundamental principle of the Constitution, II. 32; committed to prison, II. 32; set at liberty, and re-elected for Wendover, II. 33; his retirement, II. 35; his remembrance of his persecuted friends, II. 35; his letters to Sir John Eliot, II. 35; Clarendon's character of him as a debater, II. 36. 54; letter from him to Sir John Eliot, II. 36; his acquirements, II. 18. 37; death of his wife, II. 38; his resistance to the assessment for ship-money, II. 44; Strafford's hatred of him, II. 45; his intention to leave England, II. 46; his return for Buckinghamshire in the fifth parliament of Charles I., II. 48; his motion on the subject of the king's message, II. 49; his election by two constituencies to the Long Parliament, II. 53; character of his speaking, II. 54; his opinion on the bill for the attainder of Strafford, II. 56; Lord Clarendon's testimony to his moderation, II. 58; his mission to Scotland, II. 58; his conduct in the House of Commons on the passing of the Grand Remonstrance, II. 61; his impeachment ordered by the king, II. 63—69; returns in triumph to the House, II. 68; his resolution, II. 69. 74; raised a regiment in Buckinghamshire, II. 74; contrasted with Essex, II. 76; his encounter with Rupert at Chalgrove, II. 77; his death and burial, II. 78; effect of his death on his party, II. 79.

Hanover, Chatham's invective against the favour shown to, by George II., II. 243.

Harcourt, French ambassador to the court of Charles II. of Spain, II. 131.

Hardwicke, Earl of, V. 172; High Steward of the University of Cambridge, V. 194; his views of the policy of Chatham, V. 185.

Harley, Robert, I. 370; his accession to power (in 1710), II. 164; censure on him by Lord Mahon,

H. 166; his unsuccessful attempt to rally the Tories in 1707, V. 105; his advice to the queen to dismiss the Whigs, V. 123; his kindness for men of genius, IV. 194.

Harrison's Introduction to Holinshed, on the condition of the working classes in the reign of Queen Elizabeth, I. 249.

Hastings, Warren, review of Mr. Gleig's Memoirs of his Life, IV. 213—359; his pedigree, IV. 215; his birth, and the death of his father and mother, IV. 216; taken charge of by his uncle and sent to Westminster school, IV. 216; sent as a writer to Bengal, his position there, IV. 219; events which originated his greatness, IV. 220; becomes a member of council at Calcutta, IV. 221; his character in pecuniary transactions, IV. 224. 307; his return to England, generosity to his relations, and loss of his moderate fortune, IV. 223; his plan for the cultivation of Persian literature at Oxford, IV. 224; his interview with Johnson, IV. 224; his appointment as member of council at Madras, and voyage to India, IV. 225; his attachment to the Baroness Imhoff, IV. 226; his judgment and vigour at Madras, IV. 227; his nomination to the head of the government at Bengal, IV. 227; his relation with Nuncomar, IV. 233; his embarrassed finances and means to relieve them, IV. 236; his principle of dealing with his neighbours and the excuse for him, IV. 237; his proceedings towards the Nabob and the Great Mogul, IV. 238; his sale of territory to the Nabob of Oude, IV. 239; his refusal to interfere to stop the barbarities of Sujah Dowlah, IV. 243; his great talents for administration, IV. 245. 300; his disputes with the members of the new council, IV. 250; his measures reversed, and the powers of government taken from him, IV. 250; charges preferred against him, IV. 251; his painful situation, and appeal to England, IV. 253; examination of his conduct, IV. 259; his letter to Dr. Johnson, IV. 261; his condemnation by the directors, IV. 261; his resignation tendered by his agent and accepted, IV. 262; his marriage and reappointment, IV. 265; his importance to England at that conjuncture, IV. 267. 277; his duel with Francis, IV. 277; his great influence, IV. 281; his financial embarrassment and designs for relief, IV. 281; his transactions with and measures against Cheyte Sing, 622; his perilous situation in Benares, IV. 286; his treatment of the Nabob Vizier, IV. 292; his treatment of the Begums of Oude, IV. 294—299; close of his administration, IV. 299; remarks on his system, IV. 302—309; his reception in England, IV. 309; preparations for his impeachment, IV. 310—317; his defence at the bar of the House, IV. 320; brought to the bar of the Peers, IV. 327; his appearance on his trial, his counsel, and his accusers, IV. 330; his arraignment by Burke, IV. 332; narrative of the proceedings against him, IV. 383; expenses of his trial, IV. 342; his last interference in politics, IV. 344; his pursuits and amusements at Daylesford, IV. 344; his appearance and reception at the bar of the House of Commons, IV. 346; his reception at Oxford, IV. 347;

sworn of the Privy Council, and gracious reception by the Prince Regent, IV. 347; his presentation to the Emperor of Russia and King of Prussia, IV. 347; his death, IV. 347; summary of his character, IV. 349.

Hatton, Lady, III. 30; her manners and temper, III. 30; her marriage with Sir Edward Coke, III. 31.

Havannah, capture of, V. 190.

Hawke, Admiral, his victory over the French fleet under Conflans, II. 267.

"Heathens" (the) of Cromwell's time, I. 52.

Heathfield, Lord, IV. 329.

Hebrew writers (the), resemblance of Æschylus to, I. 13.

Hebrides (the), Johnson's visit to, I. 389; his letters from, I. 399.

Hedges, Sir Charles, Secretary of State, V. 105.

Helvetius, allusion to, I. 6.

Henry IV. of France, III. 273; twice abjured Protestantism from interested motives, IV. 124.

Henry VII., effects of his accession, I. 200.

Henry VIII., I. 127; his position between the Catholic and Protestant parties, II. 105.

Hephzibah, an allegory so called, II. 13.

Heresy, remarks on, III. 277—286.

Heroic couplet (the), its mechanical nature, V. 79; specimen from Ben Jonson, V. 80; from Hoole, V. 80; its rarity before the time of Pope, V. 80.

Hesiod, his complaint of the corruption of the judges of Ascra, III. 78.

Hesse Darmstadt, Prince of, commanded the land forces sent *against* Gibraltar in 1704, II. 145; *accompanies* Peterborough on his expedition, II. 148; his death at the capture of Monjuich, II. 151.

High Commission Court, its abolition, II. 55.

Highgate, death of Lord Bacon at, III. 91.

Hindoo Mythology, IV. 103.

Hindoos, their character compared with other nations, IV. 230; their position and feeling towards the people of Central Asia, IV. 239; their mendacity and perjury, IV. 251; their view of forgery, IV. 251; importance attached by them to ceremonial practices, IV. 256; their poverty compared with the people of England, IV. 272; their feelings against English law, IV. 272.

Historical romance, as distinguished from true history, I. 110.

History, as distinguished from historical romance, I. 109; its uses, I. 389; Johnson's contempt for it, I. 389; qualifications for writing it, II. 274. 280.

History of the Popes of Rome during the 16th and 17th centuries, review of Ranke's, IV. 97—143.

Hobbes, Thomas, his influence on the two succeeding generations, III. 68; Malbranche's opinion of him, V. 85.

Hohenlohe, Prince, IV. 103.

Holbach, Baron, his supper parties, IV. 142.

Holderness, Earl of, his resignation of office, V. 183.

Holkar, origin of the House of, IV. 267.

Holland, allusion to the rise of, II. 123; governed with almost regal power by John de Witt, III. 175; its apprehensions of the designs of France, III. 177; its defensive alliance with England and Sweden, III. 183. 186.

Holland House, beautiful lines addressed to it, IV. 210; its interesting associations, IV. 211; Addison's abode and death there, V. 152—159.

Holland, Lord, review of his opinions as recorded in the journals of the House of Lords, IV. 200—212; his family, IV. 203; his public life, IV. 207; his philanthropy, IV. 209; feelings with which his memory is cherished, IV. 211; his hospitality at Holland House, IV. 212; his winning manners and uprightness, IV. 212; his last lines, IV. 212.

Hollis, Mr., committed to prison by Charles I., II. 35; his impeachment, II. 63.

Holwell, Mr., his presence of mind in the Black Hole, IV. 38; cruelty of the Nabob to him, IV. 38.

Home, John, patronage of, by Bute, V. 198.

Homer, difference between his poetry and Milton's, I. 11; one of the most "correct" poets, I. 313; Pope's translation of his description of a moonlight night, I. 315; his descriptions of war, V. 109.

Hooker, his faulty style, III. 192.

Hoole, specimen of his heroic couplets, V. 80.

Horace, Bentley's notes on, III. 248.

Hosein, son of Ali, festival to his memory, IV. 22; legend of his death, IV. 22.

Hospitals, objects for which they are built, III. 314.

Hough, Bishop, V. 83.

House of Commons (the), increase of its power, I. 199. 207; change in public feeling in respect to its privileges, I. 203; its responsibility, I. 205; commencement of the practice of buying of votes in, II. 198; *corruption in, not neces-*sary to the Tudors, II. 198; increase of its influence after the Revolution, II. 198; how to be kept in order, II. 200.

Hume, David, his description of the violence of parties before the Revolution, II. 343.

Humour, that of Addison compared with that of Swift and Voltaire, V. 119.

Hungarians, their incursions into Lombardy, IV. 12.

Hunt, Leigh, review of his edition of the Dramatic Works of Wycherley, Congreve, Vanbrugh, and Farquhar, IV. 144—199; his merits and faults, IV. 144; his qualifications as an editor, IV. 144; his appreciation of Shakspeare, Spenser, Dryden, and Addison, IV. 144.

Huntingdon, Countess of, IV. 130.

Huntingdon, William, IV. 84.

Hutchinson, Mrs., III. 168.

Hyde, Mr., his conduct in the House of Commons, II. 50; at the head of the Constitutional Royalists, II. 60; voted for Strafford's attainder, II. 57; *See also* Clarendon, Lord.

Hyder Ali, his origin and character, IV. 278; his invasion of the Carnatic, and triumphant success, IV. 279; his progress arrested by Sir Eyre Coote, IV. 281.

I.

Iconoclast, Milton's, allusion to, I. 58.

Idolatry, I. 21.

Iliad (the), Pope's and Tickell's translations, V. 145.

Illustrations of Bunyan and Milton by Martin, II. 1.

Imagination, great strength of Milton's, I. 11; great power of Bunyan's, II. 7. 16.

Imhoff, Baron, his position and circumstances, IV. 225; character and attractions of his wife, and attachment between her and Hastings, IV. 226. 265.
Impeachment, of Lord Kimbolton, Hampden, Pym, and Hollis, II. 63; of Hastings, IV. 319.
Impey, Sir Elijah, IV. 218; Chief Justice of the Supreme Court at Calcutta, IV. 249; his hostility to the Council, IV. 254; remarks on his trial of Nuncomar, IV. 255—258. 273; dissolution of his friendship with Hastings, IV. 275; his interference in the proceedings against the Begums, IV. 297; his ignorance of the native dialects, IV. 297. *note;* condemnation in Parliament of the arrangement made with him by Hastings, IV. 299.
Impostors, fertile in a reforming age, I. 324.
Indemnity, bill of, to protect witnesses against Walpole, II. 243.
India, foundation of the English empire in, II. 268; high civilisation of its people, IV. 1.
Induction, method of, not invented by Bacon, III. 124; utility of its analysis greatly overrated by Bacon, III. 124; example of its leading to absurdity, III. 126.
Indulgences, IV. 111.
Infidelity, on the treatment of, I. 244; its powerlessness to disturb the peace of the world, IV. 136.
Inquisition instituted on the suppression of the Albigensian heresy, IV. 108; armed with powers to suppress the Reformation, IV. 120.
Interest, effect of attempts by government to limit the rate of, IV. 155.
*Intolerance,* religious, effects of, I. 245.

Invocation of saints, IV. 102.
Ireland, rebellion in, in 1640, II. 59; Essex's administration in, III. 31; its condition under Cromwell's government, III. 168—170; its state contrasted with that of Scotland, III. 292; its union with England compared with the Persian fable of King Zohak, III. 293; reason of its not joining in favour of the Reformation, IV. 111. 124; danger to England from its discontents, IV. 266.
Italian Masque (the), I. 15.
Italians, their character in the middle ages, I. 79; their social condition compared with that of the ancient Greeks, I. 101.
Italy, state of, in the dark ages, I. 66; progress of civilisation and refinement in, I. 65, *et seq.;* its condition under Cæsar Borgia, I. 92; its temper at the Reformation, IV. 112, *et seq.;* its slow progress owing to Catholicism, IV. 134; its subjugation, IV. 140; revival of the power of the Church in, IV. 142.

J.

"Jackboot," a popular pun on Bute's name, V. 199. 216.
Jacobin Club, its excesses, IV. 139.
Jacobins, their origin, II. 90.
Jacobitism, Addison's opinion that travelling is the best cure for it, V. 92.
James I., I. 129; his folly and weakness, II. 27; resembled Claudius Cæsar, II. 28; court paid to him by the English courtiers before the death of Elizabeth, III. 42; his twofold character, III. 44; his favourable reception of Bacon, III. 44—49; his anxiety for the union of England and Scotland, III. 49; his employment of

Bacon in perverting the laws, III. 49; his favours and attachment to Buckingham, III. 56; absoluteness of his government, III. 64; his summons of a parliament, III. 69; his political blunders, III. 69; his message to the Commons on the misconduct of Bacon, III. 72; his readiness to make concessions to Rome, IV. 124.

James II., the causes of his expulsion, I. 33; administration of the law in his time, I. 188; Varelst's portrait of him, II. 2; his death, and acknowledgment by Louis XIV. of his son as his successor, II. 138; favour towards him of the High Church party, II. 320; his misgovernment, II. 321; his claims as a supporter of toleration, II. 321—329; his conduct towards Lord Rochester, II. 324; his union with Louis XIV., II. 326; his confidential advisers, II. 326; his kindness and munificence to Wycherley, IV. 170.

Jardine, Mr., his work on the use of torture in England, III. 54.

Jeffreys, Judge, his cruelty, II. 321.

"Jemmy Twitcher," a nickname of the Earl of Sandwich, V. 216.

Jenyns, Soane, his notion of happiness in heaven, V. 321.

Jerningham, Mr., his verses, V. 23.

Jesuitism, its rise, IV. 116; its destruction of Port Royal, IV. 137; its fall and consequences, IV. 139; its doctrines, IV. 142; its theory and practice towards heretics, II. 326.

Jesuits, order of, instituted by Loyola, IV. 116; their character, IV. 116; their policy and proceedings, IV. 118; their doctrines, IV. 118; their conduct in the confessional, IV. 118; their missionary activity, IV. 118. 126.

Jews (the), review of the Civil Disabilities of, I. 285—300; argument that the Constitution would be destroyed by admitting them to power, I. 285; the argument that they are aliens, I. 288; inconsistency of the law in respect to them, I. 289; their exclusive spirit a natural consequence of their treatment, I. 293; argument against them, that they look forward to their restoration to their own country, I. 294. 297.

Job, the book of, I. 13. IV. 101.

Johnson, Dr. Samuel, review of Croker's edition of Boswell's Life of, I. 341—394; his Lives of the Poets, I. 322; his objection to Juvenal's Satires, I. 351; his peculiarities, I. 367; condition of literary men at the time of his settling in London, I. 369; his difficulties, I. 373; his elevation, I. 375; peculiarity of his intellect, I. 378; his credulity, I. 379; his religious sentiments, I. 380; his opinion on forms of government, I. 381; his judgments on books, I. 383; narrowness of his views of society, I. 386; his visit to the Hebrides, I. 389; his style, I. 390. V. 62; his club-room, I. 393; singularity of his destiny, I. 394; desultoriness of his studies, II. 4; his admiration of the Pilgrim's Progress, II. 4; his bigotry, II. 347; his definitions of Excise and Pensioner, II. 347; comparison of his political writings with those of Swift, III. 239; language he held of Lord Clive, IV. 83; his praise of Congreve's "Mourning Bride," IV. 182. 195; his interview with Hastings, IV. 224; his friendship with Dr. Burney, V. 7; his ignorancce of music, V. 7; his want of appreciation of Gray, V.

12; his position with the Thrales, V. 22; his fondness for Miss Burney, and approbation of her book, V. 22; his injustice to Fielding, V. 22; his irritability, V. 22; his benevolence, V. 22; his death, V. 26.

Johnsonese, II. 391.
Jones, Inigo, V. 66.
Jones, Sir William, I. 355.
Jonson, Ben, I. 89; his "Hermogenes," I. 332; his description of Lord Bacon's eloquence, III. 22; his verses on the celebration of Bacon's sixtieth year, III. 67; his tribute to Bacon, III. 89; his description of humours in character, V. 56; specimen of his heroic couplets, V. 80.
Judges (the), condition of their tenure of office, I. 158; formerly accustomed to receive gifts from suitors, III. 78—82; how their corruption is generally detected, III. 87; integrity required from them, III. 258.
Judgment, private, Milton's defence of the right of, I. 56.
Judicial bench, its character in the time of James II., I. 187.
Junius, Letters of, arguments in favour of their having been written by Sir Philip Francis, IV. 246; their effects, V. 253.
Juvenal's Satires, Johnson's objection to them, I. 351; their impurity, IV. 146.

### K.

Kenrick, William, V. 21.
Kimbolton, Lord, his impeachment, II. 63.
"King's Friends," the faction of the, V. 233—239. 243.
*Kit-Cat Club*, Addison's introduction to the, V. 96.

Kneller, Sir Godfrey, II. 189; Addison's lines to him, V. 118.
"Knights," comedy of the, III. 165.
Kniperdoling and Robespierre, analogy between their followers, II. 90.
Knowledge, advancement of society in, II. 166.

### L.

Labour, division of, III. 258; effect of attempts by government to limit the hours of, IV. 155.
Labouring classes (the), their condition in England and on the Continent, I. 252; in the United States, I. 254.
Labourdonnais, his talents, IV. 8; his treatment by the French government, IV. 92.
La Fontaine, allusion to, I. 364.
Lalla Rookh, III. 138.
Lally, Governor, his treatment by the French government, IV. 92.
Lamb, Charles, his defence of the dramatists of the Restoration, IV. 151. 153; his kind nature, IV. 153.
Lampoons, Pope's, V. 148.
Lancaster, Dr., his patronage of Addison, V. 72.
Langton, Mr., his admiration of Miss Burney, V. 22.
Languedoc, description of it in the 12th century, IV. 105; destruction of its prosperity and literature by the Normans, IV. 107.
Lansdowne, Lord, his friendship for Hastings, IV. 312.
Latimer, Hugh, his popularity in London, III. 80. 85.
Latin poems, Boileau's praise of, V. 88; excellence of Milton's, I. 10.
Latinity, Croker's criticisms on, I. 352.
Laud, Archbishop, his treatment by the Parliament, I. 163; his correspondence with Strafford, I.

163; his character, II. 40; his diary, II. 40; his impeachment and imprisonment, II. 55; his rigour against the Puritans, and tenderness towards the Catholics, II. 59.

Law, its administration in the time of James II., I. 188; its monstrous grievances in India, IV. 271.

Lawrence, Major, his early notice of Clive, IV. 10. 25; his abilities, IV. 10.

Lawrence, Sir Thomas, V. 53.

Laws, penal, of Elizabeth, I. 115, 116.

Lawyers, their inconsistencies as advocates and legislators, I. 383.

Learning in Italy, revival of, I. 69; causes of its decline, I. 73.

Legerdemain, III. 16.

Legge, Right Hon. H. B., II. 254; his return to the Exchequer, II. 258. V. 172; his dismissal, V. 187.

Legislation, comparative views on, by Plato and by Bacon, III. 111.

Legitimacy, I. 33.

Lemon, Mr., his discovery of Milton's Treatise on Christian Doctrine, I. 1.

Lennox, Charlotte, III. 167.

Leo X., his character, IV. 119; nature of the war between him and Luther, IV. 124, 125.

Letters of Phalaris, controversy between Sir William Temple and Christchurch College and Bentley upon their merits and genuineness, III. 244—249.

Libels on the court of George III. in Bute's time, V. 199.

Libertinism in the time of Charles II., I. 186.

Liberty, public, Milton's support of, I. 39; its rise and progress in Italy, I. 66.

Life, human, increase in the term of, I. 251.

Lingard, Dr., his account of the conduct of James II. towards Lord Rochester, II. 324; his ability as a historian, III. 184; his strictures on the Triple Alliance, III. 184.

Literary men more independent than formerly, I. 263; their influence, I. 268; abjectness of their condition during the reign of George II., I. 372; their importance to contending parties in the reign of Queen Anne, V. 107; encouragement afforded to by the Revolution, V. 82.

Literature of the Roundheads, I. 30; of the Royalists, I. 30; of Italy in the 14th century, I. 69; of the Elizabethan age, II. 113; of Spain in the 16th century, II. 119; splendid patronage of, at the close of the 17th and beginning of the 18th centuries, I. 369; discouragement of, on the accession of the House of Hanover, I. 371; importance of classical, in the 16th century, III. 14.

Literature, German, little known in England sixty or seventy years ago, V. 86.

"Little Dickey," a nickname for Norris the actor, V. 157.

Livy, Discourses on, by Machiavelli, I. 98; compared with Montesquieu's Spirit of Laws, I. 102.

Lyttelton, Lord, II. 275.

Locke, IV. 101.

Logan, Mr., his ability in defending Hastings, IV. 342.

Lollardism in England, II. 104.

London, in the 17th century, II. 65; devoted to the national cause, II. 66; its public spirit, II. 96; its prosperity during the ministry of Lord Chatham, II. 270; conduct of, at the Restoration, II. 308; effects of the Great Plague upon, III. 115; its excitement on occa-

sion of the tax on cider proposed by Bute's ministry, V. 207.
Long Parliament (the), controversy on its merits, I. 35; its first meeting, I. 131. II. 53; its early proceedings, I. 140; its conduct in reference to the civil war, I. 142; its nineteen propositions, I. 158; its faults, I. 160—164; censured by Mr. Hallam, I. 162; its errors in the conduct of the war, I. 165; treatment of it by the army, I. 166; recapitulation of its acts, II. 55; its attainder of Strafford defended, II. 56; sent Hampden to Edinburgh to watch the king, II. 58; refuses to surrender the members ordered to be impeached, II. 63; openly defies the king, II. 67; its conditions of reconciliation, II. 71.
Lope, his distinction as a writer and a soldier, II. 120.
Lords, the House of, its position previous to the Restoration, II. 307; its condition as a debating assembly in 1770, IV. 207.
Lorenzo de Medici, state of Italy in his time, I. 71.
Lorenzo de Medici (the younger), dedication of Machiavelli's Prince to him, I. 98.
Loretto, plunder of, IV. 140.
"Love for Love," by Congreve, IV. 181; its moral, IV. 191.
"Love in a Wood," when acted, IV. 163.
Louis XIV., his conduct in respect to the Spanish succession, II. 127—136, et seq.; his acknowledgement, on the death of James II., of the Prince of Wales as King of England, and its consequences, II. 138; sent an army into Spain to the assistance of his grandson, II. 144; his proceedings in support of his grandson Philip, II. 145—162; his reverses in Germany, Italy, and the Netherlands, II. 163; his policy, II. 325; character of his government, II. 327; his military exploits, III. 151; his projects and affected moderation, III. 178; his ill-humour at the Triple Alliance, III. 183; his conquest of Franche Comté, III. 184; his treaty with Charles, III. 192; the early part of his reign a time of licence, III. 194; his devotion, V. 84.
Louis XV., his government, IV. 92.
Louis XVIII., restoration of, compared with that of Charles II., II. 302.
Louisburg, fall of, II. 269.
Loyala, his energy, IV. 116. 130.
Luther, his declaration against the ancient philosophy, III. 191; sketch of the contest which began with his preaching against the Indulgences and terminated with the treaty of Westphalia, V. 110—133.
Lysias, anecdote by Plutarch of his speech for the Athenian tribunals, III. 253.

## M.

Macburney, original name of the Burney family, V. 3.
Machiavelli, his Works, by Périer, I. 60; general odiousness of his name and works, I. 60; suffered for public liberty, I. 62; his elevated sentiments and just views, I. 62; held in high estimation by his contemporaries, I. 63; state of moral feeling in Italy in his time, I. 64; his character as a man, I. 81; as a poet, I. 84; as a dramatist, I. 86; as a statesman, I. 81. 89. 98. 103. 105; his Prince, I. 98; excellence of his precepts, I. 100; his candour, I. 102; comparison between him and Montesquieu, I. 102; his style,

I. 103; his levity, I. 105; his historical works, I. 105; lived to witness the last struggle for Florentine liberty, I. 107; his works and character misrepresented, I. 107; his remains unhonoured till long after his death, I. 108; monument erected to his memory by an English nobleman, I. 108.

Mackenzie, Mr., his dismissal insisted on by Grenville, V. 225.

Mackenzie, Henry, his ridicule of the Nabob class, IV. 82.

Mackintosh, Sir James, review of his History of the Revolution in England, II. 273—349; comparison with Fox's History of James the Second, II. 274; character of his oratory, 308; his conversational powers, II. 278; his qualities as historian, II. 280; his vindication from the imputations of the editor, II. 283. 289—298; change in his opinions produced by the French Revolution, II. 286; his moderation, II. 288; his historical justice, II. 297; remembrance of him at Holland House, IV. 211.

Macleane, Colonel, agent in England for Warren Hastings, IV. 253. 262.

Madras, description of it, IV. 5; its capitulation to the French, IV. 8; restored to the English, IV. 10.

Madrid, capture of, by the English army, in 1705, II. 154.

Magdalen College, treatment of, by James II., V. 72; Addison's connection with it, V. 73.

Mahommed Reza Khan, his character, IV. 230; selected by Clive, IV. 232; his capture, confinement at Calcutta, and release, IV. 234—236.

Mahon, Lord, Review of his History of the War of the Succession in Spain, II. 114—174; his qualities as a historian, II. 114; his explanation of the financial condition of Spain, II. 122; his opinions on the Partition Treaty, II. 126—130; his representations of Cardinal Porto Carrero, II. 140; his opinion of the peace on the conclusion of the War of the Spanish Succession, II. 165; his censure of Harley, II. 166; and view of the resemblance of the Tories of the present day, to the Whigs of the Revolution, II. 165—167.

Mahrattas, sketch of their history, IV. 12. 267; expedition against them, IV. 268.

Maintenon, Madame de, IV. 157.

Malaga, naval battle near, in 1704, II. 145.

Malcolm, Sir John, review of his Life of Lord Clive, IV. 1—96; value of his work, IV. 2; his partiality for Clive, IV. 3; his defence of Clive's conduct towards Omichund, IV. 50.

Mallet, David, patronage of, by Bute, V. 198.

Manchester, Countess of, V. 84.

Manchester, Earl of, his patronage of Addison, V. 84. 95.

Mandeville, his metaphysical powers, I. 7.

Mandragola (the), of Machiavelli, I. 84.

Manilla, capitulation of, V. 190.

Mannerism of Johnson, II. 391.

Mansfield, Lord, V. 193; his character and talents, II. 248; his rejection of the overtures of Newcastle, II. 258; his elevation, II. 255; character of his speeches, V. 256; his friendship for Hastings, IV. 312.

Manso, Milton's Epistle to, I. 10.

Manufactures and commerce of Italy in the 14th century, I. 67.
Manufacturing system (the), Southey's opinion upon, I. 222; its effect on the health, I. 224.
Manufacturing and agricultural labourers, comparison of their condition, I. 223.
Marat, his bust substituted for the statues of the martyrs of Christianity, IV. 139.
Marcet, Mrs., her Dialogues on Political Economy, I. 5.
March, Lord, one of the persecutors of Wilkes, V. 245.
Marino, San, visited by Addison, V. 91.
Marlborough, Duchess of, her friendship with Congreve, IV. 197; her inscription on his monument, IV. 188; her death, II. 244.
Marlborough, Duke of, I. 197; his conversion to Whiggism, II. 163; his acquaintance with the Duchess of Cleveland, and commencement of his splendid fortune, IV. 165; notice of Addison's poem in his honour, V. 102.
Marlborough and Godolphin, their policy, V. 97.
Marsh, Bishop, his opposition to Calvinistic doctrine, III. 306.
Martinique, capture of, V. 190.
Martin's illustrations of the Pilgrim's Progress, and of Paradise Lost, II. 2.
Marvel, Andrew, V. 79.
Mary, Queen, II. 108.
Masque, the Italian, I. 15.
Massinger, allusion to his Virgin Martyr, I. 59; his fondness for the Roman Catholic Church, II. 107; indelicate writing in his dramas, IV. 149.
*Mathematics,* comparative estimate of, *by Plato and by Bacon,* III. 104.

Maximilian of Bavaria, IV. 124.
Maxims, general, their uselessness, I. 109.
Maynooth, Mr. Gladstone's objections to the vote of money for, III. 310.
Mecca, IV. 99.
Medals, Addison's Treatise on, V. 76. 95.
Medici, Lorenzo de. *See* Lorenzo de Medici.
Medicine, comparative estimate of the science of, by Plato and by Bacon, III. 109.
Meer Cossim, his talents, IV. 67; his deposition and revenge, IV. 67.
Meer Jaffier, his conspiracy, IV. 43; his conduct during the battle of Plassey, IV. 48; his pecuniary transactions with Clive, IV. 54; his proceedings on being threatened by the Great Mogul, IV. 58; his fears of the English, and intrigues with the Dutch, IV. 60; deposed and reseated by the English, IV. 67; his death, IV. 70; his large bequest to Lord Clive, IV. 78.
Melancthon, II. 86.
Memmius, compared to Sir W. Temple, III. 248.
Memoirs of Sir William Temple, review of, III. 147—251; wanting in selection and compression, III. 148.
Memoirs of the Life of Warren Hastings, review of, IV. 213—349.
Memory, comparative views of the importance of, by Plato and by Bacon, III. 109.
Menander, the lost comedies of, V. 118.
Mendoza, Hurtado de, II. 120.
Mercenaries, employment of, in Italy, I. 74; its political conse-

quences, I. 75; and moral effects, I. 76.

Metaphysical accuracy incompatible with successful poetry, I. 23.

Metcalfe, Sir Charles, his ability and disinterestedness, IV. 96.

Methodists, their early object, IV. 114.

Mexico, exactions of the Spanish viceroys exceeded by the English agents in Bengal, IV. 67.

Michell, Sir Francis, III. 61.

Middle ages, inconsistency in the schoolmen of the, I. 383.

Middlesex election, the constitutional question in relation to it, V. 253. 256.

Middleton, Dr., remarks on his Life of Cicero, III. 4; his controversies with Bentley, III. 246.

Midsummer Night's Dream, sense in which the word "translated" is therein used, V. 146.

Milan, Addison's visit to, V. 90.

Military science, studied by Machiavelli, I. 96.

Military service, relative adaptation of different classes for, I. 72.

Militia (the), control of, by Charles I. or by the Parliament, I. 160.

Mill, James, his merits as a historian, II. 297; defects of his History of British India, IV. 2; his unfairness towards Clive's character, IV. 40; his severity towards Warren Hastings, IV. 214.

Millar, Lady, her vase for verses, V. 23.

Milton, review of his Treatise on Christian Doctrine. Mr. Lemon's discovery of the MS. of it, I. 1; his style, I. 2; his theological opinions, I. 3; his poetry his great passport to general remembrance, I. 5; power of his imagination, I. 11; the most striking characteristic of his poetry, I. 11; his Allegro and Penseroso, I. 13; his Comus and Samson Agonistes, I. 13; his minor poems, I. 17; appreciated the literature of modern Italy, I. 16; his Paradise Regained, I. 16; parallel between him and Dante, I. 18, et seq.; his Sonnets most exhibit his peculiar character, I. 29; his public conduct, I. 29; his defence of the execution of Charles I., I. 41; his refutation of Salmasius, I. 43; his conduct under the Protector, I. 44; peculiarities which distinguished him from his contemporaries, I. 47; noblest qualities of every party combined in him, I. 54; his defence of the freedom of the press, and the right of private judgment, I. 55; his boldness in the maintenance of his opinions, I. 57; recapitulation of his literary merits, I. 58; one of the most "correct" poets, I. 314.

Milton and Shakspeare, character of Johnson's observations on, I. 385.

Minden, battle of, II. 269.

Mines, Spanish-American, II. 123.

Ministers, their responsibility lessened by the Revolution, I. 199; veto by Parliament on their appointment, I. 158.

Minorca, capture of, by the French, II. 256.

"Minute guns!" Charles Townshend's exclamation on hearing Bute's maiden speech, V. 191.

Missionaries, Catholic, their zeal and spirit, IV. 98.

Modern history, the period of its commencement, I. 199.

Mogul, the Great, IV. 238; plundered by Hastings, IV. 281.

Molière, IV. 111.

Mompesson, Sir Giles, conduct of Bacon in regard to his patent, III. 61; abandoned to the vengeance of the Commons, III. 71.

Monarchy, absolute, establishment of, in continental states, I. 153.

Monarchy, the English, in the 16th century, II. 94. 98.

Monjuich, capture of the fort of, by Peterborough, II. 150.

Monmouth, Duke of, II. 318; his supplication for life, III. 236.

Monopolies, English, during the latter end of Elizabeth's reign, III. 27; multiplied under James, III. 60; connived at by Bacon, III. 61.

Monson, Mr., one of the new councillors under the Regulating Act for India, IV. 250; his opposition to Hastings, IV. 250; his death, and its important consequences, IV. 263.

Montagu, Basil, review of his edition of Lord Bacon's works, III. 1—146; character of his work, III. 1—6; his explanation of Lord Burleigh's conduct towards Bacon, III. 19; his views and arguments in defence of Bacon's conduct towards Essex, III. 35—42; his excuses for Bacon's use of torture, and his tampering with the judges, III. 51; his reflections on Bacon's admonition to Buckingham, III. 62; his complaints against James for not interposing to save Bacon, III. 73; and for advising him to plead guilty, III. 74; his defence of Bacon, III. 76—88.

Montagu, Charles, notice of him, V. 83; obtains permission for Addison to retain his fellowship *during his travels*, V. 83; Addison's epistle to him, V. 94. See also Halifax.

Montague, Lord, I. 370.

Montague, Mary, her testimony to Addison's colloquial powers, V. 109.

Montague, Mrs., IV. 330.

Mont Cenis, V. 94.

Montesquieu, his style, I. 163; Horace Walpole's opinion of him, II. 186.

Montesquieu and Machiavelli, comparison between, I. 102.

Montgomery, Mr. Robert, his Omnipresence of the Deity reviewed, I. 271; character of his poetry, I. 273—284; his Satan, I. 282.

Montreal, capture of, by the British, in 1760, II. 268.

Moore, Dr., extract from his Zeluco, I. 389.

Moore's Life of Lord Byron, review of, I. 301—340; its style and matter, I. 302; similes in his Lalla Rookh, III. 138.

Moorshedabad, its situation and importance, IV. 220.

Moral feeling, state of, in Italy in the time of Machiavelli, I. 64.

Morality, political, low standard of, after the Restoration, I. 184.

More, Sir Thomas, IV. 102.

Moses, Bacon compared to, by Cowley, III. 144.

"Mountain of Light," IV. 13.

Mourad Bey, his astonishment at Buonaparte's diminutive figure, V. 101.

Mourning Bride, by Congreve, its high standing as a tragic drama, IV. 182.

Moylan, Mr., review of his Collection of the Opinions of Lord Holland as recorded in the Journals of the House of Lords, IV. 200—212.

Mühlberg, the success of the Protestant movement not checked by defeat at, IV. 122.

Munny, Begum, IV. 235. 253.
Munro, Sir Hector, IV. 280.
Munro, Sir Thomas, IV. 96.
Munster, Bishop of, III. 175.
Murphy, Mr., his knowledge of stage effect, V. 24; his opinion of "The Witlings," V. 24.
Mussulmans, their resistance to the practices of English law, IV. 273.
Mysore, IV. 279; its fierce horsemen, IV. 279.

## N.

Nabobs, class of Englishmen to whom the name was applied, IV. 79—82.
Names, in Milton, their significance, I. 12.
Naples, V. 92.
Napoleon compared with Philip II. of Spain, II. 117; devotion of his Old Guard surpassed by that of the garrison of Arcot to Clive, IV. 21; his early proof of talents for war, IV. 95; protest of Lord Holland against his detention, IV. 200; his hold on the affections of his subjects, V. 174. *See also* Buonaparte.
Nares, Rev. Dr., Review of his "Burleigh and his Times," II. 81—113.
National debt, Southey's notions of, I. 229; effect of its abrogation, I. 230; England's capabilities in respect to it, I. 259.
National feeling, low state of, after the Restoration, I. 192.
Natural history, a body of, commenced by Bacon, III. 90.
Natural religion, IV. 100.
Navy, its mismanagement in the reign of Charles II., IV. 166.
Nelson, Southey's Life of, I. 213.
New Atlantis of Bacon, remarkable passages in, III. 140.

Newbery, Mr., allusion to his pasteboard pictures, I. 12.
Newcastle, Duke of, his relation to Walpole, II. 206. 218; his character, II. 219; his appointment as head of the administration, II. 250; his negotiations with Fox, II. 251; attacked in Parliament by Chatham, II. 253; his intrigues, II. 257; his resignation of office, II. 258; sent for by the king on Chatham's dismissal, II. 261; leader of the Whig aristocracy, II. 262. V. 168; motives for his coalition with Chatham, II. 263. V. 167; his perfidy towards the king, II. 264; his jealousy of Fox, II. 265; his strong government with Chatham, II. 265; his character and borough influence, IV. 30; his contests with Henry Fox, IV. 31; his power and patronage, V. 168; his unpopularity after the resignation of Chatham, V. 192; he quits office, V. 193.
Newdigate, Sir Roger, a great critic, I. 318.
Newton, John, his connection with the slave-trade, III. 79; his attachment to the doctrines of predestination, III. 307.
Newton, Sir Isaac, I. 6; his residence in Leicester Square, V. 5; Malbranche's admiration of him, V. 85.
Niagara, conquest of, II. 267.
Nichols, Dr., IV. 219.
Nimeguen, congress at, III. 200; hollow and unsatisfactory treaty of, III. 201.
Nizam originally a deputy of the Mogul sovereign, IV. 267.
Nizam al Mulk, Viceroy of the Deccan, his death, IV. 16.
Nonconformity. *See* Dissent *and* Church of England.
Normandy, IV. 282.

Normans, their warfare against the Albigenses, IV. 107.

Norris, Henry, the nickname "Little Dickey" applied to him by Addison, V. 157.

North, Lord, his change in the constitution of the Indian government, IV. 245; his desire to obtain the removal of Hastings, IV. 261; change in his designs, and its cause, IV. 266; his sense, tact, and urbanity, IV. 331; his weight in the ministry, V. 173; Chancellor of the Exchequer, V. 253.

Northern and Southern countries, difference of moral feeling in, I. 77.

Novels, popular, character of those which preceded Miss Burney's Evelina, V. 66.

November, fifth of, I. 42.

Novum Organum, admiration excited by it before it was published, III. 48; and afterwards, III. 68; contrast between its doctrine and the ancient philosophy, III. 94. 103—120; its first book the greatest performance of Bacon, III. 144.

Noy, Attorney-General to Charles I., II. 43.

Nugent, Lord, review of his Memorials of John Hampden and his Party, II. 17.

Nugent, Robert Craggs, V. 172.

Nuncomar, his part in the revolutions in Bengal, IV. 230; his services dispensed with by Hastings, IV. 235; his rancour against Mahommed Reza Khan, IV. 234; his alliance with the majority of the new council, IV. 251; his committal for felony, trial, and sentence, IV. 254; his death, IV. 258.

## O.

Oates, Titus, remarks on his plot, II. 313—317.

Oc, language of Provence and neighbouring countries, its beauty and richness, IV. 105.

Ochino Bernardo, his sermons on fate and free will translated by Lady Bacon, III. 13.

Odd (the), the peculiar province of Horace Walpole, II. 191.

Old Bachelor, Congreve's, IV. 179.

Old Sarum, its cause pleaded by Junius, IV. 248.

Old Whig, Addison's, V. 156.

Omai, his appearance at Dr. Burney's concerts, V. 9.

Omichund, his position in India, IV. 41; his treachery towards Clive, IV. 44—50.

Omnipresence of the Deity, Robert Montgomery's, reviewed, I. 271.

Opinion, public, its power, II. 198.

Opposition, parliamentary, when it began to take a regular form, II. 22.

Orange, the Prince of, III. 188; the only hope of his country, III. 193; his success against the French, III. 194; his marriage with the Lady Mary, III. 201.

Oratory, its necessity to an English statesman, IV. 303.

Orloff, Count, his appearance at Dr. Burney's concert, V. 9.

Orme, merits and defects of his work on India, IV. 2.

Ormond, Duke of, II 143.

Orsini, the Princess, II. 141.

Orthodoxy, at one time a synonyme for ignorance and stupidity, IV. 138.

Osborne, Sir Peter, incident of Temple with the son and daughter of, III. 160. 181.

Oswald, James, V. 172.
Otway, I. 264.
Overbury, Sir Thomas, III. 83—85.
Ovid, V. 62; Addison's Notes to the 2nd and 3rd books of his Metamorphoses, V. 74.
Oxford, Earl of. *See* Harley, Robert.
Oxford, V. 36.
Oxford, University of, its inferiority to Cambridge in intellectual activity, III. 8; its disaffection to the House of Hanover, V. 143. 194; rose into favour with the government under Bute, V. 195.
Owen, Mr. Robert, I. 217.

## P.

Painting, correctness in, I. 319; causes of its decline in England after the civil wars, II. 187.
Paley, Archdeacon, Mr. Gladstone's opinion of his defence of the Church, III. 257; his reasoning the same as that by which Socrates confuted Aristodemus, IV. 100.
Paoli, his admiration of Miss Burney, V. 22.
Papacy, its influence, IV. 110; effect of Luther's public renunciation of communion with it, IV. 110.
Paper-currency, Southey's notions of, I. 226.
Papists, line of demarcation between them and Protestants, III. 25.
Papists and Puritans, persecution of, by Elizabeth, I. 114.
Paradise, picture of, in old Bibles, I. 318; painting of, by a gifted master, I. 319.
Paradise Regained, its excellence, I. 17.
Paris, *influence of its opinions* among the educated classes in Italy, IV. 138.
Parker, Archbishop, II. 108.
Parliaments of the 15th century, their condition, I. 151.
Parliament (the) of 1640, sketch of its proceedings, I. 131—208.
Parliament of James I., II. 29; Charles I., his first, II. 32; his second, II. 33; its dissolution, II. 34; his fifth, II. 48.
Parliament, effect of the publication of its proceedings, II. 199—209.
Parliament, Long. *See* Long Parliament.
Parliamentary opposition, its origin, II. 22.
Parliamentary reform, V. 181.
Parr, Dr., IV. 330.
Parties, analogy in the state of, in 1704 and 1826, V. 97; state of, in the time of Milton, I. 52; in England in 1710, I. 164—170; mixture of, at George II.'s first levee after Walpole's resignation, V. 166.
Partridge, his wrangle with Swift, V. 117.
Party, illustration of the use and abuse of, V. 288; power of, during the Reformation and the French revolution, II. 90—93.
Pascal, Blaise, III. 242. IV. 103.
Patronage of literary men, I. 262; less necessary than formerly, I. 268.
"Patriots" (the), in opposition to Sir R. Walpole, II. 205; their remedies for state evils, II. 214.
Paul IV., Pope, his zeal and devotion, IV. 114. 120.
Paulet, Sir Amias, III. 18.
Paulician theology, its doctrines and prevalence among the Albigenses, IV. 106; in Bohemia and the Lower Danube, IV. 109.
Peacham, Rev. Mr., his treatment by Bacon, III. 50. 53.

Peers, new creations of, I. 158; impolicy of limiting the number of, V. 156.

Pelham, Henry, his character, II. 217; his death, II. 249.

Pelhams (the), their ascendency, II. 215; their accession to power, II. 245; feebleness of the opposition to them, II. 245. *See also* Newcastle, Duke of.

Peninsular War, Southey's, II. 214.

Penseroso and Allegro, Milton's, I. 13.

People (the), comparison of their condition, in the 16th and 19th centuries, I. 247, *et seq.;* their welfare not considered in partition treaties, II. 127.

Pepys, his praise of the Triple Alliance, III. 187. *note.*

Pericles, his distribution of gratuities among the members of the Athenian tribunals, III. 78.

Périer, M., translator of the works of Machiavelli, I. 60.

Persecution, religious, in the reign of Elizabeth, I. 115; its reactionary effects upon churches and thrones, I. 129; in England during the progress of the Reformation, II. 92.

Personation, Johnson's want of talent for, II. 392.

Personification, Robert Montgomery's penchant for, I. 279.

Peshwa, authority and origin of, IV. 267.

Peterborough, Earl of, his expedition to Spain, II. 146; his character, II. 146. 158; his successes on the north-east coast of Spain, II. 148—154; his retirement to Valencia thwarted, II. 157; returns to Valencia as a volunteer, II. 158; his recall to England, II. 158.

*Petition of Right,* its enactment, II. 33; *violation of it,* III. 34.

Petrach, I. 10; the first restorer of polite letters into Italy, I. 69; interest excited by his loves, I. 338.

Phalaris, Letters of, controversy upon their merits and genuineness, III. 245—251.

Philarchus for Phylarchus, I. 353.

Philip II. of Spain, extent and splendour of his empire, II. 116, *et seq.*

Philip III. of Spain, his accession, II. 136; his character, II. 136. 141; his choice of a wife, II. 141; is obliged to fly from Madrid, II. 154; surrender of his arsenal and ships at Carthagena, II. 154; defeated at Almenara, and again driven from Madrid, II. 160; forms a close alliance with his late competitor, II. 169; quarrels with France, II. 171; value of his renunciation of the crown of France, II. 171.

Philip le Bel, IV. 109.

Philippeaux, Abbé, his account of Addison's mode of life at Blois, V. 85.

Philips, John, author of the Splendid Shilling, V. 101; specimen of his poetry in honour of Marlborough, V. 102; the poet of the English vintage, V. 207.

Philips, Sir Robert, III. 71.

Phillipps, Ambrose, V. 112.

Philosophy, ancient, its characteristics, III. 93; its stationary character, III. 98. 115; its alliance with Christianity, III. 99; its fall, III. 101; its merits compared with the Baconian, III. 116; reason of its barrenness, III. 131.

Philosophy, moral, its relation to the Baconian system, III. 121.

Philosophy, natural, the light in which it was viewed by the ancients, III. 92—100; chief peculiarity of Bacon's, III. 91.

# INDEX.

Pindar and the Greek drama, I. 13.
Pisistratus, Bacon's comparison of Essex to him, III. 34.
Pitt, William, (the first). *See* Chatham, Earl of.
Pitt, William, (the second), his admiration for Hastings, IV. 312. 322; his asperity towards Francis, IV. 314; his speech in support of Fox's motion against Hastings, IV. 322; his motive, IV. 325; his eloquence, IV. 331; his combination with Fox against Addington, IV. 344.
Pius V., his bigotry, III. 316; his austerity and zeal, IV. 120.
Pius VI., his captivity and death, IV. 140; his funeral rites long withheld, IV. 141.
Plagiarism, instances of R. Montgomery's, I. 271.
Plain Dealer, Wycherley's, its appearance and merit, IV. 168. 177; its libertinism, IV. 178.
Plassey, battle of, IV. 42—48; its effect in England, IV. 57.
Plato, comparison of his views with those of Bacon, III. 103—114; excelled in the art of dialogue, III. 242.
Plautus, his Casina, I. 88.
Plays, English, of the age of Elizabeth, I. 316.
Plebeian, Steele's, V. 156.
Plomer, Sir T., one of the counsel for Hastings on his trial, IV. 331.
Plutarch, his evidence of gifts being given to judges in Athens, III. 78; his anecdote of Lysias's speech before the Athenian tribunals, III. 253.
Poetry, definition of, I. 7; character of Southey's, I. 217; character of Robert Montgomery's, I. 271—284; wherein that of our times differs from that of the last century, I. 313; laws of, I. 316. 322; unities in, I. 316; its end, I. 320; alleged improvements in since the time of Dryden, I. 322; the interest excited by Byron's, I. 338; Dr. Johnson's standard of, I. 384; Addison's opinion of Tuscan, V. 104.
Poland, contest between Protestantism and Catholicism in, IV. 121. 131.
Pole, Cardinal, II. 87.
Politeness, definition of, I. 378.
Pondicherry, IV. 18; its occupation by the English, IV. 269.
Poor (the), their condition in the 16th and 19th centuries, I. 248, *et seq.*; in England and on the Continent, I. 252—256.
Poor-rates (the), lower in manufacturing than in agricultural districts, I. 223.
Pope, his independence of spirit, I. 263; his translation of Homer's description of a moonlight night, I. 315; relative "correctness" of his poetry, I. 315; Byron's admiration of him, I. 326; praise of him, by Cowper, I. 326; his character, habits, and condition, I. 374; his dislike of Bentley, III. 249; his acquaintance with Wycherley, IV. 172; his appreciation of the literary merits of Congreve, IV. 195; the originator of the heroic couplet, V. 79; his testimony to Addison's talking powers, V. 109; his Rape of the Lock his best poem, V. 135; his prologue to Cato, V. 132; his Essay on Criticism warmly praised in the Spectator, V. 135; his intercourse with Addison, V. 135; his hatred of Dennis, V. 135; his estrangement from Addison, V. 136; his suspicious nature, V. 143—148; his satire of Addison, V. 149.
Popes, review of Ranke's History of the, IV. 91—143.

Popham, Major, IV. 290.
Popish Plot, circumstances which assisted the belief in, II. 313.
Popoli, Duchess of, saved by the Earl of Peterborough, II. 151.
Portico, the doctrines of the school so called, III. 97.
Porto Carrero, Cardinal, II. 131—135; Louis XIV.'s opinion of him, II. 140; his disgrace, and reconciliation with the Queen Dowager, II. 155.
Port Royal, its destruction a disgrace to the Jesuits and to the Romish Church, IV. 137.
Portugal, its retrogression in prosperity compared with Denmark, IV. 134.
Posidonius, his eulogy of philosophy as ministering to human comfort, III. 93.
Post Nati, the great case in the Exchequer Chamber, conducted by Bacon, III. 48; doubts upon the legality of the decision, III. 48.
Power, political, religious belief ought not to exclude from, I. 285.
Pratt, Charles, V. 173; Chief Justice, V. 239; created Lord Camden, and entrusted with the seals, V. 244.
Predestination, doctrine of, I. 294.
Prerogative, royal, its advance, I. 156; in the 16th century, II. 94. 98; its curtailment by the Revolution, II. 198; proposed by Bolingbroke to be strengthened, II. 290. *See also* Crown.
Press, Milton's defence of its freedom, I. 55; its emancipation after the Revolution, I. 197; remarks on its freedom, I. 244; censorship of in the reign of Elizabeth, II. 94; its influence on the public mind after the Revolution, V. 82.
Prince, The, of Machiavelli, general condemnation of it, I. 60; dedicated *to the* younger Lorenzo de Medici, I. 98; compared with Montesquieu's Spirit of Laws, I. 102.
Princes, royal, right of Parliament to direct their education and marriage, I. 158.
Printing, its inventor and the date of its discovery unknown, III. 100.
Prior, Matthew, his modesty compared with Aristophanes and Juvenal, IV. 145.
Private judgment, Milton's defence of the right of, I. 55; Mr. Gladstone's notions of the rights and abuses of, III. 294—299.
Privileges of the House of Commons, change in public opinion in respect to them, I. 203. *See also* Parliament.
Privy Council, Temple's plan for its reconstitution, III. 204; Mr. Courtenay's opinion of its absurdity contested, III. 205. 216; Barillon's remarks upon it, III. 208.
Progress of mankind in the political and physical sciences, II. 291—296; in intellectual freedom, III. 25; the key of the Baconian doctrine, III. 91; how retarded by the unprofitableness of ancient philosophy, III. 94—110; during the last 250 years, IV. 99.
Prosperity, national, I. 232.
Protector (the), character of his administration, I. 44.
Protestant nonconformists in the reign of Charles I., their intolerance, II. 59.
Protestantism, its early history, II. 92; its doctrine touching the right of private judgment, III. 296; light which Ranke has thrown upon its movements, IV. 98; its victory in the northern parts of Europe, IV. 110; its failure in Italy, IV. 112; effect of its outbreak in any one part of Christendom, IV. 114. 121; its contest with Catholicism in

France, Poland, and Germany, IV. 121, 122. 126; its stationary character, IV. 142.

Protestants and Catholics, their relative numbers in the 16th century, II. 102.

Provence, its language, literature, and civilization in the 12th century, IV. 105.

Prussia, king of, subsidised by the Pitt and Newcastle ministry, II. 268; influence of Protestantism upon her, IV. 134.

Prynne, II. 40. 46.

Public opinion, its power, II. 198.

Public spirit an antidote against bad government, II. 96; a safeguard against legal oppression, II. 96.

Publicity (the) of parliamentary proceedings, influence of, II. 198; a remedy for corruption, V. 181.

Pulci, allusion to, I. 71.

Pulteney, William, his opposition to Walpole, II. 228; moved the address to the king on the marriage of the Prince of Wales, II. 235; his unpopularity, II. 242; accepts a peerage, II. 244; compared with Chatham, V. 245.

Pundits of Bengal, their jealousy of foreigners, IV. 304.

Punishment, warning not the only end of, I. 137.

Punishment and reward, the only means by which government can effect its ends, IV. 155.

Puritanism, effect of its prevalence upon the national taste, IV. 155; the restraints it imposed, IV. 158; reaction against it, IV. 160.

Puritans (the), character and estimate of them, I. 47—52; hatred of them by James I., I. 129; effect of their religious austerity, I. 242; Johnson's contempt for their religious scruples, I. 381; their persecution by Charles I., II. 39; settlement of, in America, II. 46; blamed for calling in the Scots, II. 51; defence of them against this accusation, II. 51; difficulty and peril of their leaders, II. 61; the austerity of their manners drove many to the royal standard, II. 73; their position at the close of the reign of Elizabeth, III. 26; violent outbreak of public feeling against them at the Restoration, IV. 81; their oppression by Whitgift, IV. 125; their faults in the day of their power, and their consequences, IV. 160.

Puritans and Papists, persecution of, by Elizabeth, I. 115.

Pym, John, his influence, II. 54; Lady Carlisle's warning to him, II. 64; his impeachment ordered by the king, II. 63.

Pynsent, Sir Wm., his legacy to Chatham, V. 219.

Pyramid, the Great, Arab fable concerning it, IV. 141.

"Pyrenees (the) have ceased to exist," II. 135.

## Q.

Quebec, conquest of, by Wolfe, II. 267.

Quince, Peter, sense in which he uses the word "translated," V. 146.

## R.

Rabbinical learning, work on, by Rev. L. Addison, V. 71.

Racine, his Greeks far less "correctly" drawn than those of Shakspeare, I. 314; his Iphigénie an[f]anachronism, I. 314; passed the close of his life in writing sacred dramas, V. 84.

Raleigh, Sir Walter, II. 113; his varied acquirements, II. 113; his position at court at the close of the reign of Elizabeth, III. 27; his execution, III. 59.

Ramsay, court painter to George III., V. 198.

Ramus, III. 102.

Ranke, Leopold, review of his History of the Popes, IV. 97—143; his qualifications as an historian, IV. 97. 141.

Rape of the Lock (The), Pope's best poem, V. 135; recast by its author, V. 144.

Reader, Steele's, V. 122.

Rebellion, the Great, and the Revolution, analogy between them, I. 33. 41.

Rebellion in Ireland in 1640, II. 59.

Reform, the process of, often necessarily attended with many evils, II. 92; its supporters sometimes unworthy, II. 92.

Reform in Parliament before the Revolution, I. 206; public desire for, I. 207; policy of it, I. 208. V. 181.

Reform Bill, II. 259; conduct of its opponents, II. 328.

Reformation (the), its history much misrepresented, I. 114; party divisions caused by it, I. 200; their consequences, I. 202; its immediate effect upon political liberty in England, II. 24; its social and political consequences, II. 90; its effect upon the Church of Rome, II. 125; vacillation which it produced in English legislation, III. 8; auspices under which it commenced, IV. 110; its effect upon the Roman court, IV. 118; its progress not affected by the event of battles or sieges, IV. 122; analogy between it and the French Revolution, II. 89; Milton's treatise of, I. 58.

*Reformers*, always unpopular in their own age, II. 293.

Refugees, V. 49.

Regicides of Charles I., disapproval of their conduct, I. 41; injustice of the imputations cast on them, I. 41.

Regium Donum, III. 307.

Regulating Act, its introduction by Lord North, and change which it made in the form of the Indian government, IV. 245. 261. 271; power which it gave to the Chief Justice, IV. 276.

Religion, national establishment of, I. 235; its connection with civil government, I. 237, *et seq.*; its effects upon the policy of Charles I., and of the Puritans, I. 243; no disqualification for the safe exercise of political power, I. 288; the religion of the English in the 16th century, II. 105; what system of should be taught by a government, III. 319; no progress made in the knowledge of natural religion, since the days of Thales, IV. 100; revealed, not of the nature of a progressive science, IV. 101.

Remonstrant, allusion to Milton's Animadversions on the, I. 58.

Representative government, decline of, I. 156.

Restoration (the), degenerated character of our statesmen and politicians in the times succeeding it, I. 181; low standard of political morality after it, I. 184; violence of party and low state of national feeling after it, I. 92; that of Charles II. and of Louis XVIII. contrasted, II. 302; its effects upon the morals and manners of the nation, IV. 158.

Retrospective law, is it ever justifiable? I. 137. 169; warranted by a certain amount of public danger, II. 56.

Revolution (the), its principles often grossly misrepresented, I. 32; analogy between it and the "Great Rebellion," I. 33. 42; its effect on the character of public men, I. 194; freedom of the press after it, I. 197; its effects, I. 197; ministerial responsibility since, I. 198; review of Mackintosh's History of, II. 273—349.

Revolution, the French, its social and political consequences, II. 90. 285; analogy between it and the Reformation, II. 89; warnings which preceded it, IV. 135.

Reynolds, Sir Joshua, IV. 330.

Richardson, V. 13.

Richelieu, Cardinal, IV. 133.

Richmond, Duke of, V. 260.

Rigby, secretary of Ireland, V. 172.

Riots, public, during Grenville's administration, V. 225.

Robertson, Dr., III. 125; Scotticisms in his works, V. 87.

Robespierre, IV. 140; analogy between his followers and those of Kniperdoling, II. 90.

Robinson, Sir Thomas, II. 252.

Rochefort, threatening of, II. 266.

Rochester, Earl of, II. 324. III. 250. V. 79. 81.

Rockingham, Marquess of, his characteristics, V. 228; parallel between his party and the Bedfords, V. 228; accepts the Treasury, V. 228; patronises Burke, V. 229; proposals of his administration on the American Stamp Act, V. 232. 237; his dismissal, V. 242; his services, V. 242; his moderation towards the new ministry, V. 246; his relation to Chatham, V. 255; advocated the independence of the United States, V. 257.

Rockinghams and Bedfords, parallel between them, V. 228.

Roe, Sir Thomas, IV. 73.

Rohillas, description of them, IV. 240; agreement between Hastings and Surajah Dowlah for their subjugation, IV. 241.

Romans and Greeks, difference between, I. 79.

Rome, ancient, bribery at, III. 78.

Rome, Church of, effect of the Reformation on it, II. 125; its encroaching disposition, II. 314; its policy, II. 326; its antiquity, IV. 98. *See also* Church of Rome.

Rooke, Sir George, his capture of Gibraltar, II. 145; his fight with a French squadron near Malaga, II. 146; his return to England, II. 146.

Rosamond, Addison's opera of, V. 104.

Roundheads (the), their literature, I. 30; their successors in the reign of George I. turned courtiers, V. 165.

Rousseau, his sufferings, I. 338; Horace Walpole's opinion of him, II. 186.

Rowe, his verses to the Chloe of Holland House, V. 152.

Royalists (the) of the time of Charles I., I. 52; many of them true friends to the Constitution, I. 155; some of the most eminent formerly in opposition to the court, II. 60.

Royalists, Constitutional, in the reign of Charles I., II. 60. 67.

Rupert, Prince, II. 76; his encounter with Hampden at Chalgrove, II. 77.

Russell, Lord, I. 194; his conduct in the new council, III. 233; his death, III. 236.

Russia and Poland, diffusion of wealth in, as compared with England, I. 255.

Rutland, Earl of, his character, III. 70.

Ruyter, Admiral de, III. 193.

Rymer, I. 385.

## S.

Sacheverell, Dr., his impeachment and conviction, II. 164. V. 106.
Sackville, the Earl of (16th century), II. 112. IV. 62.
Sackville, Lord George, V. 173.
St. Ignatius. *See* Loyola.
St. John, Henry, his accession to power in 1712, II. 164. 174. *See also* Bolingbroke, Lord.
St. John, Oliver, counsel against Charles I.'s writ for ship-money, II. 45. 50; made Solicitor-General, II. 58.
St. Louis, his persecution of heretics, III. 79.
St. Malo, ships burnt in the harbour of, II. 266.
St. Patrick, III. 303.
Sallust, III. 2.
Salmasius, Milton's refutation of, I. 43.
Salvator Rosa, V. 92.
Samson Agonistes, I. 13.
San Marino, visited by Addison, V. 91.
Sandwich, Lord, his conduct in respect to the persecution of Wilkes, V. 215.
Sanscrit, IV. 239. 304.
"Satan," Robert Montgomery's, I. 282.
Savanarola, IV. 112.
Savile, Sir George, V. 227.
Saxony, its elector the natural head of the Protestant party in Germany, IV. 124; its persecution of the Calvinists, IV. 125; invasion by the Catholic party in Germany, IV. 131.
Schism, cause of, in England, IV. 109.
Schitab Roy, IV. 234.
Schwellenberg, Madame, her position and character, V. 33. 42. 46.
*Science*, political, progress of, II. 291. 298. 348.
Scindia, origin of the House of, IV. 267.
Scotland, cruelties of James II. in, II. 323. 338; establishment of the Kirk in, II. 338. 292; her progress in wealth and intelligence owing to Protestantism, IV. 134.
Scots (the), effects of their resistance to Charles I., II. 47, *et seq.*; ill feeling excited against them by Bute's elevation to power, V. 197.
Scott, Major, his plea in defence of Hastings, IV. 242. 311; his influence, IV. 311; his challenge to Burke, IV. 319.
Scott, Sir Walter, I. 111; relative "correctness" of his poetry, I. 314; his Duke of Buckingham (in "Peveril"), I. 332; Scotticisms in his works, V. 87.
Sea, mysterious horror of it entertained by the natives of India, IV. 213.
Sedley, Sir Charles, IV. 147.
Self-denying ordinance (the), I. 166.
Seneca, his work "On Anger," III. 94; his claims as a philosopher, III. 94; his work on natural philosophy, III. 98; the Baconian system in reference to, III. 130.
Sevajee, founder of the Mahratta empire, IV. 267.
Seward, Mr., V. 22.
Sforza, Francis, I. 77.
Shaftesbury, Lord, allusion to, I. 6. III. 158; his character, III. 220—227; contrasted with Halifax, III. 227.
Shakspeare, allusion to, I. 7; one of the most "correct" poets, I. 314; relative "correctness" of his Troilus and Cressida, I. 314; contrasted with Byron, I. 333; Johnson's observations on, I. 385.
Shaw, the Lifeguardsman, V. 101.

Shebbeare, Bute's patronage of, V. 198.

Shelburne, Lord, Secretary of State in Chatham's second administration, V. 244; his dismissal, V. 252.

Shelley, Percy Bysshe, II. 7.

Sheridan, Richard Brinsley, IV. 179; his speech against Hastings, IV. 325; his encouragement to Miss Burney to write for the stage, V. 24.

Sheridan and Congreve, effect of their works upon the Comedy of England, I. 85; contrasted with Shakspeare, I. 86.

Ship-money, question of its legality, II. 44, et seq.

Shrewsbury, Duke of, V. 138.

Sienna, cathedral of, V. 93.

Sigismund of Sweden, IV. 124.

Silius Italicus, V. 101.

Simonides, his speculations on natural religion, IV. 100.

Sismondi, M., I. 110.

Sixtus V., IV. 120.

Skinner, Cyriac, I. 1.

Smith, Adam, IV. 85.

Smollett, his judgment on Lord Carteret, II. 216; his satire on the Duke of Newcastle, II. 218.

Social contract, III. 312.

Society, Mr. Southey's Colloquies on, reviewed, I. 247.

Socrates, the first martyr of intellectual liberty, III. 14; his views of the uses of astronomy, III. 107; his reasoning exactly the reasoning of Paley's Natural Theology, IV. 100.

Somers, Lord, his just acquittal IV. 328.

Somers, Lord Chancellor, his encouragement of literature, V. 83; procures a pension for Addison, V. 83; made Lord President of the Council, V. 106.

Somerset, the Protector, as a promoter of the English Reformation, I. 127; his fall, III. 56.

Somerset, Duke of, V. 155.

Sonnets, Milton's, I. 29.

Sophocles and the Greek drama, I. 14.

Soul, IV. 101.

Soult, Marshal, reference to, V. 222.

Southampton, Earl of, notice of, III. 45.

Southcote, Johanna, IV. 104. 131.

Southern and Northern countries, difference of moral feeling in, I. 78.

Southey, Robert, review of his Colloquies on Society, I. 210; his characteristics, I. 211; his poetry preferable to his prose, I. 213; his lives of Nelson and John Wesley, I. 213; his Peninsular War, I. 214; his Book of the Church, I. 214; his political system, I. 217; plan of his present work, I. 219; his opinions regarding the manufacturing system, I. 222—226; his political economy, I. 227, et seq.; the national debt, I. 229—232; his theory of the basis of government, I. 234; his remarks on public opinion, I. 235; his view of the Catholic claims, I. 244; his ideas on the prospects of society, I. 247. 256; his prophecies respecting the Corporation and Test Acts, and the removal of the Catholic disabilities, I. 247; his observations on the condition of the people in the 16th and 19th centuries, I. 249; his arguments on national wealth, I. 252; review of his edition of Bunyan's Pilgrim's Progress, II. 1. *See also* Bunyan.

South Sea bubble, II. 226.

Spain, II. 72; review of Lord Mahon's War of the Succession in, II. 114; her state under Philip, II. 118; her literature during the 16th century, II. 119; her state a century later, II. 121; effect produced on her by the Reformation, II. 125; her disputed succession, II. 126; the Partition treaty, II. 127; conduct of the French towards her, II. 131; how affected by the death of Charles, II. 134, *et seq.;* change in her favour, II. 138; designation of the War of the Spanish Succession, II. 156; no conversions to Protestantism in, IV. 142.

Spanish and Swiss soldiers in the time of Machiavelli, character of, I. 97.

Sparre, the Dutch general, II. 143.

Spectator (the), notices of it, V. 127—131. 138.

Spenser, II. 3.

Spirits, Milton's, materiality of them, I. 23.

Spurton, Dr., II. 78.

Stafford, Lord, incident at his execution, II. 318.

Stamp Act, disaffection of the American colonies on account of it, V. 230; its repeal, V. 237.

Stanhope, Earl of, II. 227.

Stanhope, General, II. 150; commands in Spain (1707), II. 160.

Star Chamber, II. 46. 51; its abolition, II. 55.

Staremberg, the imperial general in Spain (in 1707), II. 160.

Statesmanship, contrast of the Spanish and Dutch notions of, III. 179.

Statesmen, the character of, greatly affected by that of the times, I. *198; character of the first generation of professed statesmen that England produced*, III. 7—12.

State Trials, II. 316. 318. 340. III. 84.

Steele, V. 109; his character, V. 112; Addison's treatment of him, V. 112; his origination of the Tatler, V. 116; his subsequent career, V. 126. 132. 142.

Steevens, George, V. 21.

Stoicism, comparison of that of the Bengalee with the European, IV. 231.

Stoics, their philosophy, III. 98. 113. 118.

Strafford, Earl of, I. 132; his character as a statesman, I. 133; bill of attainder against him, I. 137; his character, II. 42; his impeachment, attainder, and execution, II. 55; defence of the proceedings against him, II. 56.

Strawberry Hill, II. 178. 192.

Subsidies, foreign, in the time of Charles II., I. 199.

Subsidising foreign powers, Pitt's aversion to, II. 254.

Succession in Spain, War of the, II. 114. *See also* Spain.

Sujah Dowlah, Nabob Vizier of Oude, IV. 239; his flight, IV. 243; his death, IV. 291.

Sulivan, Mr., chairman of the East India Company, his character, IV. 65; his relation to Clive, IV. 70.

Sumner, Rev. C. R., I. 2.

Sunderland, Earl of, II. 226; Secretary of State, V. 105; appointed Lord Lieutenant of Ireland, V. 139; reconstructs the ministry in 1717, V. 153.

Superstition, instances of, in the 19th century, IV. 104.

Supreme Court of Calcutta, account of, IV. 254.

Surajah Dowlah, Viceroy of Bengal, his character, IV. 34; the monster of the "Black Hole," IV. 36; his

flight and death, IV. 48. 53; investigation by the House of Commons into the circumstances of his deposition, IV. 88.
Sweden, her part in the Triple Alliance, III. 182; her relations to Catholicism, IV. 124.
Swift, Jonathan, his position at Sir William Temple's, III. 238; instance of his imitation of Addison, V. 78; his relations with Addison, V. 139; joins the Tories, V. 141.
Swiss and Spanish soldiers in the time of Machiavelli, character of, I. 97.
Sydney, Algernon, I. 193; his reproach on the scaffold to the sheriffs, II. 342.
Sydney, Sir Philip, II. 112.
Syllogistic process, analysis of, by Aristotle, III. 126.

### T.

Talleyrand, I. 183; his fine perception of character, III. 156; picture of him at Holland House, IV. 211.
Tasso, I. 328; difference of the spirit of his poem from that of Ariosto, IV. 129; specimen from Hoole's translation, V. 79.
Tatler (the), its origination, V. 116; its popularity, V. 122; change in its character, V. 126; its discontinuance, V. 127.
Taxation, principles of, I. 231.
Teignmouth, Lord, his high character and regard for Hastings, IV. 309.
Telemachus, the standard of morality in, IV. 152.
Tempest, the great, of 1703, V. 102.
Temple, Lord, First Lord of the Admiralty in the Duke of Devonshire's administration, II. 258; his parallel between Byng's behaviour at Minorca and the king's behaviour at Oudenarde, II. 261; his resignation of office, V. 188; supposed to have encouraged the assailants of Bute's administration, V. 199; dissuades Pitt from supplanting Grenville, V. 224; prevents Pitt's acceptance of George III.'s offer of the administration, V. 226; his opposition to Rockingham's ministry on the question of the Stamp Act, V. 233; quarrel between him and Pitt, V. 243.
Temple, Sir William, review of Courtenay's Memoirs of, III. 147—251; his character as a statesman, III. 148—153. 157; his family, III. 158; his early life, III. 159; his courtship of Dorothy Osborne, III. 160; historical interest of his love-letters, III. 160; his marriage, III. 168; his residence in Ireland, III. 168; his feelings towards Ireland, III. 171; attaches himself to Arlington, III. 173; his embassy to Munster, III. 175; appointed resident at the court of Brussels, III. 176; danger of his position, III. 178; his interview with De Witt, III. 179; his negotiation of the Triple Alliance, III. 180—184; his fame at home and abroad, III. 187; his recall, and farewell of De Witt, III. 189; his cold reception and dismissal, III. 189; style and character of his compositions, III. 191; charged to conclude a separate peace with the Dutch, III. 197; offered the Secretaryship of State, III. 199; his audiences of the king, III. 199. 203; his share in bringing about the marriage of the Prince of Orange with the Lady Mary, III. 201; required to sign the treaty of Nimeguen, III.

201; recalled to England, III. 202; his plan of a new privy council, III. 204. 218; his alienation from his colleagues, III. 233; his conduct on the Exclusion Question, III. 234; leaves public life and retires to the country, III. 235; his literary pursuits, III. 238; his amanuensis, Swift, III. 238; his Essay on Ancient and Modern Learning, III. 242; his Essay on the Letters of Phalaris, III. 244; his death and character, III. 249.

Tessé, Marshal, II. 152.

Thackeray, Rev. Francis, review of his Life of the Rt. Hon. William Pitt, Earl of Chatham, &c., II. 221. His style and matter, II. 221. 242; his omission to notice Chatham's conduct towards Walpole, II. 243.

Thales, IV. 100.

Theatines, IV. 115.

Theology, characteristics of the science of, IV. 100—104.

Thrale, Mrs., I. 358; her position and character, V. 21; her regard for Miss Burney, V. 21.

Thurlow, Lord, IV. 91. 312; his weight in the government, IV. 312.

Tickell, Thomas, Addison's chief favourite, V. 114; his translation of the first book of the Iliad, V. 145; character of his intercourse with Addison, V. 147; appointed by Addison Undersecretary of State, V. 155; Addison entrusts his works to him, V. 158; his elegy on the death of Addison, V. 160.

Tindal, his character of the Earl of Chatham's maiden speech, II. 235.

Toledo, admission of the Austrian troops into (in 1705), II. 155.

Toleration, religious, the safest policy for governments, I. 120; conduct of James II. as a professed supporter of it, II. 321—329.

Tories, their popularity and ascendancy in 1710, II. 164; description of them during the sixty years following the Revolution, II. 174; of Walpole's time, II. 232; mistaken reliance by James II. upon them, II. 232; their principles and conduct after the Revolution, II. 347; contempt into which they had fallen (1754), IV. 30; Clive unseated by their vote, IV. 31; their joy on the accession of Anne, V. 96; analogy between their divisions in 1704 and in 1826, V. 97; their attempt to rally in 1767, V. 105; called to office by Queen Anne in 1710, V. 124; their conduct on occasion of the first representation of Addison's Cato, V. 132; their expulsion of Steele from the House of Commons, V. 137; possessed none of the public patronage in the reign of George I., V. 165; their hatred of the House of Hanover, V. 164. 173; paucity of talent among them, V. 165; their joy on the accession of George III., V. 176; their political creed on the accession of George I., V. 180; in the ascendant for the first time since the accession of the House of Hanover, V. 194. See Whigs.

Tories and Whigs after the Revolution, I. 198.

Torture, the application of, by Bacon in Peacham's case, III. 50—53; its use forbidden by Elizabeth, III. 54; Mr. Jardine's work on the use of it, III. 54.

Tory, a modern, II. 165; his points of resemblance and of difference to a Whig of Queen Anne's time, II. 165.

Toulouse, Count of, compelled by Peterborough to raise the siege of Barcelona, II. 153.

Townshend, Lord, his quarrel with Walpole and retirement from public life, II. 229.

Townshend, Charles, V. 173; his exclamation during the Earl of Bute's maiden speech, V. 191; his opinion of the Rockingham administration, V. 229; Chancellor of the Exchequer in Pitt's second administration, V. 244; Pitt's overbearing manners towards him, V. 248; his insubordination, V. 250; his death, V. 252.

Town Talk, Steele's, V. 143.

Tragedy, how much it has lost from a false notion of what is due to its dignity, III. 164.

Trainbands of the City (the), II. 66; their public spirit, II. 96.

Transubstantiation, a doctrine of faith, IV. 103.

Travel, its uses, I. 390; Johnson's contempt for it, I. 389.

Treadmill, the study of ancient philosophy compared to labour in the, III. 97.

Treason, high, did the articles against Strafford amount to? I. 135; law passed at the Revolution respecting trials for, II. 343.

Trent, general reception of the decisions of the council of, IV. 124.

Trial of the legality of Charles I.'s writ for ship-money, II. 45; of Strafford, II. 55; of Warren Hastings, IV. 329.

Tribunals, the large jurisdiction exercised by those of Papal Rome, IV. 110.

Triennial Bill, consultation of William III. with Sir William Temple upon it, III. 240.

Triple Alliance, circumstances which led to it, III. 177—181; its speedy conclusion and importance, III. 183—187; Dr. Lingard's remarks on it, III. 184; its abandonment by the English government, III. 191; reverence for it in Parliament, III. 197.

Tudors (the), their government popular though despotic, II. 95; dependent on the public favour, II. 100; corruption not necessary to them, II. 198; parallel between the Tudors and the Cæsars not applicable, II. 99.

Turgot, M., veneration with which France cherishes his memory, IV. 96.

Turkey-carpet style of poetry, I. 271.

Turner, Colonel, the Cavalier, anecdote of him, I. 171.

Tuscan poetry, Addison's opinion of, V. 104.

## U.

Union of England with Scotland, its happy results, III. 293; of England with Ireland, its unsatisfactory results, III. 293; illustration in the Persian fable of King Zohak, III. 293.

United Provinces, Temple's account of, a masterpiece in its kind, III. 192.

Unities (the), in poetry, I. 316.

Unity, hopelessness of having, III. 295.

Universities, their principle of not withholding from the student works containing impurity, IV. 143; of Oxford and Cambridge, change in their position in relation to the government when Bute became minister, V. 194.

Usurper (a), to obtain the affection

of his subjects must deserve it, V. 174.
Utility the key of the Baconian doctrine, III. 92.
Utrecht; the treaty of, exasperation of parties on account of it, II. 169; dangers that were to be apprehended from it, II. 170; state of Europe at the time, II. 170; defence of it, II. 173.

### V.

Vandyke, his portrait of the Earl of Strafford, II. 41.
Vansittart, Mr., Governor of Bengal, his position, IV. 221; his fair intentions, feebleness, and inefficiency, IV. 221.
Varelst's portrait of James II., II. 2.
Vattel, V. 185.
Vega, Garcilasso de la, a soldier as well as a poet, II. 119.
Vendome, Duke of, takes the command of the Bourbon forces in Spain, (1710), II. 161.
Venice, republic of, next in antiquity to the line of the Supreme Pontiffs, IV. 98.
Verona, protest of Lord Holland against the course pursued by England at the Congress of, IV. 200.
Verres, extensive bribery at the trial of, III. 78.
Versification, modern, in a dead language, I. 10.
Veto, by Parliament on the appointment of ministers, I. 158; by the Crown on acts of Parliament, I. 159.
Voltaire the connecting link of the literary schools of Louis XIV. and Louis XVI., I. 329; *Horace* Walpole's opinion of him, II. 186; his partiality to England, IV. 92; meditated a history of the conquest of Bengal, IV. 92; his character and that of his compeers, IV. 137; his interview with Congreve, IV. 196; compared with Addison as a master of the art of ridicule, V. 120.
Vigo, capture of the Spanish galleons at, in 1702, II. 144.
Villani, John, his account of the state of Florence in the 14th century, I. 68.
Villa-Viciosa, battle of, 1710, II. 162.
Villiers, Sir Edward, III. 70.
Virgil not so "correct" a poet as Homer, I. 314; skill with which Addison imitated him, V. 77.
Vision of Judgment, Southey's, I. 222.

### W.

Wages, effect of attempts by government to limit the amount of, IV. 155.
Waldégrave, Lord, made First Lord of the Treasury by George II., II. 265; his attempt to form an administration, II. 265.
Wales, Frederic Prince of, joined the opposition to Walpole, II. 233; his marriage, II. 235; makes Pitt his groom of the bedchamber, II. 241; his death, II. 247; headed the opposition, V. 167; his sneer at the Earl of Bute, V. 179.
Wales, Princess Dowager of, mother of George III., V. 177; popular ribaldry against her, V. 196.
Wales, the Prince of, generally in opposition to the minister, II. 233.
Wallenstein, IV. 8.
Waller, Edmund, his conduct in the House of Commons, II. 321; similarity of his character to Lord Bacon's, III. 48.

Walpole, Lord, I. 371. 374.

Walpole, Sir Horace, review of Lord Dover's edition of his Letters to Sir Horace Mann, II. 175; eccentricity of his character, II. 178; his politics, II. 178; his affectation of philosophy, II. 180; his unwillingness to be considered a man of letters, II. 181; his love of the French language, II. 183; character of his works, II. 187—193; his sketch of Lord Carteret, II. 215.

Walpole, Sir Robert, his retaliation on the Tories for their treatment of him, II. 169; the "glory of the Whigs," II. 195; his character, II. 195, *et seq.*; the charge against him of corrupting the Parliament, II. 200; his dominant passion, II. 201; his conduct in regard to the Spanish war, II. 202; formidable character of the opposition to him, II. 204. 231; his last struggle, II. 207; outcry for his impeachment, II. 206; his conduct in reference to the South Sea bubble, II. 226; his conduct towards his colleagues, II. 229; found it necessary to resign, II. 242; bill of indemnity for witnesses brought against him, II. 243; his maxim in election questions in the House of Commons, IV. 31; his many titles to respect, IV. 203.

Walpolean battle, the great, II. 195.

Walsingham, the Earl of (16th century), II. 112.

Wanderer, Madame D'Arblay's, V. 59.

War, the Art of, by Machiavelli, I. 96.

War of the Succession in Spain, Lord Mahon's review of, II. 114—174. *See* Spain.

War, languid, condemned, I. 165; *Homer's descriptions of*, V. 100; descriptions of by Silius Italicus, V. 101; against Spain, counselled by Pitt and opposed by Bute, V. 188; found by Bute to be inevitable, V. 190; its conclusion, V. 195; debate on the treaty of peace, V. 206.

War, civil. *See* Civil War.

Warburton, Bishop, his views on the ends of government, III. 313; his social contract a fiction, III. 313; his opinion as to the religion to be taught by government, III. 319.

Warning, not the only end of punishment, I. 137.

Warwick, Countess Dowager of, V. 151; her marriage with Addison, V. 152.

Warwick, Earl of, makes mischief between Addison and Pope, V. 149; his dislike of the marriage between Addison and his mother, V. 151; his character, V. 151.

Way of the World, by Congreve, its merits, IV. 193.

Wealth, tangible and intangible, I. 226; national and private, I. 230. 253; its increase among all classes in England, I. 254—258; its diffusion in Russia and Poland as compared with England, I. 255; its accumulation and diffusion in England and in Continental states, I. 256.

Wedderburne, Alexander, his able defence of Lord Clive, IV. 91. 311; his urgency with Clive to furnish Voltaire with the materials for his meditated history of the conquest of Bengal, IV. 92.

Weekly Intelligencer (The), extract from, on Hampden's death, II. 79.

Weldon, Sir A., his story of the meanness of Bacon, III. 66.

Wellesley, Marquis, his eminence as a statesman, III. 206; his opinion as to the expediency of reducing the numbers of the Privy Council, III. 206.

Wellington, Duke of, IV. 302. V. 101.

Wendover, its recovery of the elective franchise, II. 31.

Wentworth. *See* Strafford, Earl of.

Wesley (John), Southey's Life of, I. 214; his dislike to the doctrine of predestination, III. 307.

Westminster Hall, IV. 251; the scene of the trial of Hastings, IV. 328.

Westphalia, the treaty of, IV. 110. 133.

Wharton, Earl of, lord lieutenant of Ireland, V. 114; appoints Addison chief secretary, V. 114.

Wheler, Mr., his appointment as Governor-General of India, IV. 263; his conduct in the council, IV. 265. 270. 281.

Whigs (the), their unpopularity and loss of power in 1710, II. 164; their position in Walpole's time, II. 231; doctrines and literature they patronised during the seventy years they were in power, II. 346; exclamations of George II. against them, II. 265; their violence in 1679, II. 317; the king's revenge on them, II. 319; revival of their strength, II. 321; their conduct at the Revolution, II. 334; after that event, II. 345; Mr. Courtenay's remark on those of the 17th century, III. 148; attachment of literary men to them after the Revolution, V. 82; their fall on the accession of Anne, V. 95. 123; in the ascendant in 1705, V. 105; Queen Anne's dislike of them, V. 123; their dismissal by her, V. 124; their success in the administration of the government, V. 124; dissensions and reconstruction of the *Whig* government in 1717, V. 153; *enjoyed all* the public patronage *in the reign of* George I., V. 165; *acknowledged* the Duke of Newcastle as their leader, V. 167; their power and influence at the close of the reign of George II., V. 170; their support of the Brunswick dynasty, V. 174; division of them into two classes, old and young, V. 227; superior character of the young Whig school, V. 227. *See* Tories.

Whig and Tory, inversion of the meaning of, II. 165.

Whigs and Tories after the Revolution, I. 197; their relative condition in 1710, II. 164; their essential characteristics, V. 163; their transformation in the reign of George I., V. 164; analogy presented by France, V. 165; their relative progress, II. 166; subsidence of party spirit between them, V. 165; revival under Bute's administration of the animosity between them, V. 195.

Whitgift, master of Trinity College, Cambridge, his character, III. 17; his Calvinistic doctrines, III. 306; his zeal and activity against the Puritans, IV. 125.

Wickliffe, John, juncture at which he rose, IV. 109; his influence in England, Germany, and Bohemia, IV. 109.

Wilberforce, William, IV. 324.

Wilkes, John, conduct of the government with respect to his election for Middlesex, I. 202; his comparison of the mother of George III. to the mother of Edward III., V. 199; his persecution by the Grenville administration, V. 212; description of him, V. 212; his North Britain, V. 212; his committal to the Tower, V. 212; his discharge, V. 213; his Essay on Woman laid before the House of Lords, V. 216; fights a duel with one of Lord Bute's dependants,

V. 216; flies to France, V. 216; his works ordered to be burnt by the hangman, and himself expelled the House of Commons, and outlawed, V. 216; obtains damages in an action for the seizure of his papers, V. 216; returns from exile and is elected for Middlesex, V. 253.

Wilkie, David, recollection of him at Holland House, IV. 211; failed in portrait-painting, V. 66.

William III., low state of national prosperity and national character in his reign, I. 197; his feeling in reference to the Spanish succession, II. 137; unpopularity of his person and measures, II. 137; suffered under a complication of diseases, II. 138; his death, II. 139; limitation of his prerogatives, II. 199; compact with the Convention, II. 336; his habit of consulting Temple, III. 240; coalition which he formed against Louis XIV. secretly favoured by Rome, IV. 133; his vices not obtruded on the public eye, IV. 183; his assassination planned, IV. 184; Addison's Lines to him, V. 78; reference to him, V. 222.

Williams, Dean of Westminster, his services to Buckingham, and counsel to him and the king, III. 70. 74.

Williams, John, his character, IV. 342. V. 21; employed by Hastings to write in his defence, IV. 342.

Williams, Sir William, his character as a lawyer, III. 39; his view of the duty of counsel in conducting prosecutions, III. 39.

Wimbledon Church, Lord Burleigh attended mass at, II. 85.

Wine, excess in, not a sign of ill-breeding in the reign of Queen Anne, V. 118.

"Wisdom of our ancestors," proper value of the plea of, II. 293.

Wit, Addison's compared with that of Cowley and Butler, V. 118.

Witt, John de, power with which he governed Holland, III. 175; his interview with Temple, III. 179; his manners, III. 179; his confidence in Temple and deception by Charles's court, III. 189; his violent death, III. 393.

Wolcot, V. 21.

Wolfe, General, Pitt's panegyric upon, II. 238; his conquest of Quebec, and death, II. 267; monument voted to him, II. 267.

Woodfall, Mr., his dealings with Junius, IV. 248.

Wordsworth, relative "correctness" of his poetry, I. 314; Byron's distaste for, I. 327; characteristics of his poems, I. 330, 335.

Works, public, employment of the public wealth in, I. 233; public and private, comparative value of, I. 233.

Writing, grand canon of, II. 115.

Wycherley, William, his literary merits and faults, IV. 162; his birth, family, and education, IV. 162; age at which he wrote his plays, IV. 163; his favour with the Duchess of Cleveland, IV. 164; his marriage, IV. 168; his embarrassments, IV. 169; his acquaintance with Pope, IV. 171; his character as a writer, IV. 174. 177; his severe handling by Collier, IV. 189; analogy between him and Congreve, IV. 199.

Wyndham, Mr., his opinion of Sheridan's speech against Hastings, IV. 326; his argument for retaining Francis in the impeachment against Hastings, IV. 327; his appearance at the trial, IV. 332; his adherence to Burke, IV. 339.

## X.

Xenophon, his report of the reasoning of Socrates in confutation of Aristodemus, IV. 100.

## Y.

York, Duke of, III. 263; anxiety excited by his sudden return from Holland, III. 232; detestation of him, III. 232; revival of the question of his exclusion, III. 233.

York House, the London residence of Bacon and of his father, III. 67. 89.

Yonge, Sir William, II. 231.

Young, Dr., his testimony to Addison's colloquial powers, V. 169.

## Z.

Zohak, King, Persian fable of, III. 293.

THE END.

PRINTED BY BERNH. TAUCHNITZ JUN.

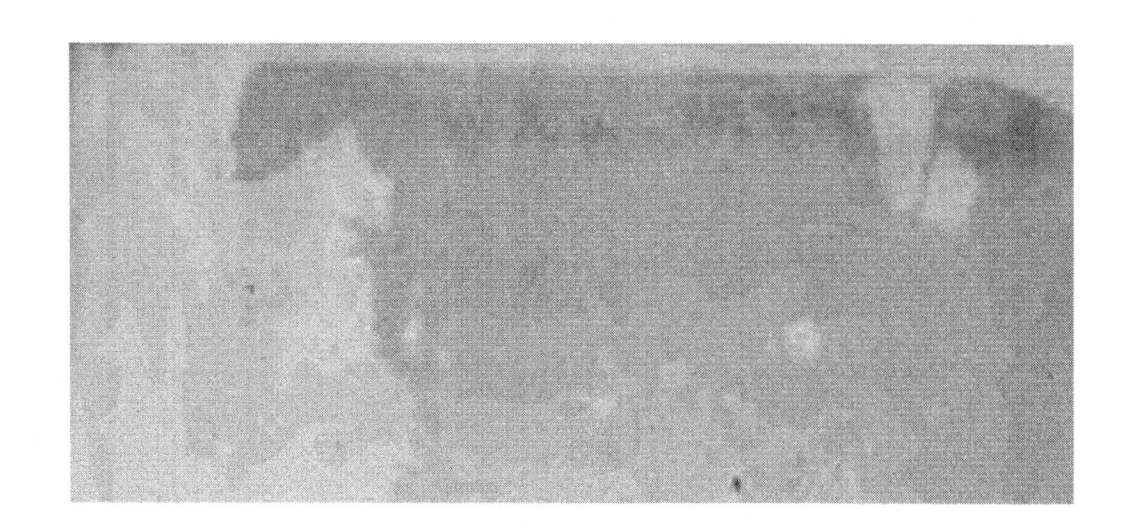

STANFORD UNIVERSITY LIBRARIES
STANFORD AUXILIARY LIBRARY
STANFORD, CALIFORNIA 94305-6004
(650) 723-9201
salcirc@sulmail.stanford.edu
All books are subject to recall.
DATE DUE

JUN 28 1999
JUN 08 1999

Lightning Source UK Ltd.
Milton Keynes UK
UKOW05f1147310816

281892UK00001B/133/P